CONTENTS

1. The Basic Requirements 1
2. The Speech and the Sentence 3
3. The Structure of an English Sentences 8
4. Parts of Sentences (Part I) 10
5. Parts of Sentences (Part II) .. 14
6. Parts of Speech .. 16
7. Kinds of Nouns .. 22
8. The Noun : Number .. 29
9. The Noun : Gender 35
10. Formation of Nouns from Adjectives 38
11. Formation of Nouns from Verbs 42
12. The Pronoun 47
13. The Usage of Pronoun 50
14. The Usage of the Pronoun 'It' 55
15. The Adjective 59
16. The Article 68
17. The Verb 79
18. The Tense 101
19. Change of Tenses 149
20. Modals 161
21. Voice 182

22. Change of Voice 187

23. The Adverb 200

24. The Conjunction 205

25. The Preposition 213

26. Interjections 227

27. Idiomatic Sentences 229

28. Translation Exercise - I (Mixed Tenses) 234

29. Translation Exercise - II [Passages in Hindi (Solved)]

30. Translation Exercise - III (Unsolved Passages with Hints) 247

31. Practice Passages 252

Chapter 1

The Basic Requirements

(A) The Important Points

Translation is an art that could be acquired through hard work and patience. The most important point is to learn the grammars of both the languages concerned. The sentences or passages ought to be translated in spirit and not according to words. In other words, the idea of literal translation should be dropped.

However, it is sad to note that much attention to this art is not being paid in the modern eudcational institutions. The result is that even the brilliant students cannot express their thoughts in another language (*e.g.*, English or Hindi) in a proper manner. The lack of knowledge of this art proves to be a wet blanket for them and they lack the qualities like of self-confidence, candour, self-expression, creativity and learning spirit.

It should be made clear that this art cannot be attained overnight; one can be perfect in this venture only through sincere and hard practice and prompted through proper guidance.

Any passage or sentence which have to be translated, must be read properly and a full experience of the study of various grammatical rules should go into the translation work. It should be realised that there is always a scope for improvement and accuracy. But it should be remembered that the task may be hard but not impossible.

(B) Steps to be Taken

The following steps should be taken while translating a passage written in Hindi (or any other modern Indian language) into English:

1. Read the given passage carefully once or twice so that you grasp its full meaning.

2. Think in your mind, of equivalent words, phrases and sentences that are comparable to those contained in the passage.
3. Be very careful about the tense, as the passage in Hindi or in any other language might connote a different tense altogether, eg,

   (i) मेरा भाई कल आया।

   (ii) मेरा भाई कल आया है।

   (iii) मेरा भाई कल आया था।

   इन तीनों वाक्यों का एक ही अंग्रेज़ी translation होगा:

   My brother came yesterday.
4. Literal tranlation should be avoided. Proverbs and idioms in Hindi should be translated into their equivalents in English.
5. Maintain the voice in English. Use the active voice as far as is possible.
6. Changes in the tense, particularly in the case of narration, should be carefully noted.
7. Very lengthy sentences may be broken down into two or more sentences—if necessary —but the original sequence of ideas must be maintained as far as is possible.
8. Translation of difficult sentences must be done with an extra care as even the slightest error in them could be too glaring.
9. All sentences and passages must be revised thoroughly to remove errors, if any.
10. The prepositions need extra attention.

Chapter 2

The Speech and The Sentence

मनुष्य जब से पैदा हुआ है, अपनी भावनाओं को लिख कर या बोल कर दूसरे के सामने प्रकट करता आ रहा है। हमारे लिखने या बोलने में जिन शब्दों का प्रयोग होता है, हम उन सभी के समूह को अथवा Speech के हर उस Minimum भाग को जो अपने आप में पूर्ण Sense देता है, Sentence (वाक्य) कहते हैं।

कोई भी Speech अगर शब्दों को ठीक जगह पर लगा कर बोली या लिखी न जाये तो वह ठीक Sentence नहीं बना सकती।

e.g., (1) He hockey plays.

अब इस Sentence में Subject 'He' के साथ Object 'hockey' आ गया और Verb 'plays' Sentence के अन्त में चला गया है। यह Sentence ठीक नहीं है।

ठीक Sentence नीचे दिया गया है:

He plays hockey.

S + V + O

KINDS OF SENTENCES

हम किसी भी वाक्य को पांच प्रकार से व्यक्त करते हैं। पांच प्रकार से बोलने से पांच प्रकार के वाक्य बनते हैं:

(A) Assertive or Declarative Sentences.
(B) Interrogative Sentences.
(C) Imperative Sentences.
(D) Exclamatory Sentences.
(E) Optative Sentences.

Note: कई भाषा विज्ञानी Exclamatory Sentences और Optative Sentences को एक ही प्रकार के मानते हैं। अतः वे Sentences चार प्रकार के बताते हैं।

(A) Assertive Sentences

यह दो प्रकार के होते हैं:

(A) Positive या Affirmative sentences.

(B) Negative sentences.

(A) *Positive Sentences* (सकारात्मक वाक्य): जो Sentence सीधे तौर पर एक Statement प्रस्तुत करता है, उसे Positive या Affirmative Sentence कहा जाता है:

(i) Ram goes to school.
राम स्कूल जाता है।

(ii) I get up early in the morning.
मैं सुबह जल्दी जागता हूँ।

(iii) He laughs all the day.
वह सारा दिन हँसता रहता है।

(iv) We sing a song.
हम गाना गाते हैं।

(B) *Negative Sentences* (नकारात्मक वाक्य): जो Sentence किसी बात को 'नहीं' में या किसी प्रकार की मनाही या 'न' को प्रकट करें, उन्हें Negative Sentences कहा जाता है:

(i) You should not pluck the flowers.
तुम्हें फूल नहीं तोड़ने चाहिए।

(ii) You should not make a noise.
तुम्हें शोर नहीं करना चाहिए।

(iii) He will not sing a song.
वह गाना नहीं गायेगा।

(iv) You should not tell a lie.
तुम्हें झूठ नहीं बोलना चाहिए।

(B) Interrogative Sentences

जिन Sentences में हम किसी से प्रश्न के तौर पर कोई बात पूछें तो उन्हें हम Interrogative Sentences कहते हैं:

(i) Do you like me?
क्या आप मुझे पसन्द करते हैं?

(ii) Will he beat you?
क्या वह तुम्हें मारेगा?

(iii) Do you like milk?
क्या आपको दूध पसन्द है?

(iv) Has she lost the bet?
क्या वह शर्त हार चुकी है?

(C) Imperative Sentences

जिन Sentences में किसी को सुझाव, प्रार्थना, आदेश या कोई अन्य शिक्षा दी जाती है, उन्हें हम Imperative Sentences कहते हैं। इन Sentences में कई बार Subject का प्रयोग नहीं किया जाता तथा वहां पर Subject 'you' लुप्त रहता है:

(i) Work hard.
खूब मेहनत करो।

(ii) Go away.
दूर चले जाओ।

(iii) Move ahead.
आगे बढ़ो।

(iv) Please help me.
कृपया मेरी सहायता करो।

इस Sentence में Subject 'you' understood है।

(D) Exclamatory Sentences

जब कोई बात बड़ी खुशी, दु:ख, हैरानी अथवा घृणा आदि में कही जाती है तो हमारी तीव्र भावनाएं भी एक साथ प्रकट हो जाती है। ऐसे Sentences को हम Exclamatory Sentences कहते हैं।

(i) Hurrah! we have won the match.
हुर्रा! हम मैच जीत चुके हैं।

(ii) Bravo! Well done.
शाबाश! बहुत अच्छा किया।

(iii) Oh! What a dull fellow you are.
ओह! तुम कितने मूर्ख हो।

(iv) How beautiful this flower is!
यह फूल कितना सुन्दर है!

(v) Hurrah! I have stood first in the examination.
हुर्रा! मैं परीक्षा में प्रथम आया हूं।

(vi) Ah! Kusum has stood first.
वाह! कुसुम प्रथम आ गई।

(E) Optative Sentences

जिन Sentences में हम किसी को वरदान अथवा अभिशाप देते हैं, किसी की आराधना करते हैं अथवा कोई इच्छा प्रकट करते हैं, ऐसे Sentences को Optative Sentences कहा जाता है:

(i) May you live long!
भगवान करे तुम्हारी आयु लम्बी हो!

(ii) May God bless you!
भगवान तुम्हें आशीर्वाद दे!

(iii) Alas! My son is no more.
कितने दु:ख की बात है कि मेरा बेटा जीवित नहीं रहा।

(iv) May you die!
भगवान करे कि तुम मर जाओ!

Note: (i) Assertive तथा Imperative Sentences के बाद Full Stop (.) का प्रयोग होता है।

(ii) Exclamatory व Optative Sentences के बाद Sign of Exclamation (!) लगता है।

(iii) Interrogative Sentences के बाद Sign of Interrogation (?) लगता है।

EXERCISE 1

नीचे दिये गये Sentences में ठीक Sentence के सामने (√) Tick का प्रयोग करें:

1. Alas! I have an intelligent son.
(a) Assertive
(b) Optative
(c) Exclamatory
(d) Imperative

2. I love you.
(a) Affirmative
(b) Exclamatory
(c) Imperative
(d) Negative

3. Sham is not a good boy.
(a) Negative
(b) Optative
(c) Affirmative
(d) Imperative

4. Do you know him?
(a) Assertive
(b) Interrogative
(c) Imperative
(d) Exclamatory

5. May you become rich!
(a) Imperative
(b) Optative
(c) Exclamatory
(d) Assertive

6. Do not pluck the flowers.
(a) Imperative
(b) Exclamatory
(c) Negative
(d) Optative

7. My name is Tony.
(a) Affirmative
(b) Optative
(c) Negative
(d) Interrogative

8. She does not work hard.
(a) Assertive
(b) Exclamatory
(c) Optative
(d) Interrogative

9. Have you ever seen the Taj?
(a) Assertive
(b) Optative
(c) Affirmative
(d) Interrogative

10. Move forward.
(a) Optative
(b) Imperative
(c) Exclamatory
(d) Affirmative

EXERCISE 2

नीचे दिये गये Sentences का English में अनुवाद करें तथा बताएं कि ये किस-किस तरह के Sentences हैं:

1. काश! मैं बूढ़ा न होता।

2. काश! मैं बहुत अमीर होता।

3. शोर मत मचाओ।

4. मैंने खाना खा लिया है।

5. हुर्रा! मेरा भाई कक्षा में प्रथम आया है।

6. तुम मुझसे बात मत करो।

7. वह हंस रहा है।

8. बच्चे खेल क्यों नहीं रहे?

9. मनजीत को किसने पीटा?

10. चोर ने कौन से घर में सेंध लगाई

Chapter 3

The Structure of an English Sentences

(अंग्रेज़ी वाक्यों की संरचना)

हर भाषा का अपना व्याकरण होता है तथा उसे बोलने व लिखने के नियम भी अलग-अलग होते हैं। इसी तरह English व्याकरण के भी अपने ही नियम हैं तथा इन नियमों का पालन करते हुए ही व्यक्ति इस भाषा को ठीक प्रकार से बोल या लिख सकता है।

English में कुल 26 अक्षर होते हैं जिनमें से पांच को स्वर (Vowels) कहते हैं तथा अन्य 21 व्यंजन (Consonants) कहलाते हैं। इन सभी को समझना इसलिये ज़रूरी है क्योंकि इसके बिना इस भाषा को सीखना असम्भव है।

Note: हम जिन शब्दों के समूह को बोल कर या लिख कर प्रकट करते हैं उसमें Subject, Object व Verb का ठीक जगह पर लगा होना अति अनिवार्य है, नहीं तो Sentence गलत हो सकता है।

English में नीचे दिये गये ढंग से प्राय: Sentence बने होते हैं:
He does his work.

वह अपना काम करता है। इस Sentence में He → Subject (कर्ता), does → Verb (क्रिया) तथा his work → Object (कर्म) है। तो इस Sentence का Structure हुआ:

S + V + O

यहां पर 'S' → Subject, 'V' → Verb तथा 'O' → Object है।

1. I take my meals.
↓ ↓ ↓
S V O
मैं अपना भोजन करता हूँ।

2. She makes no noise.
↓ ↓ ↓
S V O
वह शोर नहीं मचाती है।

3. Ram plays hockey.
↓ ↓ ↓
S V O
राम हाकी खेलता है।

Note: कई बार कुछ एक Sentences में Object का प्रयोग नहीं होता:

1. I laugh.
↓ ↓
S V
मैं हंसता हूँ।

2. She laughs.
↓ ↓
S V
वह हंसती है।

3. We play in the playground.
↓ ↓
S V
हम खेल के मैदान में खेलते हैं।

EXERCISE 1

नीचे दिये Sentences का अंग्रेजी में अनुवाद करें तथा Subject, Verb, व Object ढूंढें:

1. क्या वह गाना गाता है?
2. वह सोता है।
3. हम सब फर्श पर नाचते हैं।
4. चपरासी घण्टी बजाता है।
5. मुर्गियां अण्डे देती हैं।
6. वह रोता है।
7. सोहन हंसता है।
8. सूर्य रोशनी देता है।
9. पानी जीवन देता है।
10. बढ़ई कुर्सी बनाता है।

Hints for Translation

3. फर्श = floor. **10.** बढ़ई = Carpenter.

Note: ऊपर दिये गये सब वाक्य Present Indefinite Tense में हैं। अब कुछ और वाक्यों (मिश्रित Terms) का भी अंग्रेजी में अनुवाद करें।

EXERCISE 2

1. वह गाना गा रही है।
2. उसकी बहन अपने बालों को कंघी कर रही है।
3. उसने पत्र नहीं लिखा है।
4. आपकी बहुत प्रशंसा की गई है।
5. आप कहां गये थे?
6. मैंने पहले बब्बर शेर कभी नहीं देखा था।
7. मैं आपके साथ नहीं जाऊंगा।
8. मैंने कोई गलत काम नहीं किया है।
9. कल वर्षा हो रही होगी।
10. अब वर्षा नहीं होगी।

Hints for Translation

2. अपने बालों को कंघी करना = combing her hair **4.** बहुत प्रशंसा = much praised.

Chapter 4

Parts of Sentences (Part I)

वाक्यों के भाग (भाग I)

जब कोई सही Sentence बोला या लिखा जाता है तो इसके दो भाग होते हैं:

(1) The Subject (उद्देश्य अथवा कर्त्ता)

(2) The Predicate (विधेय)

The Subject: Sentence के एक भाग में हम किसी व्यक्ति, स्थान या वस्तु का कर्त्ता के रूप में वर्णन करते हैं। इसे Subject कहा जाता है। यह Noun या Pronoun का एक वचन या बहु-वचन भी हो सकता है। यह सब Sentence के Nature पर आधारित है।

The Predicate: (1) यह Sentence का वह भाग है जो Subject के बारे में जानकारी देता है। यह एक Word भी हो सकता है तथा एक से अधिक Words भी हो सकते हैं।

(2) नीचे दिए गए उदाहरण से Subject और Predicate का अन्तर स्पष्ट हो जाता है:

The cow is black.
गाय काली है।

इस Sentence में The cow एक Noun है तथा यह Subject का काम कर रहा है। बाकी सब Predicate है।

The Cow = Subject
is black = Predicate

कई बार कुछ Sentences में It का भी प्रयोग किया जाता है।

(i) It is bright day.
बाहर खुला दिन है।

(ii) It is too hot outside.
बाहर बहुत गर्मी है।

(iii) It is raining.
वर्षा हो रही है।

Imperative Sentences: Imperative Sentences में प्राय: Subject का प्रयोग नहीं होता। अत: यह केवल मान लिया जाता है कि Subject 'you' है:

(i) Walk fast. तेज़ चलो।

यहाँ "walk fast" किसी न किसी को तो कहा गया है। भले ही इसमें Subject नहीं है, फिर भी ऐसे Sentence में मान लिया जाता है कि इसका अर्थ है = (you walk fast) = (order).

(ii) Move ahead.
आगे बढ़ो।
(*i.e.,* you are commanded to move forward)

(iii) Always speak the truth.
सदा सच बोलो।
(*i.e.,* you are advised to speak the truth always)

कुछ Sentences में 'there' का प्रयोग Sentence के आरम्भ में किया जाता है तथा Subject Sentence के बीच कहीं स्थापित हो जाता हो।

(i) There is a *good number of students* in my class.
मेरी कक्षा में काफी (बहुत से) विद्यार्थी हैं।

(ii) There is a *little milk* in this glass.
इस गिलास में थोड़ा सा दूध है।

Exclamatory Sentences: Exclamatory Sentences में आमतौर पर Subject को Predicate के बाद प्रयोग में लाया जाता है।

Examples

(a) What a solid man *he* is!
वह कितना ताकतवर आदमी है!

(b) How beautiful the rainbow is!
इन्द्रधनुष कितना सुन्दर है!

इन वाक्यों में क्रमश: 'he' और 'the rainbow' Subject हैं और वाक्य का बाकी भाग Predicate है।

Interrogative Sentences: Interrogative Sentences में भी Subject प्राय: Predicate के बाद में या बीच में प्रयोग में लाया जाता है।

Examples

(a) Are you dumb? क्या तुम गूंगे हो?

इस Sentence में 'Are' तथा 'dumb' Predicates हैं जबकि 'you' शब्द Subject है।

(b) *Who* will play with me?
मेरे साथ कौन खेलेगा ?

(c) Do you like him?
क्या आप उसे पसन्द करते हैं।

Note: यह देखा गया है कि आम बोलचाल में लोग Double Subject का प्रयोग करते है जो कि avoid करना चाहिए।

(i) You fetch a glass of water for me.

(ii) You, please go away.

लेकिन कई बार Double Subject का प्रयोग भी हो जाता है।

(i) You, the cheat! Go away.
तुम, धोखेबाज ! दूर हटो।

(ii) I tell you, you never try to come near me.
मैं तुम्हें बता रहा हूं कि कभी मेरे निकट आने का यत्न मत करो।

EXERCISE 1

नीचे दिये गये, Sentences में से Subject व Predicate ढूंढ़ें:

1. You are a good boy.
   तुम एक अच्छे लड़के हो।
2. Go away!
   दूर हटो !
3. Do not pluck flowers.
   फूल मत तोड़ो।
4. Take it seriously.
   इसे गम्भीरता से लो।
5. He is telling a white lie.
   वह सफेद झूठ बोल रहा है।
6. There is something wrong at the bottom.
   दाल में कुछ काला है।
7. The lion is roaring in his den.
   बब्बर शेर अपनी गुफा में दहाड़ रहा है।
8. She was turning pale.
   उसका रंग पीला पड़ रहा था।
9. Who are you?
   आप कौन हैं ?
10. What are you doing?
    आप क्या कर रहे हैं ?
11. There is a little ink in this inkpot.
    स्याही की दवात में थोड़ी सी स्याही है।
12. The rabbit was running down the way into the bushes.
    खरगोश बडी तेज़ी से झाड़ियों में जा रहा था।
13. He makes no noise.
    वह शोर नहीं करता।

EXERCISE 2

Complete the following sentences by filling in the Subject or the Predicate:

1. ...... am waiting for them.
2. You ......
3. ..... made me laugh.
4. She .....
5. Are .... coming tomorrow?
6. Where is .... going?
7. They .....
8. Why are ..... laughing.
9. How are ..... to blame for this?
10. ... is waiting for you?
11. Where does .... want me to stay?
12. Can there be more .... :
13. When can .... be reformed?
14. He ....
15. Shall .... go there together?
16. ..... never come alone.
17. What can .... do for you?
18. You .....
19. He and his friends ....
20. We ....
21. All of us ....
22. Have....come to much a pass?
23. .... has beaten?
24. Where are .... who had sacrificed their lives for the country?
25. ..... in India is there who is not ready to die for the mother-land?
26. .... do not know his where-abouts.
27. Am ..... responsible for this mess?

Chapter 5

Parts of Sentences (Part II)
वाक्यों के भाग (भाग II)

किसी भी Sentence को Subject तथा Predicate का मिश्रण कह कर ही बात खत्म नहीं हो जाती। इस मिश्रण में और भी कई प्रकार् की चीज़ें छिपी होती हैं जिनकी जानकारी होना अति आवश्यक है। इनका वर्णन नीचे किया गया है।

Subject(कर्ता): हम पहले भी पढ़ चुके हैं कि यह Noun या Pronoun, Singular or Plural form में होता है। यह Sentence का Performing Person या Place होता है, जैसे कि:

He sings a song. (He - subject)

Verb (क्रिया): यह Sentence में वह शब्द है जो Subject पर हो रहे, हो चुके या होने वाले Action के बारे में बताता है, जैसे कि:

He sings a song. (sings - verb)

Direct Object: यह Sentence में वह शब्द होता है जो कि सीधे तौर पर कर्म के रूप में आता है जैसे कि:

He sings a song. (a song - object)

Complement: यह वह शब्द है जो कि किसी Sentence में Sense को पूरा करता है।

Examples

They made *him King.*

उन्होंने उसे राजा बनाया।

इस वाक्य में King लिखे बिना Sense पूरा नहीं होता।

Complement and Object: कई बार complement or object एक जैसे ही प्रतीत होते हैं:

Examples

(a) He is playing hockey.
वह हाकी खेल रहा है।
He - Subject
is playing - Verb
hockey - Object

(b) He made no speech.
उसने कोई भाषण नहीं दिया।
He - Subject
made - Verb
no speech - Object complement

इस वाक्य में Speech शब्द के बिना वाक्य का कोई अर्थ नहीं निकलता। यहां हम Speech को Object Complement कह सकते हैं।

Indirect Object: जब किसी वाक्य में दो Objects हों तो Person Object को Indirect Object कहते हैं और Thing Object को Direct Object कहते हैं :

Examples

(a) Narinder gave me a pen.
↓ ↓ ↓ ↓
S V IO DO
नरेन्द्र ने मुझे एक पेन दिया।

इस वाक्य में Narinder Subject है और बाकी सारा वाक्य Predicate है। इस Predicate में gave एक Verb है, me Indirect Object (IO) है और a pen यहां पर Direct Object (DO) है।

(b) अब एक और वाक्य देखिये:
You called him names.
↓ ↓ ↓ ↓
S V IO DO
आपने उसे गालियां निकालीं।

Chapter 6

Parts of Speech
(भाषा के भाग)

प्रति दिन की Speech में हम Different Sentences बोलते हैं। प्रत्येक Sentence कई Words का समूह होता है। हर एक word किसी न किसी class को belong करता है। हम Speech को आठ अलग-अलग भागों में बांट सकते हैं जो कि इस प्रकार हैं:

(A) Noun
(B) Pronoun
(C) Verb
(D) Adjective
(E) Adverb
(F) Conjunction
(G) Interjection
(H) Preposition

(A) Noun (संज्ञा): Noun वह शब्द होता है जिससे किसी व्यक्ति, जगह या वस्तु के नाम का बोध होता है। यह Singular अथवा Plural भी हो सकता है।

(i) Moti is a nice boy.
मोती एक अच्छा लड़का है।

(ii) Ramesh takes tea.
रमेश चाय पीता है।

इस subject में Ramesh व tea दोनों Nouns हैं।

(iii) He is my brother.
वह मेरा भाई है।

इस Sentence में brother शब्द Noun है।

(iv) The birds fly in the *air*.
इस Sentence में birds Plural रूप में Noun है जबकि air भी Noun है।

(B) Pronoun (सर्वनाम): Pronoun वह शब्द होता है जो किसी Noun के स्थान पर Use होकर उसको Represent करता है। जैसे मैं, तुम, वे, हम आदि।

(i) Mohan is a good boy. *He* has lost *his* book.
मोहन एक अच्छा लड़का है। उसने अपनी किताब खो दी है।

इस Sentence में He तथा his दोनों शब्द मोहन को ही Represent करते हैं। अतः दोनों Pronouns हैं।

(ii) Satish was punished because *he* was making a noise.
सतीश को सज़ा दी गई क्योंकि वह शोर मचा रहा था।

(iii) Lucky has got back *his* coin.
लक्की को उसका सिक्का वापिस मिल चुका है।

(C) Verb (क्रिया): Verb वह शब्द होता है जो Noun या Pronoun पर हो रहे, होने वाले या हो चुके Actions के बारे में जानकारी देता है:

(i) He *flies* a kite.
वह पतंग उड़ाता है।

(ii) She *talks* too much.
वह बहुत अधिक बातें करती है।

(iii) The fish *swam* in fresh water.
मछली ताज़े पानी में तैरी।

(iv) He *hit* the ball.
उसने गेंद को मारा।

(v) The lion *pounced* upon the stag.
उसने गेंद मारा।

(vi) Sonu *slept* on the bed.
सोनू पलंग पर सो गया।

(D) Adjective (विशेषण): Adjective वह शब्द होता है जो Noun या Pronoun की विशेषता बताता है। नीचे Italicised किये गये शब्द Adjectives हैं।

(i) He is a *clever* boy.
वह एक चालाक लड़का है।

इस Sentence में boy Noun है तथा clever उस boy की विशेषता बताता है कि वह चालाक है।

(ii) He is a *classical* player.
वह एक बहुत अच्छा खिलाड़ी है।

(iii) He is a *brilliant* student.
वह बहुत होशियार विद्यार्थी है।

(E) Adverb (क्रिया विशेषण): Adverb वह शब्द है जो किसी Adjective, Verb या किसी और Adverb की विशेषता बताता है। नीचे Italicise किये गये शब्द Adverb हैं।

(i) He is a *very* clever boy.
वह बहुत चालाक लड़का है।

(ii) She works *quite well*.
वह काफी अच्छा काम करती है।

(iii) He can run *very fast*.
वह बड़ी तेज़ दौड़ सकता है।

(iv) She talkes *very quickly*.
वह बड़ी तेज़ी से बात करती है।

(F) Conjunction (संयोजक अव्यय): Conjunction वह Word होता है जो दो

शब्दों, Phrases, Clauses या Sentences को आपस में जोड़ता है। नीचे Italicise किये गये शब्द Conjunctions हैं।

(i) I know him *but* I do not like him.
मैं उसे जानता हूँ पर मैं उसे पसन्द नहीं करता।

(ii) Mohan *and* Sohan are brothers.
मोहन व सोहन भाई हैं।

(G) Interjection (विस्मयादिबोधक शब्द): Interjection वह शब्द होता है जो अचानक उठने वाली भावना को प्रकट करे, जैसे गुस्सा, खुशी, दु:ख, हैरानगी आदि।

(i) Hurrah! We have won the match.
हुर्रा! हम मैच जीत चुके हैं।
यहां पर हुर्रा शब्द खुशी प्रकट करता है।

(ii) Oh! What a dull boy you are.
ओह! तुम कितने बुद्धू लड़के हो।

(iii) Ah! What a deep wound this is.
आह! यह कितना गहरा घाव है।

(H) Prepositions (सम्बन्धसूचक अव्यय): यह वह शब्द होते हैं जो किसी **Noun,** Pronoun या Sentence के दूसरे भागों से सम्बन्ध व्यक्त करते हैं। नीचे Italicised किये गये शब्द Prepositions हैं।

(i) The frog jumped *into* the pond.
मेंढक तालाब में कूद गया।

(ii) He sat *on* the bench.
वह बैंच पर बैठा।

(iii) He jumped *over* the wall.
वह दीवार फाँद गया।

(iv) He went *with* his brother.
वह अपने भाई के साथ गया।

(v) A carpet *of* red colours was spread across the floor.
लाल रंग का गलीचा फर्श पर बिछाया गया था।

(vi) The dog was lying *under* the table.
कुत्ता मेज के नीचे सो रहा था।

(vii) The birds were chirping *on* the trees.
पक्षी पेड़ों पर चहचहा रहे थे।

EXERCISE 1

Italicise किये गये Word के ठीक उत्तर के सामने Tick (√) का निशान लगाएं:

1. He talks *very* slowly.
(a) Adjective (b) Adverb (c) Interjection (d) Verb
(e) Noun

2. He *rides* a horse.
(a) Interjection
(b) Conjunction
(c) Preposition
(d) Noun
(e) Verb

3. Mohan *and* Satish are friends.
(a) Preposition
(b) Conjunction
(c) Interjection
(d) Verb
(e) Noun

4. Mohan and Lovely are *fast* friends.
(a) Preposition
(b) Conjunction
(c) Adverb
(d) Adjective
(e) Noun

5. *Oh*! How old I have become.
(a) Interjection
(b) Conjunction
(c) Adverb
(d) Adjective
(e) Preposition

6. *Satish* has a cow; it is black.
(a) Noun
(b) Pronoun
(c) Interjection
(d) Adverb
(e) Adjective

7. *We* should take care of the children.
(a) Noun
(b) Adverb
(c) Adjective
(d) Verb
(e) Pronoun

8. He *slapped* across her face.
(a) Noun
(b) Pronoun
(c) Adverb
(d) Verb
(e) Adjective

9. She played *extremely* well.
(a) Adverb
(b) Verb
(c) Adjective
(d) Interjection
(e) Preposition

10. He ran fast *but* could not win the race.
(a) Interjection
(b) Conjunction
(c) Preposition
(d) Noun
(e) Verb

EXERCISE 2

नीचे दिये गये Sentences में से Verb, Noun, Pronoun, Interjection, Conjunction, Preposition, Adverb तथा Adjective ढूंढ़े:

1. He ran very fast.
वह बहुत तेज़ दौड़ा।

2. She made no mistake.
उसने कोई गलती नहीं की।

3. **He is singing a song.**
वह गाना गा रहा है।

4. **Sunita and Geeta walk out for school together.**
सुनीता व गीता स्कूल जाने के लिये इकट्ठी बाहर निकलती हैं।

5. He struck the ball with his bat.
उसने गेंद को अपने बैट से मारा।

6. Ahoy! What a girl she is.
वाह ! वह क्या लड़की है।

7. Who will break the door?
दरवाज़ा कौन तोड़ेगा ?

8. Bravo! Well done.
शाबाश ! बहुत अच्छे।

9. He told me about your problem.
उसने मुझे आपकी समस्या के बारे में बताया।

10. **I always find him in a good spirit.**
मैं उसे हमेशा खुश देखता हूँ।

11. She is my mother.
वह मेरी माता जी हैं।

12. Good! I love you, my son.
अच्छा ! मैं तुमसे प्यार करता हूँ, मेरे बच्चे।

13. Well! You have done quite well.
अच्छा ! आपने बहुत अच्छा काम किया है।

14. He is a damned fool.
वह बिल्कुल मूर्ख है।

15. She ran after a bus.
वह एक बस के पीछे भागी।

EXERCISE 3

नीचे दिये गये वाक्यों का अंग्रेजी में अनुवाद करें तथा सभी Parts of Speech को अलग से लिखें:

Example

वह खेल के मैदान में खेल रहा है।
He is playing in the playground.
He = Pronoun
is playing = Verb
in = Preposition
the = Article
playground = Noun

1. वह जल्दी में है।
2. आपको ज्यादा नहीं बोलना चाहिए।

3. वह कल घर से भाग गया।
4. उसका भाई मेरा पक्का मित्र है।
5. हम दो दिन बाद ताजमहल देखने जायेंगे।
6. उसकी घड़ी समय नहीं बताती।
7. सोनू की मम्मी ने उसे कल डांटा था।
8. मनदीप सबसे प्यार से बात करता है।
9. वे सब कहां चले गये?
10. मैं कल फिल्म देखने जाऊंगा।
11. हमारा कल नतीजा निकलेगा।
12. उसने सिगरेट पीना छोड़ दिया है।
13. तुम्हारा भाई बहुत शराब पीता है।
14. उसे मत मारो।
15. कौन कहता है कि तुम कुछ नहीं कर सकते?
16. आपके सामने वह क्या है?
17. उसका नाम रामू है।
18. माली पौधों को पानी दे रहा है।
19. वह हंसता है।
20. तुमसे मेरा कोई लेना-देना नहीं है।
21. मैं इस बात को झूठ मानता हूँ।
22. क्या भूत होते हैं?
23. वह चूहों से बहुत डरता है।
24. वह बहुत सा भोजन एक बार में खा जाता है।
25. संदीप ने मेरी बात की ओर कोई ध्यान नहीं दिया।
26. पवन चोर नहीं है।
27. आप कहां जा रहे हैं।
28. शोर किसने मचाया था?

Hints for Translation:

4. पक्का मित्र = fast friend. 7. डांटना = to reprimand. 12. छोड़ देना = to give up. 22. भूत = ghosts.

Chapter 7

Kinds of Nouns

(संज्ञा के प्रकार)

---

(1) किसी व्यक्ति, जगह अथवा चीज को Noun कहा जाता है। यह Singular व Plural भी हो सकता है।

(2) *Kinds of Noun :* Noun पांच प्रकार के कहे जा सकते हैं:

(A) Proper Noun
(B) Common Noun
(C) Collective Noun
(D) Abstract Noun
(E) Material Noun

(A) Proper Noun: किसी खास जगह, वस्तु या आदमी के नाम को Proper Noun कहते हैं:

(i) *Soma* is a good girl.
सोमा अच्छी लड़की है।

(ii) *New Delhi* is the capital of India.
नई दिल्ली भारत की राजधानी है।

(iii) *The Tajmahal* is a wonderful building.
ताजमहल एक अद्भुत इमारत है।

ऊपर दिये गये Sentences में Soma एक लड़की का नाम है। इसी तरह New Delhi एक खास शहर का नाम है जो India —एक खास Country—की राजधानी है। इसी प्रकार The Taj एक खास इमारत का नाम है।

अगर हम इन Sentences को ध्यान से देखेंगे तो हमें पता चलेगा कि Proper Noun का पहला अक्षर हमेशा Capital Letter से शुरू होता है।

कई बार Proper Noun भी Common Noun की तरह Use होता है लेकिन यहां भी इसका पहला letter Capital ही लिखा जाता है:

(iv) Tony is the Denis Lilly of our team.
टोनी हमारी टीम का डैनिस लिली है।

(v) Mohan is the Newton of our school.
मोहन हमारे स्कूल का न्यूटन है।

(B) Common Noun: जब दिए गए Noun से किसी खास व्यक्ति या वस्तु का बोध नहीं होता तो उसे Common Noun कहते हैं:

(i) He is a good *boy*.
वह एक अच्छा लड़का है।

(ii) It is a *book*.
यह एक किताब है।

ऊपर दिये गये Sentence में लड़का (Boy) तथा किताब (Book) दोनों शब्द Common Noun हैं क्योंकि यह किसी खास व्यक्ति या किसी खास वस्तु को प्रकट नहीं करते। Common Noun होने के कारण इनका पहला अक्षर Small Letter लिखा जाता है।

(C) Collective Noun: किसी चीज अथवा जगह के झुण्ड को सम्बोधित करने वाले जानवरों, फूलों, अन्य पौधों या व्यक्तियों की पूरी जाति को प्रकट करने वाले Noun को Collective Noun कहा जाता है:

(i) A school of dolphins.
डॉलफिन (मछली) का समूह

(ii) A bunch of keys.
चाबियों का गुच्छा

(iii) A bunch of grapes.
अंगूर का गुच्छा

(iv) A gang of robbers.
लुटेरों का गिरोह

(v) An army of soldiers.
सिपाहियों की सेना

(vi) A herd of cattle.
जानवरों का समूह

(vii) A team of scientists.
वैज्ञानिकों की टीम

(viii) A big crowd of people.
लोगों की एक बड़ी भीड़

(ix) A jury of judges.
अभिनिर्णायक मंडल

(x) A bag of wheat.
गेहूं का थैला

(xi) A basket of fruits.
फलों की टोकरी

(xii) A galaxy of stars.
तारों का समूह

(xiii) A flock of sheep.
भेड़ों का झुंड

(xiv) A class of (fifty) students.
(पचास) बच्चों की क्लास

(xv) A committee of one hundred members.
सौ सदस्यों की एक कमेटी

(xvi) A group of companies.
कम्पनियों का ग्रुप

(xvii) An archipelago of islands.
द्वीपों का एक समूह

(D) Abstract Noun: Abstract Noun निम्नलिखित बातों को बताता है:

(i) *Quality :* truth, honesty, foolishness, loudness, cruelty, softness, dullness, wisdom, bravery, cunningness etc.

(ii) *Action :* actvity, theft, action, behaviour, movement etc.

(iii) *State :* boyhood, childhood, infancy, freedom, sickness youth, soundness, old age, death, sleep etc.

(iv) Name of various professions, arts and sciences *e.g.,* history, economics, grammar, chemistry, geology, botany, pharmacy etc.

Abstract Noun किसी भी Proper Noun, Common Noun अथवा Collective Noun— बेशक वह व्यक्ति हो, जगह हो या कोई वस्तु हो, के सुक्ष्म गुण अथवा भाव को प्रकट करता है।

(i) Truthfulness एक Quality है जो कि किसी व्यक्ति के एक गुण को प्रकट करती है लेकिन इसे हम देख या छू नहीं सकते।

(ii) Honesty ईमानदारी

(iii) Goodness अच्छाई

(iv) Cleverness चुस्ती

Article 'the' का प्रयोग कुछ एक खास Abstract Nouns के पहले होता है जब हम किसी Abstract Noun को किसी खास आदमी, वस्तु एवं जगह के लिए प्रयोग में लाते हैं:

(i) Youth is a golder. period.
जवानी एक स्वर्णिम समय होता है।
यह एक साधारण सा Sentence है।

(ii) The youth of Sandeep was full of happiness.
संदीप की जवानी का समय बड़ा खुशियों भरा था।

इस Sentence में एक Proper Noun Sandeep की जवानी के समय का वर्णन किया गया है।

नीचे कुछ Sentences दिये गये हैं जिनमें Abstract Noun का प्रयोग किया गया है:

(i) Cunningness never wins.
धूर्तता कभी नहीं जीतती।

(ii) Wisdom always wins.
अक्लमंदी हमेशा जीतती है।

(iii) Truthfulness makes a man God.
सच्चाई आदमी को देवता बना देती है।

(E) Material Noun: Material Noun धातुओं तथा अन्य प्राकृतिक पदार्थों को संबोधित करता है, जैसे:- milk, iron, lead, copper, honey, sugar, glucose, oil, cotton, silk, water, wheat, rice etc.

(i) Wheat is the main crop of Punjab?
गेहूँ पंजाब की मुख्य फसल है।

(ii) Rice is the main crop of Bihar.
चावल बिहार की मुख्य फसल है।

(iii) Milk keeps us healthy.
दूध हमें स्वस्थ रखता है।

(iv) Sugar tastes sweet.
चीनी मीठी होती है।

(v) Mercury is a liquid metal.
पारा एक तरल धातु है।

(**Note I:** Article 'the' का प्रयोग प्राय: Material Noun से पहले नहीं होता।)

(i) Milk is good for health.
दूध स्वास्थ्य के लिये अच्छा होता है।

(ii) Coal is black.
कोयला काला होता है।

(iii) Honey is sweet in taste.
शहद मीठी होती है।

(**Note II:** Article 'the' का प्रयोग तब होता है जब Material Noun किसी खास जगह, आदमी या वस्तु से सम्बन्ध रखता है।)

(i) The milk of this cow is very tasty.
इस गाय का दूध बहुत मीठा है।

(ii) The rice from this field is good.
इस खेत का चावल अच्छा है।

(iii) The water of this well is rich in minerals.
इस कुएं के पानी में बहुत से खनिज पदार्थ हैं।

EXERCISE 1

नीचे दिये गये Sentences में जो शब्द Italicise किए गए हैं, उनके सही उत्तर के सामने Tick (√) का निशान लगायें।

1. *Ram* goes to school.
राम स्कूल जाता है।
(a) Collective Noun
(b) Proper Noun
(c) Common Noun
(d) Abstract Noun
(e) Material Noun

2. One needs *copper* to make a coin.
सिक्का बनाने के लिये ताँबे की जरूरत होती है।
(a) Collective Noun
(b) Proper Noun
(c) Common Noun
(d) Abstract Noun
(e) Material Noun

3. *Chandigarh* is the capital of Punjab.
चण्डीगढ़ पंजाब की राजधानी है।
(a) Collective Noun
(b) Proper Noun
(c) Common Noun
(d) Abstract Noun
(d) Material Noun

4. The *hen* lays eggs.
मुर्गी अण्डे देती है।
(a) Collective Noun
(b) Common Noun
(c) Proper Noun
(d) Abstract Noun
(e) Material Noun

5. *Gold* is a precious metal.
सोना एक महंगी धातु है।
(a) Collective Noun
(b) Common Noun
(c) Proper Noun
(d) Abstract Noun
(e) Material Noun

6. *A bend* of imps has beaten him.
शरारती बच्चों के एक झुण्ड ने उसकी पिटाई की है।
(a) Collective Noun
(b) Common Noun
(c) Proper Noun
(d) Abstract Noun
(e) Material Noun

7. Dinesh is *the Kapil Dev* of our team.
दिनेश हमारी टीम का कपिल देव है।
(a) Collective Noun
(b) Common Noun
(c) Proper Noun
(d) Abstract Noun
(e) Material Noun

8. The *Bible* is a holy book.
बाइबिल एक पवित्र किताब है।
(a) Collective Noun
(b) Common Noun

(c) Proper Noun
(d) Abstract Noun
(e) Material Noun

9. The *Committee* has changed its decission.
कमेटी ने अपना फैसला बदल लिया है।
(a) Collective Noun
(b) Common Noun
(c) Proper Noun
(d) Abstract Noun
(e) Material Noun

10. *Mango* is the king among all fruits.
आम सभी फलों का राजा है।
(a) Collective Noun
(b) Common Noun
(c) Proper Noun
(d) Abstract Noun
(e) Material Noun.

EXERCISE 2

नीचे दिये गये Sentences में विभिन्न प्रकार के Nouns को ढूंढें:

1. He is an honest man.
वह एक ईमानदार आदमी है।

2. Monkeys swing their buttocks in the trees.
वृक्षों पर बैठे बन्दर अपने चूतड़ों को हिलाते हैं।

3. I have a cow which gives a lot of milk.
मेरे पास एक गाय है जो बहुत दूध देती है।

4. Pratap works in a laboratory.
प्रताप एक प्रयोगशाला में काम करता है।

5. He lost his gold ring.
उसने अपनी सोने की अंगूठी खो दी।

6. A bunch of flowers falls down.
फूलों का एक गुच्छा नीचे गिरता है।

7. The rabbit runs very fast.
खरगोश बहुत तेज दौड़ता है।

8. A life of honesty paid him in the end.
ज़िन्दगी भर की ईमानदारी का फल उसे अन्ततः मिला।

9. Lead is a poisonous metal.
सीसा एक जहरीली धातु है।

10. Mr. JK Sharma is the Hitler of our school.
श्री जे.के. शर्मा हमारे स्कूल के हिटलर हैं।

11. Pawan drives in a rash manner.
पवन अन्धाधुन्ध गाड़ी चलाता है।

12. The citrus fruits are full of vitamin C.
खट्टे फल विटामिन C से भरपूर होते हैं।

EXERCISE 3

नीचे दिये गये Sentences का अंग्रेजी में अनुवाद करें:

1. शेर सबसे शक्तिशाली जानवर है।
2. वह आग से नहीं डरता।
3. वह सांप से डरता है।
4. दरवाजा किसने खटखटाया?
5. दूध से दही बनता है।
6. वह बहुत अच्छा लड़का है।
7. वह एक ईमानदार बूढ़ी औरत है।
8. कमेटी ने उसकी बात मान ली।
9. कल एक चोरों का गिरोह पकड़ा गया।
10. उसने चाभियों का एक गुच्छा मेरी तरफ फेंका।
11. मेरा भाई बाज़ार चला गया है।
12. वर्षा हो रही है।

Hints for Translation

4. खटखटाया = Knocked. 5. दही = curd.

Chapters 8

The Noun : Number

(संज्ञा : वचन)

There are three types of numbers in Sanskrit.

अंग्रेज़ी में दो प्रकार के Numbers होते हैं:

(1) Singular Number एकवचन

(2) Plural Number बहुवचन

Singular केवल एक ही व्यक्ति या वस्तु को प्रकट करता है जबकि Plural एक से अधिक वस्तुओं या व्यक्तियों को प्रकट करता है।

Examples

(a) There is a dog playing in the garden.
बाग में एक कुत्ता खेल रहा है।

(b) There are dogs playing in the garden.
बाग में कुत्ते खेल रहे हैं।

— Sentence No (a) से स्पष्ट पता चलता है कि एक कुत्ता है जो खेल रहा है।

— Sentence No (b) से कुत्तों की पूरी संख्या का पता नहीं चलता परन्तु इस बात का पक्का पता चल रहा है कि कुत्ते एक से अधिक हैं जो उद्यान में खेल रहे हैं। इसलिए यहां dogs Plural Number है।

नीचे कुछ और Singular Numbers के Plural Numbers बनाये गए हैं।

	Singular	*Meaning*	*Plural*
1.	Actor	अभिनेता	Actors
2.	Antenna	एंटीना	Antennae
3.	Arm	बाजू	Arms
4.	Article	वस्तु	Articles

	Singular	Meaning	Plural
5.	Ass	गधा	Asses
6.	Bamboo	बांस	Bamboos
7.	Base	आधार	Bases
8.	Bed	बिस्तरा	Beds
9.	Bee	मधुमक्खी	Bees
10.	Beggar	भिखारी	Beggars
11.	Boat	नाव	Boats
12.	Boy	लड़का	Boys
13.	Brief	संक्षिप्त, जांघिया	Briefs
14.	Brush	ब्रश	Brushes
15.	Buffalo	भैंस	Buffaloes
16.	Calf	बछड़ा	Calves
17.	Camel	ऊंट	Camels
18.	Cargo	सामान (समुद्री जहाज में)	Cargoes
19.	Chair	कुर्सी	Chairs
20.	Chairman	प्रधान	Chairmen
21.	Chief	मुख्य	Chiefs
22.	Church	गिरजाघर	Churches
23.	Circus	सर्कस	Circuses
24.	City	नगर	Cities
25.	Cliff	ऊंची चोटी, चट्टान	Cliffs
26.	Coach	गाड़ी	Coaches
27.	Coachman	गाड़ीवान	Coachmen
28.	Cock	मुर्गा	Cocks
29.	Cook	बावरची	Cooks
30.	Cow	गाय	Cows
31.	Cry	चीख	Cries
32.	Day	दिन	Days

	Singular	Meaning	Plural
33.	Deer	हिरण	Deer
34.	Dish	तश्तरी	Dishes
35.	Ditch	खाई	Ditches
36.	Duty	कर्त्तव्य	Duties
37.	Dwarf	बौना	Dwarfs
38.	Echo	गूंज	Echoes
39.	Egg	अण्डा	Eggs
40.	Essay	निबन्ध	Essays
41.	Examiner	परीक्षक	Examiners
42.	Farmer	कृषक	Farmers
43.	Father-in-law	ससुर	Fathers-in-law
44.	Fly	मक्खी	Flies
45.	Foot	पांव	Feet
46.	Gallery	गलियारा	Galleries
47.	Gas	गैस	Gases
48.	Gentleman	भद्रपुरुष	Gentlemen
49.	Gentleman-farmer	भद्र कृषक	Gentlemen-farmers
50.	Girl	लड़की	Girls
51.	Glass	शीशा	Glasses
52.	Goose	बत्तख	Geese
53.	Grief	दुःख	Griefs
54.	Half	आधा	Halves
55.	Halo	गोल चक्र (सिर पर)	Halos
56.	Hand	हाथ	Hands
57.	Hat	हैट	Hats
58.	Hero	नायक	Heroes
59.	Key	चाभी	Keys
60.	Kid	भेड़ का बच्चा, छोटा बच्चा (मनुष्य का)	Kids

	Singular	Meaning	Plural
61.	Kiss	चुम्बन	Kisses
62.	Kite	पतंग, चील	Kites
63.	Knife	चाकू	Knives
64.	Lady	स्त्री	Ladies
65.	Library	लाइब्रेरी	Libraries
66.	Life	जीवन	Lives
67.	Loaf	रोटी का टुकड़ा	Loaves
68.	Loss	हानि	Losses
69.	Louse	जूं	Lice
70.	Man	पुरुष	Men
71.	Man-of-war	सैनिक, जांबाज़	Men-of-war
72.	Man-servant	नौकर	Men-servants
73.	Mango	आम	Mangoes
74.	Match	मैच	Matches
75.	Monkey	बन्दर	Monkeys
76.	Month	मास	Months
77.	Mosquito	मच्छर	Mosquitoes
78.	Mother-in-law	सास	Mothers-in-law
79.	Mouse	चूहा	Mice
80.	Mouth	मुंह	Mouths
81.	Negro	हब्शी	Negroes
82.	Night	रात्रि	Nights
83.	Owl	उल्लू	Owls
84.	Page	पृष्ठ	Pages
85.	**Parrot**	तोता	**Parrots**
86.	**Pen**	**कलम**	**Pens**
87.	Photo	फोटो	Photos
88.	Play	खेल, नाटक	Plays

	Singular	*Meaning*	*Plural*
89.	Potato	आलू	Potatoes
90.	Princess	राजकुमारी	Princesses
91.	Proof	प्रमाण	Proofs
92.	Radio	रेडियो	Radios
93.	Ray	किरण	Rays
94.	Roof	छत	Roofs
95.	Root	जड़	Roots
96.	Shelf	शेल्फ	Shelves
97.	Speech	भाषण	Speeches
98.	Storey	मंजिल	Storeys
99.	Story	कथा	Stories
100.	Strike	हड़ताल	Strikes
101.	Studio	स्टूडियो	Studios
102.	Table	मेज	Tables
103.	Tailor	दर्ज़ी	Tailors
104.	Temple	मन्दिर	Temples
105.	Thief	चोर	Thieves
106.	Tomato	टमाटर	Tomatoes
107.	Tooth	दांत	Teeth
108.	Town	नगर	Towns
109.	Toy	खिलौना	Toys
110.	Tree	पेड़	Trees
111.	Volcano	ज्वालामुखी पर्वत	Volcanoes
112.	Watch	घड़ी	Watches
113.	Week	सप्ताह	Weeks
114.	Wife	पत्नी	Wives
115.	Woe	दुःख	Woes
116.	Wolf	भेड़िया	Wolves

	Singular	*Meaning*	*Plural*
117.	Woman	स्त्री	Women
118.	Woman-servant	नौकरानी	Women-servants
119.	Zoo	चिड़ियाघर	Zoos

Note: जैसा कि दिये गये Singular-Plural से स्पष्ट है :

(1) प्रायः Singular को हम केवल 's' लगाकर Plural में बदल देते हैं।

(2) जिन शब्दों के अन्त में 'ss,' 'ch', 'sh' आदि हों—जैसे ass, match, brush आदि—उनको Plural में बदलते समय 'es' लगते हैं।

(3) जिन शब्दों के अन्त में 'o' होता है—जैसे कि mango, potato आदि—उनके अन्त में 'es' जोड़कर इसे Plural में बदल देते हैं।

(4) कई Nouns के अन्त में 'o' लगा होने पर भी—जैसे कि photo, radio आदि—उनके Plural में केवल 's' लगता है।

(5) कुछ Nouns के अन्त में 'f' या 'fe' लगा रहता है—जैसे knife, loaf, life, etc. इसका Plural f या fe को ves में बदलकर करते हैं।

(6) शब्दों के अन्त में 'f' लगा होने पर Plural में केवल 's' लगेगा। *e.g.*, dwarf, hoof, etc.

(**Note:** Dwarves और hooves भी ठीक माने जाते हैं।)

(7) यदि किसी Noun के अन्त में 'y' हो और उससे पहले Vowel न हो तो, Plural बनाते समय, 'y,' 'ies' में बदल देते हैं जैसे city, story, lady etc.

(8) यदि 'y' से पहले Vowel लगा हो जैसे कि storey, day, key, toy आदि में, तो इन Nouns के Plurals केवल 's' लगाने से बन जायेंगे।

(9) कुछ शब्दों की Plural form internal vowels के बदलने से बन जाती है। जैसे man, mouse etc.

(10) अधिकतर Compound Nouns में—जैसे son-in-law, passer-by etc. में —प्रथम शब्द के साथ 's' जोड़ा जाता है।

(11) कुछ Compound Nouns में—जैसे कि stand-by, lady doctor etc में—'s' बाद के शब्द के साथ लगता है।

(12) कुछ Compound Nouns में—जैसेकि man-servant, gentleman-farmer आदि में—'s' दोनों शब्दों के साथ लगता है।

Chapter 9

The Noun : Gender

(संज्ञा : लिंग)

Gender चार प्रकार के होते हैं :

(A) Feminine Gender (C) Common Gender

(B) Masculine Gender (D) Neuter Gender

(A) Feminine Gender: जो Noun Female (स्त्रीलिंग) को प्रकट करता है, उसे Feminine Gender कहते हैं, *e.g.*, Mother, Sister, Woman, Queen, etc.

(B) Masculine Gender: जो Noun Male (पुल्लिग) को प्रकट करता है, उसे Masculine Gender कहते हैं, *e.g.*, Father, Brother, Man, King etc.

(C) Common Gender: जो Noun दोनों स्त्रीलिंग व पुल्लिग के लिये प्रयोग में लाया जाता है, उसे Common Gender कहते हैं, *e.g.*, Baby, Friend, Student, Person etc.

(D) Neuter Gender: जो Noun किसी निर्जीव वस्तु के लिये प्रयोग में लाया जाये, उसे Neuter Gender कहते हैं। *e.g.*, Book, Table, Pen, Copy etc.

कुछ Commonly Use होने वाले Nouns के Masculine Genders और Feminine Genders नीचे दिये गये हैं :

	Masculine	*Meaning*	*Feminine*
1.	Abbot	पादरी	Abbess
2.	Actor	अभिनेता	Actress
3.	Boy	लड़का	Girl
4.	Brother	भाई	Sister
5.	Bull	बैल	Cow
6.	Count	नवाब	Countess

	Masculine	Meaning	Feminine
7.	Deer	हिरण	Doe
8.	Dog	कुत्ता	Bitch
9.	Drake	बतख	Duck
10.	Drone	मधुमक्खी	Bee
11.	Duke	नवाब	Duchess
12.	Father	पिता	Mother
13.	Father-in-law	ससुर	Mother-in-law
14.	Fisherman	मछुआ	Fisherwoman
15.	Fox	लोमड़	Vixen

(Note : अब 'Vixen' शब्द अधिकतर किसी झगड़ालू स्त्री के लिए प्रयोग होता है।)

	Masculine	Meaning	Feminine
16.	Gander	बतख (पु.)	Goose
17.	Gentleman	भद्रपुरुष	(Gentle) Lady
18.	Giant	देव, राक्षस	Giantess
19.	God	परमात्मा	Goddess
20.	Grandfather	दादा	Grandmother
21.	Grandson	पोता	Granddaughter
22.	He-goat	बकरा	She-goat
23.	Headmaster	मुख्याध्यापक	Headmistress
24.	Hero	नायक	Heroine
25.	Horse	घोड़ा	Mare
26.	Host	यजमान	Hostess
27.	Hunter	शिकारी	Huntress
28.	Husband	पति	Wife
29.	Jew	यहूदी	Jewess
30.	King	राजा	Queen
31.	Lion	बब्बर शेर	Lioness
32.	Man	पुरुष	Woman
33.	Master	मालिक	Mistress
34.	Milkman	गोपी	Milkmaid
35.	Mr.	श्रीमान	Mrs

	Masculine	Meaning	Feminine
36.	Negro	हब्शी	Negress
37.	Ox	बैल	Cow
38.	Pappa	पापा	Mamma
39.	Peacock	मोर	Peahen
40.	Poet	कवि	Poetess
41.	Priest	पुजारी	Priestess
42.	Prince	राजकुमार	Princess
43.	**Prophet**	**अवतार**	**Prophetess**
44.	**Shepherd**	**गडेरिया/मेषपाल**	**Shepherdess**
45.	Sir	श्रीमान	Madam
46.	Son-in-law	दामाद	Daughter-in-law
47.	Stag	बारहसिंघा	Hind
48.	Uncle	चाचा	Aunt

Note: (1) English में Grammarians तीन प्रकार के genders ही बताते हैं; अर्थात् Masculine, Feminine and Neuter. Masculine और Feminine Genders के लिए प्रयोग होने वाले Common शब्दों को Neuter Gender में सम्मिलित करना अधिक उचित नहीं लगता। इसलिए इन्हें Common Gender के रूप में माना जाना चाहिए। इस बात का प्रावधान English के कोशों में भी है।

(2) नीचे Common Genders के उदाहरण दिये जा रहे हैं—अर्थात् वह शब्द जो Masculine Gender और Feminine Gender दोनों के लिए प्रयोग किये जाते हैं। वास्तव में, अब इसका Trend दिन-प्रतिदिन बढ़ रहा है:

Infant, baby, child, student, doctor, lawyer, judge, client, customer, director, nurse, advocate, patient, inspector, teacher, professor, governor, president, minister, beggar, thief, robber, pickpocket, culprit, saint, sage, criminal, preacher, dancer, producer, musician, singer, worshipper, engineer, architect, technician, manager, operator, mechanic, accountant, clerk, librarian, supervisor.

(3) हम देखते हैं कि Common Gender का प्रयोग बहुत से Professions में होता है।

(4) प्राय: हम He-cat को भी 'Cat' कह देते हैं।

(5) बहुत से Animals जैसे elephant, fox, jackal आदि का वर्णन करते समय Gender को विशेष महत्त्व नहीं दिया जाता। इसी प्रकार छोटे जीवों rat, squirrel, lizard, spider etc. के बारे में विशेष नियम नहीं है।

Chapter 10

Formation of Nouns from Adjectives

(विशेषण से संज्ञा बनाना)

	Adjective	Meaning	Noun
1.	Able	योग्य	Ability
2.	Active	काम में व्यस्त, चुस्त	Activity
3.	Actual	वास्तविक	Actuality
4.	Adequate	पर्याप्त	Adequacy
5.	Advisable	परामर्श देने योग्य	Advice
6.	Alert	सतर्क	Alertness
7.	Amusing	मनोरंजक	Amusement
8.	Angry	क्रोधित	Anger
9.	Anxious	चिन्तित	Anxiety
10.	Arrogant	घमण्डी	Arrogance
11.	Attractive	आकर्षक	Attraction
12.	**Awful, awesome**	**भयानक/विस्मयकारी**	**Awe**
13.	**Beautiful**	**सुन्दर**	**Beauty**
14.	**Bitter**	**कड़वा**	**Bitterness**
15.	**Bold**	**निडर**	**Boldness**
16.	**Brave**	**बहादुर**	**Bravery**
17.	**Brilliant**	**प्रतिभाशाली**	**Brilliance**
18.	**Calm**	**शांत**	**Calmness**
19.	**Capable**	**योग्य**	**Capacity**
20.	**Careful**	**सावधान**	**Care**
21.	**Certain**	**निश्चित**	**Certainty**

	Adjective	*Meaning*	*Noun*
22.	Cheerful	प्रसन्न	Cheerfulness
23.	Clever	चालाक	Cleverness
24.	**Cloudy**	**धुंधला, बदली**	**Cloud**
25.	**Cold**	**ठंडा**	**Coldness**
26.	**Complete**	**पूर्ण**	**Completion**
27.	**Confident**	**विश्वास रखने वाला**	**Confidence**
28.	**Cruel**	**निर्दयी, कठोर**	**Cruelity**
29.	Deep	गहरा	Depth
30.	**Desirous**	**इच्छुक**	**Desire**
31.	**Difficult**	**कठिन**	**Difficulty**
32.	Eager	उत्सुक	Eagerness
33.	Efficient	निपुण	Efficiency
34.	**Eligible**	**चुने जाने योग्य/उपयुक्त**	**Eligibility**
35.	**Eminent**	**प्रसिद्ध**	**Eminence**
36.	**Exact**	**ठीक**	**Exactness**
37.	**Exclusive**	**अकेला**	**Exclusion**
38.	**Faithful**	**विश्वासी**	**Faith. Faithfulness**
39.	Firm	मज़बूत	Firmness
40.	**Fit**	**योग्य**	**Fitness**
41.	**Free**	**आजाद**	**Freedom**
42.	Generous	उदार	Generosity
43.	Gentle	भद्र	Gentleness
44.	Great	महान	Greatness
45.	Harmful	हानिकारक	Harm
46.	Healthy	स्वस्थ	Health, Healthfulness
47.	Hearty, cordial	हार्दिक	Heart
48.	Helpful	सहायक	Help
49.	Honest	ईमानदार	Honesty
50.	Honourable	माननीय	Honour

	Adjective	Meaning	Noun
51.	Ill	बीमार	Illness
52.	Important	महत्त्वपूर्ण	Importance
53.	Injurious	हानिकारक	Injury
54.	**Innocent**	**मासूम/निदोष**	Innocence
55.	**Intelligent**	**बुद्धिमान**	Intelligence
56.	**Kind**	**दयालु**	Kindness
57.	**Legible**	**पठनीय**	**Legibility**
58.	Long	लम्बा	Length
59.	Loyal	स्वामिभक्त	Loyalty
60.	Lucid	स्पष्ट	Lucidity
61.	Lucky, luckless	(अ) भाग्यशाली	Luck
62.	Modest	नम्र	Modesty
63.	Natural	प्राकृतिक	Nature, Naturalism
64.	Neat	साफ	Neatness
65.	New	नया	Newness
66.	Nice	बढ़िया	Nicety, Niceness
67.	Noble	अच्छा	Nobility
68.	Novel	नया	Novelty
69.	Obedient	आज्ञाकारी	Obedience
70.	Painful	दु:खदायी	Pain
71.	Partial	अधूरा, पछपातपूर्ण	Partiality
72.	Patient	संतोषी	Patience
73.	Perfect	पूर्ण	Perfection
74.	Poor	गरीब	Poverty
75.	Popular	सर्वप्रिय	Popularity
76.	Possible	सम्भव	Possibility
77.	Present	वर्तमान, उपस्थित	Presence
78.	**Prudent**	**विवेकी**	Prudence
79.	**Pure**	**निर्मल**	**Purity**
80.	**Rapid**	**तेज**	Rapidity
81.	**Real**	**वास्तविक**	**Reality**

	Adjective	Meaning	Noun
82.	Regular	नियमपूर्वक, नियमात्मक	Regularity
83.	Religious	धार्मिक	Religion
84.	Rich	धनी	Richness, Riches
85.	Risky	खतरनाक	Risk
86.	Rude	अशिष्ट	Rudeness
87.	Sad	उदास	Sadness
88.	Secret	गुप्त	Secrecy
89.	Serious	गम्भीर	Seriousness
90.	Sharp	तेज़	Sharpness
91.	Shy	शर्मीला	Shyness
92.	Silent	शांत	Silence
93.	Sincere	सच्चा	Sincerity
94.	Skilful	निपुण	Skill
95.	Smart	चुस्त	Smartness
96.	Solemn	गम्भीर	Solemnity
97.	Sorry	खेद	Sorrow
98.	Speedy	तेज़	Speed
99.	Strong	मजबूत	Strength
100.	Stupid	मूर्ख	Stupidity
101.	Successful	सफल	Success
102.	Tasty, tasteful	स्वादिष्ट	Taste
103.	Terrible	भयानक	Terror
104.	Tolerable	सहनीय	Tolerance, Toleration
105.	Tragic	दुःखदायी, दुःखित	Tragedy
106.	True, truthful	सच्चा	Truth, Truthfulness
107.	Urgent	आवश्यक	Urgency
108.	Valid	ठीक	Validity
109.	Wealthy	धनी	Wealth
110.	Wise	बुद्धिमान	Wisdom
111.	Young	नवयुवक	Youth
112.	Zonal	क्षेत्रीय	Zone

Chapter 11

Formation of Nouns from Verbs
(क्रिया से संज्ञा बनाना)

(**Note:** Verbs से बनने वाले Common Nouns Brackets में दिये गये हैं।)

	Verb	*Meaning*	*Nouns*
1.	Add	जोड़ना	Addition
2.	Admire	प्रशंसा करना	Admiration
3.	Adopt	ग्रहण करना	Adoption
4.	Advise	परामर्श देना	Advice
5.	Agree	सहमत होना	Agreement
6.	Alter	बदलना	Alteration
7.	Appoint	नियुक्त करना	Appointment
8.	Approve	स्वीकृति देना	Approval
9.	Arrive	पहुंचना	Arrival
10.	Attach	बाँधना, जोड़ना	Attachment
11.	Attract	आकर्षित करना	Attraction
12.	Avoid	बचना	Avoidance
13.	Beautify	सुन्दर बनाना	Beauty
14.	Believe	विश्वास करना	Belief
15.	Calculate	गिनना	Calculation
16.	Cancel	समाप्त करना	Cancellation
17.	Celebrate	मनाना	Celebration
18.	Certify	सिद्ध करना	Certification, (Certificate)

	Verb	*Meaning*	*Nouns*
19.	Collect	इकट्ठा करना	Collection (Collector)
20.	Combine	इकट्ठा करना	Combination
21.	Compete	मुकाबला करना	Competition
22.	Confess	स्वीकार करना	Confession
23.	Confirm	पक्का करना	Confirmation
24.	Congratulate	बधाई देना	Congratulation(s)
25.	Connect	जोड़ना	Connection
26.	Consult	परामर्श लेना	(Consultant) Consultation, Consultancy
27.	Continue	जारी रखना	Continuation, Continuity
28.	Correct	ठीक करना	Correction
29.	Correspond	पत्रव्यवहार करना	Corespondence
30.	Decide	निर्णय लेना	Decision
31.	Demolish	गिराना	Demolition
32.	Deny	इन्कार करना	Denial
33.	Depart	जुदा होना	Departure
34.	Die	मरना	Death
35.	Discuss	विवाद करना	Discussion
36.	Dismiss	बर्खास्त करना	Dismissal
37.	Donate	दान देना	Donation, (Donor)
38.	Enclose	बन्द करना	Enclosure
39.	**Enjoy**	**आनन्द मनाना**	**Enjoyment**
40.	**Exist**	**जीवित रहना**	**Existence**
41.	**Explain**	**व्यवहार करना**	**Explanation**
42.	**Fascinate**	**मोहित करना/होना**	**Fascination**
43.	Flatter	चापलूसी करना	Flattery, (Flatterer)
44.	Follow	अनुसरण करना	(Follower), Following
45.	Found	नींव रखना	Foundation

	Verb	*Meaning*	*Nouns*
46.	Gamble	जुआ खेलना	(Gambler), Gambling
47.	Grieve	दुःख मनाना	Grief
48.	Grow	बढ़ना	Growth
49.	Guide	पथप्रदर्शन करना	Guidance, (Guide)
50.	Harass	तंग करना	Harrassment
51.	Hate	घृणा करना	Hatred
52.	Imagine	कल्पना करना	Imagination
53.	Impress	प्रभावित करना	Impression
54.	Improve	बेहतर करना	Improvement
55.	**Include**	**शामिल करना**	**Inclusion**
56.	**Infect**	**संक्रामक रोग फैलाना**	**Infection**
57.	Inform	सूचित करना	Information
58.	Insist	बल देना, जिद करना	Insistence
59.	Inspect	निरीक्षण करना	Inspection
60.	Invite	निमन्त्रण देना	Invitation
61.	Know	जानना	Knowledge
62.	Live	जीवित रहना	Life
63.	Locate	पता लगाना	Location
64.	Maintain	कायम रखना	Maintenance
65.	Marry	विवाह करना	Marriage
66.	Mix	मिलाना	Mixture
67.	Modify	बदलना	Modification
68.	Move	हिलाना	Movement
69.	Murder	क़त्ल करना	Murder
70.	Negotiate	सौदा करना	Negotiation, (Negotiator)
71.	Notify	नोटिस निकालना	Notification
72.	Obey	आदेश मानना	Obedience
73.	Objecte	एतराज़ करना	Objection

	Verb	Meaning	Nouns
74.	Omit	छोड़ देना	Omission
75.	Oppose	विरोध करना	Opposition
76.	Originate	आरम्भ होना	Origin
77.	Participate	भाग लेना	Participation
78.	Perform	करना	Performance
79.	Permit	आज्ञा लेना	Permission
80.	Please	प्रसन्न करना	Pleasure
81.	Pray	प्रार्थना करना	Prayer
82.	Press	बल लगाना	Pressure
83.	Prohibit	रोकना, मना करना	Prohibiton
84.	Propose	सुझाव देना	Proposal
85.	Protect	रक्षा करना	Protection
86.	Prove	सिद्ध करना	Proof
87.	Punish	दण्ड देना	Punishment
88.	Quicken	तेज करना	Quickness
89.	Realise	महसूस करना	Realisation
90.	Recommend	सिफारिश करना	Recommendation
91.	Recover	दुबारा प्राप्त करना, स्वास्थ्य ठीक होना	Recovery
92.	Refuse	इन्कार करना	Refusal
93.	Reject	नामंजूर करना	Rejection
94.	Relieve	छोड़ देना, आराम देना	Relief
95.	Rely	निर्भर होना	Reliance
96.	Remove	हटाना	Removal
97.	Resign	त्यागपत्र देना	Resignation
98.	Rob	लूटना	Robber
99.	Select	चुनना	Selection

	Verb	Meaning	Nouns
100.	Settle	रहना	Settlement
101.	Speak	बोलना	Speech
102.	State	कहना	Statement
103.	Stop	रुकना	Stoppage
104.	Stregthen	शक्तिशाली बनाना	Strength
105.	Succeed	सफल होना	Success
106.	Suppose	अनुमान लगाना	Supposition
107.	Survive	बच निकलना	Survival
108.	Teach	पढ़ाना	Teaching
109.	Think	सोचना	Thought
110.	Threaten	धमकी देना	Threat
111.	Treat	व्यवहार करना	Treatment
112.	Unite	इकट्ठे होना	Unity, union
113.	Vex	तंग करना	Vexation

Chapter 12

The Pronoun

(सर्वनाम)

(1) Pronoun वे शब्द होते हैं जो किसी Noun (संज्ञा) की जगह पर प्रयुक्त होते हैं।

(i) Rakesh belongs to a noble family. *He* is an honest boy.

इस Sentence में 'He' शब्द 'Rakesh' शब्द (Noun) की जगह पर Use किया गया है। अत: 'He' word एक Pronoun है।

(ii) Laxmi is a very sweet girl. *She* lives two doors ahead of my house.

इस Sentence में 'She' शब्द 'Laxmi', जो कि एक Noun है, की जगह पर Use किया गया है। अत: 'She' word एक Pronoun है।

(2) (a) अगर मैं आपको (You) अपने बारे में कुछ कहता हूँ, अर्थात् अगर 'I' शब्द 'you' को कुछ कहे तो 'I' First Person कहलाता है, जबकि 'You' Second Person कहलाता है। इस तरह जब 'I' किसी 'You' से 'He' या 'She' के बारे में बात करता है, ('He' तथा 'She' वहां पर नहीं हैं या दूर कहीं हैं) तो 'He व She' को Third Person कहा जाता है।

अगले पृष्ठ पर दिये गये Table में यह सब कुछ समझाया गया है।

Note: सभी Pronouns के Plural forms भी होते हैं।

Personal Pronouns Possessive Cases में Nouns से पहले आते हैं तथा कुछ Nouns को Qualify करते हैं। इस तरह Pronouns होने के साथ-साथ वे Possessive Adjective अथवा कभी-कभी Pronominal Adjective का भी काम करते हैं।

(i) This is your pen. (ii) This is my book.

(iii) This is his bag. (iv) This is her bag.

(v) These are your bags. (vi) These are their bags.

Table I: Cases of Personal Pronouns

	Cases	*Nominative*	*Possessive or Genitive*	*Objective or Accusative*
First Person	Masculine (Singular)	I	my, mine	me
	Feminine (Singular)	I	my, mine	me
	Plural	We	ours, our	us
Second Person	Masculine (Singular)	you	your, yours	you
	Feminine (Singular)	you	your, yours	you
	Plural	you	your, yours	you
Third Person	Masculine (Singular)	He	his	him
	Neuter (Singular)	It	its	it
	Feminine (Singular)	She	her, hers	her
	Plural (All Genders)	They	their, theirs	them

ऊपर दिये गये Sentences में my, his, her, your, their etc. Pronoun के साथ "Possessive Adjective" या कभी कभी "Pronominal Adjective" का भी काम करते हैं।

(4) कई बार Possessive Case में Pronouns Nouns के एकदम साथ नहीं आते:

(i) This bag is mine. (ii) That bag is yours.
(iii) This book is hers. (iv) Those books are theirs.
(v) These pencils are ours.

इस तरह के Pronouns को "Possessive Pronouns" कहते हैं।

EXERCISE 1

नीचे दिये गये Sentences को ध्यान से पढ़ें व बतायें कि कौन सा Pronoun कौन से Noun के लिये Use किया गया है। The first sentence has been done for you.

(i) In the match, Ravi reached the extreme of brilliance and *he* managed to get a win for *his* team.

इस Sentence में He तथा His दोनों Pronoun हैं तथा ये Ravi—जो कि एक

Proper Noun है—की जगह पर प्रयोग में लाये गये हैं।

(ii) Jagdish is a naughty boy. He befools others with his naughty tricks.

(iii) It can never be a good day for those who try to make a noise in the classroom.

(iv) Mohan! Stand up on the bench. You cannot be spared for such follies.

(v) Dinesh seems to be a gentle boy. He never quibbles whenever I point out his weakness.

(vi) You, Tarsem. Why are you bent upon losing your credit by making a fool of yourself through your foolish act? Remember, it will not lead you anywhere?

Chapter 13

The Usage of Pronouns

(सर्वनाम का प्रयोग)

(1) पहले बताया गया है कि Pronouns वे शब्द होते हैं जो Noun की जगह पर प्रयोग में लाये जाते हैं, जैसे कि:

Ram is a gentle boy. He is intellegent also.

इस Sentence में 'He' word Ram को ही प्रकट करता है क्योंकि Ram Masculine है तथा Singular है, इसलिये 'He'–जो एक Singular Masculine को प्रकट करता है–प्रयोग किया गया है।

(2) जब एक Singular Noun तथा एक Singular Pronoun (और दो Singular Pronouns) को 'and' शब्द से जोड़ा जाता है, तो जो Pronoun हम उनको प्रकट करने के लिये प्रयोग में लायेंगे, वह Plural होगा।

Examples

(a) Ram and I are good friends. We always go to the school together.
राम तथा मैं पक्के मित्र हैं। हम स्कूल हमेशा इकट्ठे जाते हैं।

(b) He and she are talking to each other. They sometimes laugh in between.
वह तथा वह (महिला) आपस में बातें कर रहे हैं। वे कभी-कभी बीच में हंस पड़ते हैं।

(3) जब दो या दो से अधिक Singular Nouns का प्रयोग and शब्द से जोड़ कर किया जाता है, तो इनका Pronoun, जो इनको प्रकट करता है, हमेशा Plural Form में होता है।

Examples

(a) Pawan and Girish make a noise in the class. They are naughty boys.
पवन और गिरीश कक्षा में शोर मचाते हैं। दोनों शरारती लड़के हैं।

(b) Ravi and Sheela are fast friends. They do their home-work together.
रवि व शीला पक्के मित्र हैं। वे दोनों घर का काम इकट्ठे करते हैं।

(4) Singular Nouns—जो कि 'and' Word द्वारा जोड़े गये हों लेकिन 'Every' या 'Each,' शब्द Noun से पहले Use में लाया गया हो—में Singular Pronoun का प्रयोग होता है।

Examples

(a) Every boy and girl of this class, Please listen to me carefully. Otherwise, I shall not spare him or her.
इस कक्षा का हर एक लड़का व लड़की मेरी बात को ध्यान से सुने। नहीं तो, उसे क्षमा नहीं करूँगा।

(b) Every man and woman of this country is ready to sacrifice his or her life.
इस देश का हर एक आदमी व औरत अपने जीवन का बलिदान देने को तैयार है।

Collective Noun

(5) जब कोई Pronoun Collective Noun को प्रकट करता है तो वह Neuter Gender की Form में Use होता है।

Examples

(a) The cabinet has given its first decision.
कैबिनेट ने अपना पहला निर्णय सुना दिया है (सामूहिक रूप में)।

(b) The committee has shown its disagreement with the customers.
कमेटी ग्राहकों से अपनी असहमति व्यक्त कर चुकी है (सामूहिक रूप में)।

(c) The Air Force has shown its mettle to the enemy.
हवाई सेना दुश्मन को अपना अदम्य साहस दिखा चुकी है (सामूहिक रूप में)।

Plural Numbers

Plural Number में जब Collective Noun एक-एक व्यक्ति के रूप में काम करता है, तो Pronoun भी Plural Form में ही Use होता है।

Examples

(a) The cabinet have given their first decision.
कैबिनेट ने अपना पहला फैसला सुना दिया है (हर एक मैम्बर ने)।

(b) The police have done well with their jobs during the past few months.
पुलिस ने पिछले कुछ महीनों में (हर एक मैम्बर ने) बहुत अच्छे काम किये हैं।

(6) Plural Pronoun का प्रयोग समय के अनुसार होता है जबकि Singular Noun तथा एक Plural Noun दोनों 'or' शब्द से जुड़े हों, जिसमें Plural Noun बाद में आता हो।

Examples

(a) Either Shyam or his friends can do their jobs upto the mark.
श्याम या उसके मित्र अपने कामों को सही ढंग से कर सकते हैं।

(b) Either Reeta or her friends have shown their skills in this type of job.
रीटा या उसकी सहेलियां इस तरह के काम में अपनी कला दिखा चुकी हैं।

(7) 'Than' शब्द के प्रयोग के तुरन्त बाद Nominative Case में Pronoun का प्रयोग होता है।

Examples

(a) Mohan is more handsome than I.
मोहन मुझसे ज़्यादा सुन्दर है।

Note: आजकल व्यावहारिक रूप में 'I' के स्थान पर 'me' का प्रयोग होता है।

(b) Renu is taller than you.
रेणु आप से ज्यादा लम्बी है।

(8) जिन Sentences में Pronoun, Object के रूप में सामने आता है, वहां Accusative Case का प्रयोग अनिवार्य होता है।

Examples

(a) These pens are for you and me.
यह पैन तुम्हारे व मेरे लिये हैं।

(b) These bags are for you and me.
यह बैग तुम्हारे व मेरे लिये है।

(9) जिस Sentence में सभी Persons (I, II and III) को Nominative Case में प्रयोग में लाया जाता है, ऐसे Sentence में प्राय: Second Person पहले, इसके बाद Third Person तथा अन्त में First Person का प्रयोग होता है।

Examples

(a) You, he and I, would go for a walk.
तुम, वह तथा मैं सैर के लिये जायेंगे।

(b) You, Tony and I would not talk to him.
तुम, टोनी व मैं उससे बात नहीं करेंगे।

(c) You and he do not make a noise.
तुम व वह शोर नहीं मचाते।

(10) जब कोई काम गलत हो जाता है, तो ऊपर दिये गये Pronouns का Order बदल जाता है।

Examples

(a) I, he and you made so many blunders.
मैंने, उसने व तुमने बहुत सी गल्तियां कीं।

(b) I, Sandeep and you have not behaved properly.
मैंने, संदीप और तुमने अच्छी तरह से व्यवहार नहीं किया है।

(11) जिन Sentences में Pronoun एक से अधिक Noun और Pronoun of Different Persons को प्रकट करता है, इस प्रकार के Sentences में—(A) यदि Pronoun First Person के साथ-साथ Noun या Pronoun Second या Third Person है तो Pronoun First Person Plural होगा।

Examples

(a) Mukesh and I have made our decisions.
मुकेश व मैं अपना फैसला कर चुके हैं।

(b) Tony and I have changed our minds.
टोनी व मैं अपने विचार बदल चुके हैं।

(B) यदि Pronoun Second Person के साथ-साथ Noun or Pronoun Third Person भी होता है तो इन सभी को प्रकट करने वाला Pronoun ज़रूर Second Plural होगा।

Examples

(a) You and he take your meal together.
तुम तथा वह अपना भोजन एक साथ खाते हो।

(b) You and Kartar are stuck to your work.
तुम व करतार अपने काम में लगे हुए हैं।

EXERCISE

नीचे दिये गये वाक्यों का अंग्रेजी में अनुवाद करो:

1. वह आपसे अधिक ताकतवर है।
2. इस क्लास का कोई भी लड़का या लड़की शोर करता हुआ न पकड़ा जाये।
3. सोनू व मोनू दोनों भाई हैं। वे किसी की बात नहीं सुनते।

4. कमेटी ने सही फैसला किया है।
5. ज्यूरी को आज सुनवाई करनी है।
6. तुम तथा वह क्यों अपनी बात मनवाने पर तुले हो?
7. राजेश हरी से ज़्यादा चालाक है।
8. हमारी सेनाओं ने दुश्मन को नाकों चने चबवा दिये।
9. मैं, तुम व वह झूठ बोलते हुए पकड़े गये।
10. मोहन या उसके दोस्त लोगों से लड़ाई मोल लेते हैं।
11. वह मुझसे अधिक मोटी है।
12. मैं तथा गणेश पक्के मित्र हैं। हम एक दूसरे के घर में ही सो जाते हैं।
13. हर आदमी व औरत इस बात को ध्यान से सुने कि उसे देश के लिये मर मिटने को सदा तैयार रहना चाहिए।
14. गणेश मुकेश से पतला है।
15. तुम, वह तथा मैं बाज़ार में अपने लिये खाने-पीने का सामान लेने जायेंगे।
16. पुलिस ने कल शहर में छापे मारे तथा उन्होंने काफी हथियार बरामद किये।
17. वह आपसे ज़्यादा गोरा है।
18. वह आपसे ज्यादा बुद्धिमान है।
19. मनजीत व रणजीत दोनों भाई हैं। वे सबसे झूठ बोलते हैं।
20. तुम्हें तथा मुझे कोई भी अलग नहीं कर सकता।
21. जो भी नकल करता पकड़ा जायेगा, उसे दण्ड मिलेगा।
22. तुम्हें आपस में भाइयों की तरह रहना चाहिए।
23. हमें अपने देश को कभी धोखा नहीं देना चाहिए।
24. जो दूसरों के लिए गड्ढा खोदता है, स्वयं उसमें गिरता है।
25. कभी किसी से डरो नहीं, चाहे वह कोई भी हो।

Chapter 14

The Usage of the Pronoun 'It'

(सर्वनाम 'It' का प्रयोग)

(1) 'It' Impersonel Pronoun के रूप में उस समय Use होता है, जब यह Impersonal Verb का Subject बन जाता है।

Examples

(a) It hailed and hailed.
ओले पड़ते ही रह गये।

(b) It barks and barks.
वह भौंकता ही रहता है।
(कुत्ता लगातार भौंकता है।)

(c) It roars and roars.
वह (अर्थात् बादल) गरजता ही रहता है।

(2) 'It' का प्रयोग किसी Lifeless वस्तु या छोटे जीव के लिए किया जाता है।

Examples

(a) I returned his umbrella because it was full of holes.
मैंने उसका छाता लौटा दिया क्योंकि यह सुराख़ों से भरा पड़ा था।

(b) My friend has broken my bicycle and so, I have sent it for repair.
मेरे दोस्त ने मेरी साइकिल तोड़ दी है और इसलिए, मैंने इसे मरम्मत के लिये भेज दिया है।

(c) He sent me a letter but it was not neatly written.
उसने मुझे एक पत्र भेजा लेकिन यह साफ नहीं लिखा गया था।

EXERCISE 1

1. बर्फ पड़ती ही जा रही है।

2. इससे कोई अन्तर नहीं पड़ता।

3. यह चमकता ही जाता है।

4. मैंने उसकी किताब वापिस कर दी

क्योंकि यह फटी हुई थी।

5. उसने मेरी कलम मुझे वापिस दिया क्योंकि यह लिखती नहीं थी।

6. बाहर वर्षा हो रही है।

7. वह मेरा बैग वापिस कर देगी क्योंकि यह छोटा है।

8. वर्षा होती ही जाती है।

9. मैंने उसकी कापी वापिस कर दी क्योंकि उसमें कुछ नहीं लिखा था।

10. उसे मनाने का यत्न करना व्यर्थ है।

(3) 'It' शब्द का प्रयोग प्राय: छोटे जानवरों या Domestic Animals के लिए भी किया जाता है।

Examples

(a) I like the rabbit when it jumps.
मुझे खरगोश अच्छा लगता है जब वह कूदता है।

(b) I hate a snake because it can never be a friend to man.
मैं सांप से घृणा करता हूँ क्योंकि यह मनुष्य का मित्र कभी नहीं बन सकता।

(c) I love a puppy when it is bouncing.
मैं पिल्ले से प्यार करता हूँ जब यह छलांग लगाता है।

(4) 'It' शब्द का प्रयोग छोटे बच्चे को सम्बोधित करने के लिये भी किया जाता है।

Examples

(a) The baby was smiling and so, I lifted it up.
बच्चा मुस्करा रहा था और इसलिए मैंने इसे उठा लिया।

(b) I did not look at the baby as it was playing.
मैंने बच्चे की तरफ नहीं देखा क्योंकि वह खेल रहा था।

Note: ऊपर दिये गये Sentences में 'it' शब्द Baby के 'Sex' के बारे में नहीं बताता। अगर बच्चे का Sex भी जानना हो तो Sentence इस तरह बनेगा।

(i) The baby was smiling, I lifted him up.
बच्चा मुस्करा रहा था और इसलिए मैंने उसे उठा लिया।
'him' शब्द का प्रयोग Male बच्चे के लिये हुआ है।

(ii) I did not look at the baby as she was playing.
मैंने बच्ची की ओर नहीं देखा क्योंकि वह खेल रही थी।

'she' Word Female के लिये Pronoun से पहले Emphasiser के तौर पर प्रयुक्त किया जाता है।

Noun या Pronoun को अधिक प्रभावशाली बनाने के लिये कुछ उदाहरण दिये गये हैं:

Examples

(a) It is he who has broken your jaws.
यह वही आदमी है जिसने तुम्हारे जबड़े तोड़े हैं।

(b) It was the police that caught the criminal.
यह वही पुलिस थी जिसने अपराधी को पकड़ा।

(c) It is I who have broken all the previous records.
यह मैं ही हूँ जिसने पहले सारे रिकार्ड तोड़ दिये हैं।

(6) जब हम दिन, समय या मौसम के बारे में बात करते हैं, तो भी 'it' का प्रयोग किया जा सकता है।

Examples

(a) It is five past nine.
नौ बज कर पांच मिनट हो गये हैं।

(b) It is Sunday today.
आज रविवार है।

(c) It is bitterly cold outside.
बाहर बड़े कड़ाके की सर्दी है।

EXERCISE 2

नीचे दिये गये Sentences का अंग्रेजी में अनुवाद करें:

1. मुझे कॉकरोच अच्छा नहीं लगता क्योंकि यह भद्दा सा दिखाई पड़ता है।

2. दस बज कर दस मिनट हो गये हैं।

3. यह वही कुत्ता है जिसने आपको काटा था।

4. यह वही लड़का है जिसने आप पर पानी फेंका था।

5. यह वही लड़की है जो हमारी क्लास में प्रथम आई है।

6. यह प्रधानमंत्री ही थे जिन्होंने सही बात अपने भाषण में बताई।

7. आज शनिवार है।

8. बाहर बड़ी गर्मी है।

9. कमरे में बहुत ठण्ड है।

10. बच्चा रो रहा था और इसलिए मैंने उसे झूले में डाल दिया।

Hints for Translation

1. कॉकरोज = cockroach, भद्दा = ugly. **10.** झूला = cradle.

EXERCISE 3

नीचे दिये गये Sentences का अंग्रेजी में अनुवाद करें:

1. लोमड़ी अंगूरों तक पहुंचने के लिए छलांगें लगाती गई परन्तु इसका कोई लाभ नहीं हुआ।
2. यह क्या है?
3. वह क्या है जो आपके पास पड़ा है?
4. यह कोई महत्त्वपूर्ण मामला नहीं है।
5. इसने मुझे परेशान कर दिया है।
6. एक हाथ से ताली नहीं बजती।
7. अब पछताए होत क्या जब चिड़िया चुग गई खेत।
8. यह एक महत्त्वपूर्ण मामला है।
9. यह कैसे सम्भव है?
10. इसमें मैं कुछ नहीं कर सकता।
11. क्या यह आकाश में इन्द्रधनुष है?
12. मेरी भैंस दस किलो दूध देती है परन्तु यह घास बहुत खाती है।
13. क्या इस समय दस बजे हैं?
14. क्या इसका कोई लाभ है?
15. यह मेरा काम नहीं है।
16. बाहर तेज़ हवा चल रही है।
17. मेरा इससे तनिक भी सम्बन्ध नहीं है।
18. आप किस बात से परेशान हैं?
19. अब बसन्त ऋतु है।

Hints for Translation

1. इसका कोई लाभ नहीं हुआ = It was of no use. **5.** परेशान = Puzzled. **6.** एक हाथ से ताली नहीं बजती = It takes two to make a quarrel. **7.** अब पछताए होत क्या जब चिड़िया चुग गई खेत = It is no use crying over splitmilk. **16.** तेज हवा = Blowing hard. **16.** मेरा काम नहीं है = None of my business. **17.** मेरा इससे तनिक भी सम्बन्ध नहीं है = I'm least concerned with it.

Chapter 15

The Adjective

(विशेषण)

विशेषण वह शब्द होता है जो किसी कर्त्ता या कर्म की विशेषता बताता है।

Examples

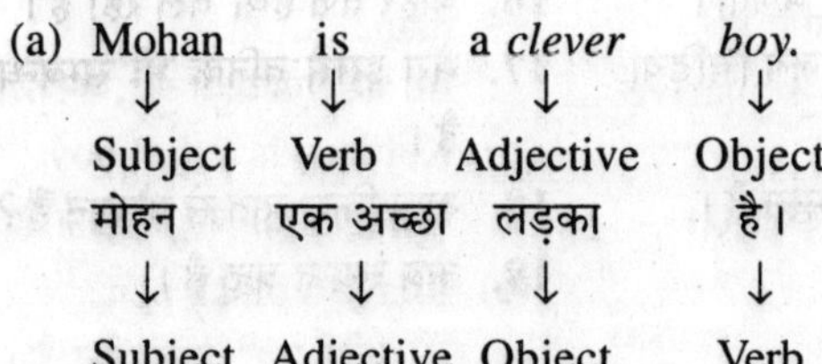

(a) Mohan → Subject, is → Verb, a *clever* → Adjective, *boy.* → Object

मोहन → Subject, एक अच्छा → Adjective, लड़का → Object, है। → Verb

(b) Ram → Subject, is → Verb, an intelligent → Adjective, boy. → Object

राम → Subject, एक होशियार → Adjective, लड़का → Object, है। → Verb

(i) इन दोनों वाक्यों को अगर हम ध्यान से पढ़ें, तो साफ पता चलता है कि 'clever' word एक लड़के के बारे में बताता है जो कि Mohan है।

(ii) इसी तरह, दूसरे वाक्य में 'intelligent' word एक लड़के, जिसका नाम राम है, के बारे में बताता है।

और भी कई Adjective हो सकते हैं जैसे nice, honest, sweet, brilliant etc. जो किसी व्यक्ति या वस्तु की कोई विशेषता बता सकते हैं।

KINDS OF ADJECTIVES

Adjectives निम्नलिखित प्रकार के होते हैं:

(A) Adjectives of Quality
(B) Adjectives of Quantity
(C) Adjectives of Number
(D) Interrogative Adjectives
(E) Possessive Adjectives
(F) Demonstrative Adjectives
(G) Exclamatory Adjectives
(H) Emphatic Adjectives.

(A) Adjectives of Quality: इस तरह के Adjectives किसी Noun या Pronoun की qualities जैसे अच्छा, बुरा, चालाक, सुस्त, चुस्त, भारतीय, पाकिस्तानी आदि के बारे में बताते हैं।

Examples

(a) Ram is a good boy.
राम एक अच्छा लड़का है।

(b) Dinesh is a very sensitive boy.
दिनेश बड़ा भावुक लड़का है।

(c) My brother is a very wise man.
मेरा भाई एक बहुत बुद्धिमान व्यक्ति है।

(d) Kuldeep is a dull boy.
कुलदीप एक बुद्धू लड़का है।

(e) I have a black pen.
मेरे पास एक काला पेन है।

EXERCISE 1

नीचे दिये गये Sentences का अंग्रेजी में अनुवाद करें व उसमें लगे Adjectives को Underline करें:

1. वह एक चुस्त लड़की है।
2. वह एक हंसमुख लड़का है।
3. उसके पास एक काली गाय है।
4. उसके पास एक सफेद स्कूटर है।
5. वह एक हिम्मती लड़का है।
6. वह काफी अक्लमंद है।
7. उसके भूरे बाल जल्दी टूट जाते हैं।
8. उसकी लम्बी जुबान चुप नहीं रह सकती।
9. उसकी तोतली बोली मुझे अच्छी लगी।
10. उसकी ईमानदारी का कोई और उदाहरण नहीं है।

(B) Adjectives of Quantity: जैसे, **enough, sufficient, great,** insufficient, any etc सभी Adjectives of Quantity हैं।

Examples

(a) There is a little milk in the pot.
बर्तन में थोड़ा सा दूध है।

(b) He has sufficient knowledge to compete with you.
तुम्हारे साथ मुकाबला करने के लिये उसके पास काफी ज्ञान है।

(c) He has a great sense of humour.
उसमें हास्य-विनोद का गुण है।

(d) There is a lot of ink in the inkpot.
स्याही की दवात में काफी स्याही है।

(e) He has little sense of understanding.
उसकी समझने की शक्ति बहुत कम है।

EXERCISE 2

नीचे दिये गये Sentences का अंग्रेज़ी में अनुवाद करें तथा Adjective of Quantity को Underline करें:

1. उसके पास काफी धन है।

2. उसके पास पर्याप्त धन नहीं है।

3. उसने काफी पानी पिया।

4. उसने थोड़ी सी चाय पी।

5. मैंने ज़्यादा नहीं खाया।

6. उसे थोड़ा सा बुखार है।

7. रामू ने काफी व्यायाम किया।

8. रेखा बहुत दूर तक दौड़ी।

9. कल ठण्ड बहुत थी।

10. गर्मी काफी कम हो गई थी।

(C) Adjectives of Number: यह तीन प्रकार के होते हैं:

(C1) Definite Adjectives of Number

(C2) Indefinite Adjectives of Number

(C3) Distributive Adjectives of Number

(C1) Definitive Adjectives of Number: (a) ये वो Adjectives हैं जिनमें सही Count किया गया हो। जैसे दो, चार, छ: एवम् दस, इनको Cardinals कहते हैं।

(b) First, second, third.... इनको Ordinals कहते हैं।

(C2) Indefinitive Adjectives of Number: ये Exact Number बताने में असमर्थ होते हैं। जैसे many, a few, all, no, several etc.

(C3) Distributive Adjectives of Number: Each, every, neither, either etc.इनके अन्तर्गत आते हैं।

Examples

(a) He has many pencils to write with.

उसके पास लिखने के लिये बहुत सी पेंसिलें हैं।
(Indefinite Adjectives of Number)

(b) Mohan has two pens to write with.
मोहन के पास लिखने के लिये दो पेन हैं।
(Definite Adjectives of Number)

(c) Every boy of your street is a fool.
तुम्हारी गली का हर एक लड़का मूर्ख है।
(Distributive Adjectives of Number)

(d) A few students of my class are good.
मेरी कक्षा के थोड़े से लड़के अच्छे हैं।
(Indefinite Adjectives of Number)

(e) He has five rooms to live in his house.
उसके घर में रहने के लिये पांच कमरे हैं।
(Definite Adiectives of Number)

EXERCISE 3

नीचे दिये गये वाक्यों का अंग्रेज़ी में अनुवाद करें तथा अलग-अलग Adjectives को Underline करें तथा उन्हें Classify करें:

1. वह तीन बार ताजमहल देखने गया।
2. उसकी कक्षा में बहुत से लड़के पढ़ते हैं।
3. आकाश में बहुत से तारे हैं।
4. हमारे स्कूल का हर एक बच्चा आज रोया।
5. उनमें से हर एक शोर कर रहा था।
6. उसकी मुर्गी ने तीन अण्डे दिये।
7. मैंने दो दर्जन आम खरीदे।
8. थोड़े से आम खराब थे।
9. वह गिलास भर पानी एक ही घूंट में पी गया।
10. क्या आकाश में एक ही सूरज है?

(D) Interrogative Adjectives: जो Adjective Nouns के साथ मिलकर Question के रूप में प्रकट होते हैं, उन्हें Interrogative Adjectives कहते हैं।

Examples

(a) Which book is yours?
आपकी कौन सी किताब है?

(b) Which bag is mine?
मेरा कौन सा बैग है?

(c) Whose brother are you?
तुम किसके भाई हो?

(d) Which boy has made you a fool?
किस लड़के ने तुम्हें मूर्ख बनाया है?

(e) What thing are you looking for?
तुम क्या ढूंढ़ रहे हो?

EXERCISE 4

नीचे दिये गये Sentences का अंग्रेजी में अनुवाद करें:

1. कौन तुम्हारी बहन है?
2. कौन सा रास्ता दिल्ली जाता है?
3. कौन सी खाने वाली चीज तुम्हें अच्छी लगती है?
4. कौन सा पैन तुम्हारा है?
5. कौन लड़का तुम्हें मार रहा था?
6. लड़के तुम पर क्यों चिल्ला रहे थे?
7. तुमने किसका नाम नहीं सुना?
8. तुमने कौन सी फिल्म कल देखी?
9. कौन सा छाता अच्छा है?
10. कौन सा स्कूल गंदा है?

(E) Possessive Adjectives: जैसे, मेरी, तुम्हारी, उसकी, हमारी कमीज़ etc. (his, your, her, their, our, yours, etc.)

Examples

(a) Your pants are good.
तुम्हारी पतलूनें अच्छी हैं।

(b) Her brother is my fast friend.
उसका भाई मेरा पक्का मित्र है।

(c) My book is on the table.
मेरी किताब मेज़ पर पड़ी है।

(d) His father likes to talk to me.
उसके पिता मुझसे बात करना पसन्द करते हैं।

(e) They should do their work well.
उन्हें अपना काम ठीक से करना चाहिए।

(F) Demonstrative Adjectives: यह Adjectives सीधे तौर पर किसी वस्तु या व्यक्ति की ओर संकेत करते हैं। ये हैं They, these, those, that, such, etc.

Examples

(a) This shirt is mine.
यह कमीज मेरी है।

(b) These books are yours.
ये किताबें आपकी हैं।

(c) That bag is hers.
वह बैग उसका है।

(d) These keys are ours.
ये चाभियां हमारी हैं।

(e) These boys are clever.
ये लड़के चालाक हैं।

EXERCISE 5

नीचे दिये गये वाक्यों का अंग्रेजी में अनुवाद करें :

1. यह उसकी गुड़िया है।
2. यह तुम्हारी गलती है।
3. वह तुम्हारा कुत्ता है।
4. मैंने इस तरह का मूर्ख पहले नहीं देखा।
5. यह छाता मेरा है।
6. वह छाता हमारा है।
7. वह छाता तुम्हारा है।
8. ये लड़के शरारती हैं।
9. ये किताबें हमारी हैं।
10. वह पुस्तक तुम्हारी है।

(G) Exclamatory Adjectives: 'What' का प्रयोग Exclamatory Adjective के तौर पर होता है:

(i) What a beautiful flower it is!
यह कितना सुन्दर फूल है!

EXERCISE 6

नीचे दिये गये वाक्यों का अंग्रेजी में अनुवाद करें:

1. कितना सुन्दर दृश्य है!
2. कितना अच्छा मौसम है!
3. मोर कितना सुन्दर नाच रहा है!
4. इन्द्रधनुष कितना सुन्दर लग रहा है!
5. यह कितना प्यारा फूल है!
6. मेमना कितना मासूम है!
7. तकिया कितना नर्म है!
8. तुम कितने मूर्ख हो!
9. कितनी ऊंची इमारत है!
10. तुम भी क्या अजीब आदमी हो!

(8) Emphatic Adjectives: 'own' तथा 'Very' Emphatic Adjectives के तौर पर प्रयोग में लाये जाते हैं।

(i) This is the very bag I was looking for.
यह वही बैग है जिसे मैं ढूंढ रहा था।

(ii) Mind your own business.
अपना काम करो।

EXERCISE 7

नीचे दिये गये वाक्यों का अंग्रेज़ी में अनुवाद करो:

1. यह मेरा अपना छाता है।
2. यह मेरा अपना पैन है।

3. यह वही खास बात है जो आपके अपने हक में है।

4. यह वही कुत्ता है जिसने तुम्हें काटा था।

5. वह वही नेता है जिसने झूठ बोला था।

Formation of Adjectives from Verbs

	Verb	*Meaning*	*Adjective*
1.	Abuse	बुरा भला कहना	Abusive
2.	Admire	प्रशंसा करना	Admirable
3.	Advise	सलाह देना	Advisable
4.	Amuse	मनोरंजन करना	Amusing
5.	Assert	दृढ़तापूर्वक कहना	Assertive
6.	**Attend**	हाज़िर होना	Attentive
7.	Clarify	स्पष्ट करना	Clear
8.	Collect	इकट्ठा करना	Collective
9.	**Control**	नियन्त्रण करना	Controllable
10.	Convince	विश्वास दिलाना	Convincing
11.	**Create**	बनाना/उत्पन्न करना	Creature
12.	Cure	ठीक करना	Curable
13.	Decide	निर्णय करना	Decisive
14.	Deny	इन्कार करना	Deniable
15.	End	समाप्त करना	Endless
16.	Enjoy	आनन्द मनाना	Enjoyable
17.	Enlarge	बड़ा करना	Large
18.	Enrich	धनी बनाना	Rich
19.	Excel	आगे निकल जाना	Excellent
20.	Fear	डरना	Fearful
21.	Fill	भरना	Full
22.	Force	मजबूर करना	Forceful
23.	Gain	लाभ प्राप्त करना	Gainful
24.	Honour	सम्मान करना	Honourable
25.	Hope	आशा करना	Hopeless, hopeful

	Verb	Meaning	Adjective
26.	Ignore	ध्यान न देना	Ignorant
27.	Insult	अपमान करना	Insulting
28.	Laugh	हंसना	Laughable
29.	Learn	सीखना	Learnable
30.	Like	पसन्द करना	Likeable
31.	Obey	आज्ञा मानना	Obedient
32.	Play	खेलना	Playful
33.	Please	प्रसन्न करना	Pleasant
34.	Punish	दण्ड देना	Punishable
35.	Purify	साफ करना	Pure
36.	Read	पढ़ना	Readable
37.	Redden	लाल करना	Red
38.	Rely	विश्वास (या निर्भर) करना	Reliable
39.	Shorten	कम करना	Short
40.	Sleep	सोना	Sleepy
41.	Soften	नर्म करना	Soft
42.	Talk	बात करना	Talkative
43.	**Thank**	**धन्यवाद देना**	**Thankful**
44.	**Trouble**	**दुःख देना**	**Troublesome**
45.	Use	प्रयोग करना	Useful
46.	Vacate	खाली करना	Vacant
47.	Wish	इच्छा करना	Wishful

Formation of Adjectives from Nouns

	Noun	Meaning	Adjective
1.	Glory	शान	Glorious
2.	Salt	नमक	Saltish
3.	Sand	रेत	Sandy

	Noun	Meaning	Adjective
4.	Scholar	विद्वान	Scholarly
5.	Science	विज्ञान	Scientific
6.	Season	मौसम	Seasonal
7.	Service	सेवा	Serviceable
8.	Silence	शान्ति	Silent
9.	Silk	रेशम	Silky, silken
10.	Silver	चांदी	Silvery
11.	Skin	चमड़ी	Skinny
12.	Slave	दास	Slavish
13.	Smoke	धुआं	Smoky
14.	Snow	बर्फ	Snowy, snow-covered
15.	Society	समाज	Sociable, societal
16.	Solitude	अकेलापन	Solitary
17.	Sorrow	दु:ख	Sorowful, sorry
18.	Splendour	शान	Splendid
19.	Study	अध्ययन	Studious
20.	Success	सफलता	Successful
21.	Sun	सूर्य	Sunny, solar
22.	**Superstition**	**वहम/अंधविश्वास**	**Superstitious**
23.	Sympathy	सहानुभूति	Sympathetic
24.	System	प्रणाली	Systematic
25.	Table	मेज	Tabular
26.	Taste	स्वाद	Tasty, tastful
27.	Thief	चोर	Thievish
28.	Time	समय	Timely
29.	**Title**	**ओहदा/पदवी**	**Titular**
30.	Tooth	दांत	Toothy
31.	Tribe	कबीला	Tribal
32.	Type	प्रकार, किस्म	Typical

Chapter 16

The Article

1. Articles वास्तव में Demonstrative Adjective होते हैं। इनको Use किये बिना English में ठीक Sentences बना पाना Possible नहीं है। इसलिये इनके महत्त्व को समझते हुए इनको अलग से पढ़ाया जाता है।

2. *Kinds of Articles*: Articles केवल तीन प्रकार के होते हैं—'a, an, तथा the.' इनके महत्त्व को समझने के लिये इनको दो भागों में बांटा गया है:

(A) Indefinite Article (B) Definite Article

USAGE OF ARTICLES

(A) Indefinite Article: 'A' व 'an' ये दोनों ही Indefinite Articles हैं। ये दोनों किसी एक साधारण वस्तु या व्यक्ति के बारे में बताते हैं।

(i) A boy — (एक लड़का) कौन सा?

(ii) A man — (एक आदमी) कौन सा?

(iii) An orange — (एक सन्तरा) कौन सा?

(iv) An honest man — (एक ईमानदार आदमी) कौन सा?

ऊपर के सभी Sentences यह नहीं बताते–कौन सा लड़का, कौन सा आदमी, कौन सा संतरा etc.

(B) Definite Article: 'the' शब्द को Definite Article कहा जाता है। यह किसी खास वस्तु या व्यक्ति के बारे में बताता है।

(i) **The boy who was punished, was my fast friend.**

वह लड़का, जिसको सजा मिली थी, मेरा पक्का मित्र था।

Explanation: यह Sentence इस बात की पुष्टि करता है कि मेरा Fast Friend कौन सा था। वही मेरा Fast Friend था जिस लड़के को सज़ा मिली थी।

(ii) The man with a sharp nose is my uncle.
तीखी नाक वाले आदमी मेरे चाचा हैं।

Explanation: इस Sentence में भी वह आदमी, जिसकी नाक तीखी है, एक खास आदमी है और जो मेरे चाचा हैं।

Usage of Indefinite Article

(A) Indefinite Articles 'a' और 'an' किसी भी Sentences में Noun से पहले Use किए जाते हैं:

(i) This is a pen.
यह एक पेन है।

(ii) She is a girl.
वह एक लड़की है।

(iii) It is an apple.
यह एक सेब है।

(iv) This is a chair.
यह एक कुर्सी है।

(B) जब एक Noun किसी पूरी Class को Represent करता है। *e.g.*,

(i) A goat can never be a lion.
एक बकरी कभी बब्बर शेर नहीं हो सकती।

Note: इस Sentence में 'A goat' पूरी goat class को represent करता है। इसी तरह 'a lion' पूरी Lion Class का बोध कराता है।

(ii) A man can never be immortal.
आदमी कभी भी अनश्वर नहीं हो सकता।

Note: इस Sentence में 'A man' पूरी इन्सानी कौम को सम्बोधित करता है। **'A man'** किसी एक आदमी के लिये नहीं बल्कि दुनिया के सभी इन्सानों के लिये प्रयुक्त किया गया है। इस Sentence से साफ पता चलता है कि 'A man' केवल पुरुषों को ही नहीं, बल्कि सभी स्त्रियों को भी (अर्थात् पूरी मनुष्य जाति को) सम्बोधित करता है।

Examples

(a) A dog can bark for a long time.
एक कुत्ता बहुत देर तक भौंक सकता है।

(b) A fox can be clever than any other animal in the world.
लोमड़ी दुनिया के किसी भी जानवर से अधिक चालाक हो सकती है।

(C) किसी Unfamiliar Person, Animal या वस्तु के बारे में बताता है:

(i) Not even a dog was barking in the street.
गली में एक कुत्ता नहीं भौंक रहा था।

Note: इस Sentence में 'a dog' हमें कुत्ते से ही परिचित नहीं करवाता बल्कि बात की जानकारी देता है कि गली में बिल्कुल शान्ति थी।

(ii) A boy, named Satish was asking about you in the morning.
सतीश नामक एक लड़का सुबह तुम्हारे बारे में पूछ रहा था।

Note: इस Sentence में 'A boy, named Satish' इस बात की पुष्टि करता है कि **बताने वाला व्यक्ति Satish को नहीं जानता था लेकिन अब वह नाम से परिचित हो चुका है।**

(iii) I saw a tiger in the zoo.
मैंने चिड़ियाघर में एक चीता **देखा।**

(D) ये Proper Noun को Common Noun में Change **कर सकते हैं:**

(i) The world needs a Gandhi to learn the lesson of non-violence.
अहिंसा का पाठ सीखने के लिए संसार को एक गांधी की आवश्यकता है।

(ii) The cricket team of our school needs a Sachin to win the matches.
मैचों को जीतने के लिये हमारे स्कूल की क्रिकेट टीम को एक सचिन की जरूरत है।

(iii) The world needs a Mother Teresa to learn the lesson of self-sacrifice.
आत्म–बलिदान का पाठ सीखने के लिए संसार को मदर टैरेसा की आवश्यकता है।

Distinction Between the Usage of 'a' and 'an'

(A) 'a' article का प्रयोग प्रायः तब होता है जब कोई शब्द Consonant Sound **से** शुरू होता है; जैसेः-

(i) A chair	(iv) A table
(ii) A cow	(v) A mango
(iii) A donkey	(vi) A university

(B) 'an' article का प्रयोग तब होता है जब कोई शब्द Vowel Sound से **शुरू होता है; जैसेः-**

(i) An inkpot	(v) An hour
(ii) An apple	(vi) An umbrella
(iii) An animal	(vii) An actor
(iv) An orange	

Note: जैसा कि ऊपर कहा गया है, 'An' शब्द का प्रयोग केवल वहां होता है जहां **Vowel** का Sound पैदा होता है। ज़रूरी नहीं है कि वह Vowel शब्द से शुरू हो।

(i) An honest man.

यहां 'honest' शब्द O Vowel की आवाज़ से बोला जाता है क्योंकि इसमें **'h'** Silent है।

(b) इसी तरह 'a' शब्द का प्रयोग जहां Consonant Sound पैदा होता है (शब्द चाहे Vowel Word से शुरू होता हो) वहां होता है:

A European (एक यूरोपिअन)

A University. (एक यूनिवर्सिटी)

यहां शब्द Vowel Sound से आरम्भ नहीं होते।

इसी प्रकार, 'a' और 'an' का प्रयोग Sound के अनुसार abbreviation से पहले होता है:

(i) an MP
(ii) a BA
(iii) an LLB
(iv) a CA

Usage of the Definite Article

Definite Article 'the' नीचे दी गई स्थितियों में Use किया जाता है:

(A) कोई Singular Noun जब पूरी Class को Represent करता हो। ***e.g.,***

(i) The lion roars very horribly.

बब्बर शेर बड़ी भयानकता से दहाड़ता है।

Note (1): इस Sentence में 'The lion' किसी एक 'lion' को नहीं बल्कि पूरी Class को Represent करता है। दूसरे शब्दों में दुनिया में जितने भी lions हैं वह भयानकता से दहाड़ते हैं।

Note (2): ध्यान रहे कि Plural Nouns के साथ 'the' का प्रयोग नहीं होता है। जैसेः-

(i) Lions roar very horribly.
बब्बर शेर बड़ी भयानकता से दहाड़ते हैं।

(ii) The rose smells sweet.
गुलाब की खुशबू बहुत मधुर होती है।

Note (1): Sentence (i) की तरह अगर हम इसे Plural Form में लिखते हैं तो 'the' का प्रयोग नहीं होगा।

Roses smell sweet.

Note (2): कई शब्द जैसे 'man' तथा 'woman' पूरी Class को Represent करते हैं।

इनकी Singular Form में ही 'the' नहीं लगाया जाता है।

(i) Man can be extremely kind to animals but can never be God.

इन्सान पशुओं के लिए बहुत दयालु हो सकता है परन्तु भगवान नहीं बन सकता।

Note: इस Sentence में 'man' पूरी 'man' Class अर्थात्, Mankind को represent करता है।

(ii) Woman is the mother of this world.

स्त्री दुनिया की माता है।

(B) जब हम किसी खास वस्तु या व्यक्ति की बात करते हैं।

(i) I liked the boy very much who jumped over the wall.

मुझे वह लड़का बहुत अच्छा लगा जो दीवार के ऊपर से कूदा।

Note: इस Sentence में 'the boy' शब्द एक खास लड़के के लिये प्रयोग में लाया गया है।

(ii) The man, who solved this sum, must be very intelligent.

जिस व्यक्ति ने यह प्रश्न हल किया, अवश्य ही बहुत बुद्धिमान होगा।

(iii) The girl, who is wearing a black skirt, looks beautiful.

वह लड़की जिसने एक काली स्कर्ट पहनी हुई है सुन्दर दिखाई पड़ती है।

(C) जब हम किसी Classical Book या Holy Book का वर्णन करते हैं:

(i) The Gita

(ii) The Bible

(iii) The Ramayana

लेकिन जब किताब से पहले उसके Author का नाम लगता है तो शब्द 'the' का प्रयोग नहीं होता:

(i) Shakespear, Hamlet

(ii) Ved Vyas, Mahabharata

(D) जब हम पहाड़ी, चोटी, Rivers, Canals, Ocean, Island इत्यादि का वर्णन करते हैं:

(i) The Ganges
(ii) The Godavari
(iii) The Suez Canal
(iv) The Mount Everest
(v) The Eiffel Tower
(vi) The Bay of Bengal
(vii) The Nile
(viii) The Arabian Sea

(E) जब Newspapers व Journals के बारे में चर्चा होती है:

(i) The Hindustan Times
(ii) The Economic Times
(iii) The Hindu
(iv) The New York Times

(F) जब पहले कहीं ज़िक्र में आई किसी वस्तु या व्यक्ति के बारे में बात करें:

(i) The man we were talking about is coming across the way to us.
जिस आदमी की हम बात कर रहे थे वह हमारी तरफ आ रहा है।

(ii) The boy, who beat you, was a compactly built up figure.
जिस लड़के ने तुम्हें पीटा, वह बहुत ही गठे हुए शरीर का मालिक था।

(G) कुछ Proper Nouns से पहले भी 'the' Article का प्रयोग होता है:

(i) The United States of America
(ii) The United Kingdom
(iii) The Punjab
(iv) The Deccan

Note: उपरलिखित शब्दों में Geographical Portion or Situation एक Major Point हैं।

(H) 'The' Article का प्रयोग Races, Organisation, Political Parties, Communities इत्यादि के पहले भी किया जाता है:

(i) The Bhartiya Janta Party
(ii) The Janata Dal
(iii) The Indian National Congress
(iv) The Hindus
(v) The Jews
(vi) The Sikhs
(vii) The U.N.O.

(I) Imaginary Geographical Lines के साथ भी 'the' Article का प्रयोग होता है:

(i) The Meridian (of Greenwich)
(ii) The Latitude
(iii) The Longitude
(iv) The Equator
(v) The Tropic of Cancer
(vi) The Tropic of Capricorn

(J) 'The' Article का प्रयोग Adjective से पहले जिस किसी Class को वह Represent करता हो, वहां भी होता है:

(i) The poor can never express themselves fully in the modern

society.

गरीब अपने आपको इस आधुनिक समाज में पूरी तरह कभी व्यक्त नहीं कर सकते।

(K) 'The' Article का प्रयोग Unique Common Nouns से पहले भी किया जाता है:

(i) The sky
(ii) The earth
(iii) The Sun
(iv) The moon

(L) 'The' Article का प्रयोग किसी Adjective से पहले, जो किसी, Proper Noun को Qualify करता हो, भी किया जाता है:

(i) The peace-loving Gandhi
(ii) The self-sacrificing Mother Teresa
(iii) The cruel Hitler

(M) 'The' Article का प्रयोग Superlative degree से पहले भी होता है:

(i) Surinder is the best boy of our school.
सुरिन्द्र हमारे स्कूल का सबसे अच्छा विद्यार्थी है।

(ii) Moti is the wisest man among us.
मोती हम सबसे अधिक बुद्धिमान है।

(iii) Madan is the strongest boy of our school.
मदन हमारे स्कूल का सबसे शक्तिशाली लड़का है।

(N) 'The' Article का प्रयोग Comparative degree से पहले भी होता है जब वह एक comparision के रूप में आता है: जैसे:-

(i) The more we read, the more we learn.
हम जितना अधिक पढ़ते हैं उतना ही सीखते हैं।

(ii) The higher we go, the cooler it becomes.
हम जितना ऊंचाई पर जाते हैं, उतनी ही ठंड बढ़ती जाती है।

(O) जब किसी Noun के प्रभाव पर जोर डालना हो, तब भी 'the' Article का प्रयोग होता है:

(i) He is the man who can open a lock without a key.
यह वह आदमी है जो किसी भी ताले को बिना चाभी से खोल सकता है।

(ii) Gandhi was the Saint who won the hearts with non-violence.
गांधी वह संत थे जिन्होंने दिलों को अंहिसा से जीत लिया।

Omission of 'the'

निम्नलिखित दशाओं में 'the' का प्रयोग नहीं होता:

(a) *Proper Noun* से पहले इसका प्रयोग नहीं होता है।

(i) Chandigarh is the capital of Punjab.
चण्डीगढ़ पंजाब की राजधानी है।

Note: Punjab शब्द Geography पर आधारित है।

(ii) Satish is a good singer.
सतीश एक अच्छा गायक है।

Note: Proper Noun से पहले प्राय: 'the' Article का प्रयोग उस समय होता है जब इसको Common Noun में Change किया जाता है।

(i) **She is the Lata Mangeshker of our class.**
वह हमारी कक्षा की लता मंगेशकर है।

(ii) **He is the Sachin Tendulkar of our team.**
वह हमारी टीम का सचिन तेंदुलकर है।

(b) *Material Noun* से पहले the का प्रयोग नहीं होता है।

(i) Platinum does not need varnish for glitter.
प्लेटिनम को चमकाने के लिये वार्निश की जरुरत नहीं होती।

(ii) Gold is a precious metal.
सोना एक कीमती धातु है।

(iii) Iron is a cheap metal.
लोहा एक सस्ती धातु है।

(c) *Abstract Nouns* से पहले the का प्रयोग नहीं होता है।

(i) Honesty always wins.
ईमानदारी हमेशा जीतती है।

(ii) **Sweetness results in a good crop in the end.**
मीठा बोलने का परिणाम अन्ततः अच्छा होता है।

Note: 'the' Article का प्रयोग उस समय Material Noun व Abstract Noun से पहले होता है जब वह Adjective या Adjectival Clause या Phrase को qualify करे।

(i) The milk of this buffalo is very tasty.
इस भैंस का दूध बहुत स्वादिष्ट है।

(ii) The gold used in this ring seems to be alloyed.
इस अंगूठी के सोने में मिलावट लगती है।

(iii) The honesty in his work he had shown to us was nothing but a trick.
जो ईमानदारी उसने अपने काम में दिखाई थी, कुछ नहीं था, बस उसकी एक चालाकी थी।

(d) Phrases में जहां Transitive Verb Object के तुरन्त बाद आये:

(i) I sent him a word.
(ii) They made him the chairman.

(e) जब किसी एक ही व्यक्ति या वस्तु के गुणों का वर्णन किया जाये, तो 'the' Article केवल पहले गुण के साथ ही लगाया जाता है:

(i) The black and white dog.
काला तथा सफेद कुत्ता।

Note: यह Sentence एक ही कुत्ते के दो रंगों—काले व सफेद—के बारे में बताता है। लेकिन 'the' Article केवल पहले Adjective से पहले लगा है।

(ii) The black and the white dog.
काला तथा सफेद कुत्ता।

Note: इस Sentence में दो कुत्ते बताये गये हैं—एक काला तथा दूसरा सफेद।

(iii) The writer and singer.
लेखक व गायक।

(एक ही व्यक्ति के पास दो गुण हैं—वह लेखक भी है व गायक भी)

(iv) The writer and the singer.
लेखक तथा गायक।

(यहां पर दो व्यक्ति अलग-अलग गुणों वाले हैं। एक लेखक व दूसरा गायक है)

(f) जब कोई Title Complement of the Sentence के तौर पर या Proper Noun का Apposition होता है तो Article प्रयोग में नहीं लाया जाता।

(i) Mother Teresa, the greatest self-sacrificer in the world, was a great lover of mankind.
मदरं टेरेसा, जो महानतम आत्म-बलिदान करने वाली थी, इन्सानों से बहुत प्यार करती थी।

(ii) JL Nehru, a great leader of India, was a great lover of peace.

जवाहर लाल नेहरू, जो भारत के एक महान नेता थे, शांति के बहुत बड़े पुजारी थे।

EXERCISE 1

निम्नलिखित वाक्यों का a/an, the का प्रयोग करके English में अनुवाद करें:

1. यह एक काला कुत्ता है।
2. यह एक अच्छी कलम है।
3. यह किताब, जो आप पढ़ रहे हैं, बड़ी मोटी है।
4. मैंने ताजमहल देखा है।
5. मैं कल एक चिड़ियाघर देखने जाऊँगा।
6. वह एक उपन्यासकार तथा चित्र-कार है।
7. उसके पास एक बहुत सुन्दर पेंसिल है।
8. वह एक संतरा खा रहा है।
9. वह लड़का जो हमारी कक्षा में शोर करता है आज अध्यापक के द्वारा पीटा गया।
10. कल भारत वेस्ट इण्डीज़ से मैच जीत गया।
11. वह एक ईमानदार लड़का है।
12. कल मेरा भाई सेना में भर्ती हो गया।
13. क्या तुम मूर्ख हो?
14. मेरे पिताजी, एम एल ए बन गये हैं।
15. वह धनवान है।
16. उसके पास गरीबों के लिये कोई दया नहीं है।
17. वही लड़का मैंने अभी देखा है जिसने तुम्हें पत्थर मारा था।
18. हवा का एक झोंका तक नहीं चल रहा था।
19. क्या तुम उस पागल को जानते हो?
20. वह बी ए पास है।

EXERCISE 2

1. उसकी कमीज़ का एक बटन टूट गया।
2. चोर घर में था।
3. वह एक स्याही की दवात खरीद लाया।
4. मेरे भाई ने कल एक छाता खरीदा।
5. वह अच्छा छाता नहीं था।
6. सोहन हमारी कक्षा का सबसे लम्बा लड़का है।
7. वह गरीबों पर हंसता है।
8. वह एक धनवान आदमी है।
9. जो आदमी हमें कल बाजार में मिला था वो आज सुबह मर गया।
10. इस नल का पानी बहुत स्वादिष्ट है।

11. जो ताम्बा इस मोटर में लगा है, उसमें जस्ता की मिलावट नहीं है।

12. मैं गाना गाता हूँ।

13. पृथ्वी सूर्य के चारों ओर चक्कर कटती है।

14. आकाश में तारे टिमटिमाते हैं।

15. वह मुझे रास्ते में मिला।

16. वहां एक मोर नाच रहा था।

17. वह एक यूरोपियन है।

18. लोहा जंग लगने से भद्दा लगता है।

19. जो शराब आपने पी वह जहरीली थी।

20. उसने मेरे साथ एक वादा किया है।

21. उसका भाई बी एड कर चुका है।

22. वह एक सेब खा रहा था।

23. वह पानी में डूब गया।

Chapter 17

The Verb
(क्रिया)

I. किसी भी भाषा को ठीक पढ़ने या लिखने के लिये उसके सभी नियमों को जान लेना अति अनिवार्य है। Enlgish में हम Noun, Pronoun, Adjective आदि के बारे में पढ़ चुके हैं। इसी तरह, Verb भी Sentence (वाक्य) का ही एक भाग है।

Kinds of Verbs: यह दो प्रकार के होते हैं:

(1) अकर्मक—Intransitive अर्थात् वह Verb, जो अपने साथ Object नहीं लेता या उस पर निर्भर नहीं करता।

(2) सकर्मक—Transitive अर्थात् वह Verb, जो कर्म (Object) लेता है या उस पर निर्भर करता है।

Examples

(1) *Intransitive Verb*

(a) She sings.
वह गांती है।

यह वाक्य बिना Object के भी ठीक है। अत: इसकी Verb किसी Object पर निर्भर नहीं करती। अत: यहां 'sings' Intransitive Verb है।

(b) The birds fly.
पक्षी उड़ते हैं।

यह वाक्य भी कर्म (Object) पर निर्भर नहीं करता तथा उसके बिना ही पूरी बात समझा देता है। यहां भी Verb 'fly' Intransitive है।

(2) *Transitive Verb*

(a) He sings a song.
वह गाना गाता है।

इस वाक्य में गाने की क्रिया कर्म गाने अथवा 'song' पर निर्भर करती है। अत: यहां

'sings' Transitive Verb है।

(b) He reads a book.
वह किताब पढ़ता है।
इस वाक्य में पढ़ने की क्रिया किताब पर निर्भर करती है। अतः यहां 'reads' एक Transitive Verb है।

EXERCISE 1

दिये गये वाक्यों का English में अनुवाद करें व अलग से दिखाएं की कौन से Verbs Intransitive हैं और कौन से Verbs Transitive हैं:

1. बच्चे पतंग उड़ाते हैं।
2. पक्षी हवा में उड़ते हैं।
3. वह हंसता है।
4. राम सदा सच बोलता है।
5. मोहन अखबार पढ़ता है।
6. वह झूला झूल रहा है।
7. सूर्य चमकता है।
8. तारे निकल आये हैं।
9. मैं स्कूल जाता हूँ।
10. हम इकट्ठे हॉकी खेलते हैं।

II. अंग्रेजी भाषा में बहुत से Verbs ऐसे हैं जिनके बाद Infinitive या Gerund भी लगाया जाता है। कुछ के बाद Infinitive व Gerund दोनों ही आते हैं।

III. अलग-अलग Tense में Verb भी अलग-अलग ढंग से प्रयोग में लाये जाते हैं जो कि हम Chapter 'The Tense' में पढ़ सकते हैं। कुछ ऐसे Auxiliary Verbs हैं जिनके पश्चात् Verb की First Form ही लगती है।

IV. English में Verb के तीन रूप होते हैं: Present, Past और Past Participle इसके अतिरिक्त 'ing' वाले Verb को Continuous Tense या Gerund के रूप में भी प्रयोग में लाया जाता है।

नीचे प्रायः प्रयोग में किये जाने वाले Verbs की Conjugations दी गई हैं।

Conjugation of Verbs

Present Indefinite	*Past Indefinite*	*Past Participle*
Agree	agreed	agreed
Allow	allowed	allowed
Apply	applied	applied
Arise	arose	arisen

Present Indefinite	Past Indefinite	Past Participle
Awake	awoke	awaken
Be	was	been
Beat	beat	beaten
Become	became	become
Begin	began	begun
Behold	beheld	beheld, beholden
Bend	bent	bent
Beset	beset	beset
Bid	bade, bid	bidden, bid
Bleed	bled	bled
Blow	blew	blown
Breed	bred	bred
Bring	brought	brought
Build	built	built
Burn	burnt	burnt
Burst	burst	burst
Bury	buried	buried
Buy	bought	bought
Call	called	called
Cast	cast	cast
Catch	caught	caught
Chide	chid, chided	chid, chidden
Choose	chose	chosen
Cleave	clove, cleft	cloven, cleft
Cling	clung	clung
Come	came	come
Creep	crept	crept
Cry	cried	cried
Cut	cut	cut
Deal	dealt	dealt
Delay	delayed	delayed
Deny	denied	denied
Dig	dug	dug

Present Indefinite	*Past Indefinite*	*Past Participle*
Do	did	done
Dream	dreamt	dreamt
Drink	drank	drunk
Drive	drove	driven
Dry	dried	dried
Dwell	dwelt	dwelt
Eat	ate	eaten
Ensure	ensured	ensured
Fail	failed	failed
Feel	felt	felt
Fell	felled	felled
Fight	fought	fought
Find	found	found
Flee	fled	fled
Fling	flung	flung
Flow	flowed	flowed
Fly	flew	flown
Follow	followed	followed
Forbid	forbade	forbidden
Forgive	forgave	forgiven
Forsake	forsook	forsaken
Free	freed	freed
Fulfil	fulfilled	fulfilled
Gather	gathered	gathered
Get	got	got
Give	gave	given
Go	went	gone
Halt	**halted**	**halted**
Hang	**hanged/hung**	**hanged/hung**
Hate	**hated**	**hated**
Have	**had**	**had**
Heat	**heated**	**heated**
Heave	**heaved/hove**	**heaved/hove**

Present Indefinite	*Past Indefinite*	*Past Participle*
Help	helped	helped
Hide	hid	hidden
Hit	hit	hit
Hold	held	held
Hope	hoped	hoped
Hurt	hurt	hurt
Injure	injured	injured
Insure	insured	insured
Join	joined	joined
Keep	kept	kept
Kill	killed	killed
Kneel	knelt	knelt
Lay	laid	laid
Lead	led	led
Learn	learned	learnt
Leave	left	left
Let	let	let
Lie	lied/lay	lied/lain
Lose	lost	lost
Lost	lost	lost
Low	lowered	lowered
Lower	lowered	lowered
Make	made	made
Mean	meant	meant
Meet	met	met
Mistake	mistook	mistaken
Operate	operated	operated
Overcome	overcame	overcome
Pay	paid	paid
Pick	picked	picked
Play	played	played
Pray	prayed	prayed
Prepare	prepared	prepared

Present Indefinite	*Past Indefinite*	*Past Participle*
Price	priced	priced
Pull	pulled	pulled
Push	pushed	pushed
Put	put	put
Rate	rated	rated
Read	read	read
Rid	rid	rid
Ride	rode	ridden
Rim	rimmed	rimmed
Ring	rang	rung
Rise	rose	risen
Run	ran	run
See	saw	seen
Set	set	set
Shed	shed	shed
Shut	shut	shut
Sing	sang	sung
Sit	sat	sat
Slay	slew	slain
Speak	spoke	spoken
Split	split	split
Spread	spread	spread
Spring	sprang	sprung
Stand	stood	stood
Steal	stole	stolen
Stick	stuck	stuck
Stride	strode	stridden
Strike	struck	stricken
Swear	swore	sworn
Sweep	swept	swept
Swim	swam	swum
Swing	swung	swung

Present Indefinite	*Past Indefinite*	*Past Participle*
Tackle	tackled	tackled
Take	took	taken
Tear	tore	torn
Term	termed	termed
Thrive	thrived/throve	thrived/thriven
Throw	threw	thrown
Thrust	thrust	thrust
Trace	traced	traced
Travel	travelled	travelled
Tread	trod	trodden
Trim	trimmed	trimmed
Try	tried	tried
Turn	turned	turned
Understand	understood	understood
Wait	waited	waited
Wake	woke	woken
Waste	wasted	wasted
Wave	waved	waved
Waver	wavered	wavered
Weaken	weakened	weakened
Weave	wove	woven
Weep	wept	wept
Win	won	won
Wind	wound	wound
Wipe	wiped	wiped
Withdraw	withdrew	withdrawn
Wither	withered	withered
Wring	wrung	wrung
Write	wrote	written

PHRASAL VERBS

ACT

1. *Act upon*
I acted upon his advice.
मैंने उसकी सलाह पर अमल किया।
2. *Act with*
He acted with courage.
उसने साहस से काम किया।
3. *Act upto*
Let him act upto his conscience.
उसे अपनी आत्मा के अनुसार काम करने दें।
4. *Act for*
In the absence of the principal, I acted for him.
मुख्याध्यापक की अनुपस्थिति में मैंने उनकी जगह काम क़िया।
5. *Act against*
We should not act against the interests of our country.
हमें अपने देश के हितों के विरुद्ध काम नहीं करना चाहिए।

BEAR

1. *Bear away*
I bore away the first prize.
मैंने प्रथम पुरस्कार जीता।
2. *Bear up*
Please bear up with me in this matter.
कृपया इस मामले में थोड़ा कष्ट सहन करें (क्योंकि मेरी मजबूरी है)।
3. *Bear out*
Do you bear out what I have said?
मैंने जो कहा है क्या आप उसको पक्का करते हो(अर्थात् उसकी गवाही देते हो)।
4. *Bear well*
You have to behave well in the party.
आपको पार्टी में सही तरीके से व्यवहार करना होगा।

5. *Bear down*
The government bore down all opposition.
सरकार ने सारे विरोध को दबा दिया।

6. *Bear with*
Please bear with us for the increase in the prices of goods.
कृपया कीमतों के बढ़ाये जाने के लिये हमारे साथ यह कष्ट सहन करें।

BREAK

1. *Break into*
The burglars broke into my house last night.
कल रात को मेरे घर में चोरों ने सेंध लगाई।

2. *Break in*
The new apprentices have to be broken in by the officers.
नये भर्ती किये प्रशिक्षुओं को अफसरों द्वारा सिखाना (सीखाना) होता है।

3. *Break with*
I have broken with him for his cunningness.
मैंने उसकी चालाकी के कारण उससे सम्बन्ध तोड़ दिये हैं।

4. *Break up*
The meeting broke up at 5 p.m.
सभा शाम पांच बजे खत्म हुई।

5. *Break open*
They broke open the door.
उन्होंने दरवाज़ा तोड़ कर खोला।

6. *Break down*
His health broke down at last.
अन्त में उसकी सेहत खराब हो गई।

7. *Break away*
Last night, a buffalo broke away from the shed.
कल रात एक भैंस तबेला तोड़कर भाग गई।

BRING

1. *Bring out*
This is the third edition of this book that my publisher has brought

out.

यह किताब का तीसरा संस्करण है जो मेरे प्रकाशक ने प्रकाशित किया है।

2. *Bring about*

Gambling brought about his ruin.

जुए ने उसे बर्बाद कर दिया।

3. *Bring up*

She was brought up by her aunt.

उसका पालन-पोषण उसकी चाची ने किया।

4. *Bring someone round to*

I brought her round to my idea.

मैंने उससे अपना विचार मनवा लिया।

5. *Bring on*

A balanced diet brings on all the required elements.

एक संतुलित भोजन में सारे जरूरी तत्व होते हैं।

BEAT

1. *To beat black and blue*

He was beaten black and blue.

वह बुरी तरह से पीटा गया।

2. *To beat about the bush*

I do not like those boys who always beat about the bush.

मैं हमेशा इधर-उधर की हांकने वाले लड़कों को पसंद नहीं करता।

3. *To beat hollow*

The Pakistani army was beaten hollow in Kargil.

पाकिस्तान की फौज कारगिल में बुरी तरह पिट गई।

BLOW

1. *Blow out*

He blew out the candle.

उसने मोमबत्ती बुझा दी।

2. *Blow up*

The Indian army has blown up the bridge.

भारतीय सेना पुल को उड़ा चुकी है।

3. *Blow over*
The moment the storm blows over, we would be out for a walk.
जिस समय तूफान रूक जायेगा, हम सैर के लिये बाहर जायेंगे।

CARRY

1. *Carry on*
Please carry on the work.
कृपया काम चलता रहने दीजिये।
2. *Carry out*
He carried out my orders.
उसने मेरे हुक्म का पालन किया।
3. *Carry away*
A stroke of current carried him away to the shore.
एक ज़ोरदार लहर उसे किनारे पर ले गई।
4. *Carry off*
I am sure to carry off the first prize.
मुझे विश्वास है कि मैं प्रथम पुरस्कार पाऊंगा।
5. *Carry off*
Many children were carried off due to plague.
बहुत से बच्चे प्लेग से मर गये।
6. *Carry the day*
I carried the day in the contest.
मुकाबले में मैं जीत गया।

COME

1. *Come on*
Come on, let us celebrate the day.
आओ, हम खुशी मनाएं।
2. *Come in*
Please come in.
कृपया अन्दर आयें।
3. *Come round*
He came round to my proposal (view).
वह मेरी बात से सहमत हुआ।

4. *Come of*
He comes of a gentle family.
वह एक अच्छे खानदान का है।

5. *Come back*
I shall come back in a minute.
मैं एक मिनट में वापिस आ जाऊंगा।

6. *Come out*
He opened his lips but no word came out of his mouth.
उसने अपने होंठ खोले लेकिन उसके मुख से कोई भी शब्द नहीं निकला।

7. *Come about*
It came about in the early hours of the morning.
यह सुबह-सुबह हुआ।

8. *Come to light*
The whole matter came to light only when he was caught by the police.
सारी बात उस समय पता लगी जब पुलिस ने उसे पकड़ लिया।

9. *Come over*
He could not come over the obstacle even in his full life.
वह ज़िन्दगी भर बाधाओं से उबर नहीं सका।

10. *Come by*
He came by this pen from his uncle.
उसने यह पेन अपने अंकल से लिया।

11. *Come up*
This point can come up in every mind.
यह बात सभी के दिमाग में आ सकती है।

12. *Come off*
My sister's marriage comes off next month.
अगले महीने मेरी बहन की शादी है।

13. *Come to the point*
Please come to the point. I am not interested in wasting time.
कृपया मुद्दे पर आयें। मैं समय नष्ट करने का इच्छुक नहीं हूँ।

14. *Come upon*
When I was on my way home, a mad man suddenly came upon

me.
मैं जब अपने घर जा रहा था, तो रास्ते में एक पागल आदमी अचानक मेरे ऊपर झपटा।

15. *Come up*
The price of wheat has come up.
गेहूँ के दाम बढ़ गये हैं।

16. *Come down*
The price of gold has come down.
सोने का भाव गिर गया है।
I saw him coming down to the foot of the mountain.
मैंने देखा कि वह पहाड़ के आधार (या निचले भाग) की ओर आ रहा था।

CALL

1. *Call on*
I called on her in her house.
मैं उससे मिलने उसके घर गया।

2. *Call up*
Tony called up the full detail.
टोनी ने सारी बात दुबारा सुनाई।
(या टोनी को सारी बात दुबारा याद आई)

3. *Called off*
The students called off the strike.
विद्यार्थियों ने हड़ताल खत्म कर दी।

4. *To call a spade a spade*
We should always call a spade a spade.
हमें सदा सच बोलना चाहिए।

5. *Call in*
Let us call in the doctor at once.
आइये हमलोग डॉक्टर को तुरंत बुलाएं।

6. *Call at*
I called at her house in the morning.
मैं सुबह उसके घर गया।

7. *Call out*
He called out my name.
उसने मेरा नाम पुकारा।

CUT

1. *Cut off*
The intruders tried their best to cut off the supply line.
घुसपैठियों ने सप्लाई लाइन को काटने का पूरा यत्न किया।
2. *Cut up*
She feels much cut up after the death of her brother.
वह अपने भाई की मौत के बाद बहुत दुःखी महसूस करती है।
3. *Cut down*
Cut down your expenses.
अपने खर्चों को कम करो।
4. *Cut out*
He is cut out for this kind of job.
वह इस तरह की नौकरी के लिये ठीक है।
5. *Cutting in*
He kept cutting in when I was talking.
वह बीच में बोलता रहा जब मैं बात कर रहा था।

FALL

1. *Fall in*
I have fallen in love with this girl.
मुझे इस लड़की से प्यार हो गया है।
2. *Fall down*
She fell down from the horse.
वह घोड़े से नीचे गिर गई।
3. *Fall out*
You should not fall out with each other.
तुम्हें एक दूसरे से नहीं लड़ना चाहिए।
4. *Fall in (with)*
(a) Many trees fell in the storm.
तूफान में बहुत से पेड़ गिर गये।

(b) I fell in with one of my friends on my way home.
घर आते समय रास्ते में मुझे मेरा एक दोस्त मिल गया।

5. *Fall flat*
My advice fell flat on him.
मेरी सलाह का उस पर कोई असर नहीं हुआ।

6. *Fall among*
He has fallen among gamblers.
वह जुआरियों के चक्कर में फंस गया है।

7. *Fall from*
The cup fell from his hand.
उसके हाथ से कप गिर गया।

GIVE

1. *Give way*
The bridge gave way.
पुल टूट गया।

2. *Give in*
The child gave in to the taste of cold drink and so, he drank a bottle full in one go.
बच्चे को कोल्ड ड्रिंक का स्वाद बहुत अच्छा लगा और इसलिए, वह इसे एक ही बार में पी गया।

3. *Give out*
It was given out that the minister was coming.
यह घोषणा की गई कि मंत्री जी पधार रहे हैं।

4. *Give over*
I was given over the charge of this office.
मुझे इस कार्यालय का कार्य-भार सौंपा गया था।

5. *Give away*
The principal gave away the prizes.
प्रधानाध्यापक ने ईनाम बांटे।

GO

1. *Go for*
He is going for a big deal.
वह बहुत बड़े धन्धे के लिये जा रहा है।

2. *Go without saying*
   It goes without saying that he will be the next Prime Minister.
   यह कहने की जरूरत नहीं है कि वह अगला प्रधानमंत्री होगा।

3. *Go up*
   Rice has gone up.
   चावल के भाव बढ़ गये हैं।

4. *Go down*
   Gold has gone down.
   सोने के भाव गिर गये हैं।

5. *Go off*
   The gun went off.
   बन्दूक चल गई।

6. *Go through*
   He went through the papers.
   उसने कागजात पढ़े।

7. *To go without*
   She can go without water for long.
   वह बिना पानी पिये काफी देर तक जिन्दा रह सकती है।

8. *Go out*
   The light has gone out.
   बत्ती बुझ गई है।

9. *Go into*
   He is a wise man and will definitely go into the matter before making up his mind.
   वह बहुत समझदार आदमी है तथा अपना मन बनाने से पहले मामले का निश्चित रूप से अध्ययन करेगा।

GET

1. *Get about*
   (a) It is getting about that he is to be put behind the bars.
   यह अफवाह फैल रही है कि उसे जेल में बन्द कर दिया जायेगा।
   (b) He has been getting about for long.
   वह बहुत देर से यात्रा कर रहा है।

(c) The patient is now getting about.
रोगी अब ठीक है।

2. *Get on with*
He is getting on with his hard work.
वह अपनी सख्त मेहनत के कारण उन्नति कर रहा है।

3. *Get off*
Get off your ring.
अपनी अंगूठी उतार दो।

4. *Get out*
Get out of the class-room.
क्लास रूम से बाहर निकलो।

5. *Get someone round*
She got her mother round to her idea.
वह अपनी माताजी को अपनी बात मनवाने में सफल हो गई।

6. *Get through*
He got through the whole matter.
उसने सारी बात समझ ली।

7. *Get over*
He got over all his problems.
उसने अपनी सब समस्याओं पर काबू पा लिया।

8. *Get at*
His hand could not get at my collars.
उसका हाथ मेरी गिरेबान तक नहीं पहुँच सका।

HOLD

1. *Hold on*
Please hold on, he would be on the line in a minute.
कृपया रिसीवर पकड़े रखें, वह एक मिनट में आपसे बात करेगा।

2. *Hold one's tongue*
Hold your tongue.
अपनी जुबान को लगाम दो।

3. *Hold over*
The meeting has been held over.
सभा को आगे कर दिया गया है।

4. *Hold out*
She tries to hold out false hopes to me.
वह मुझे झूठी आशाएं देने की कोशिश करती है।

KEEP

1. *To keep*
She keeps a lot of money.
उसके पास बहुत पैसा है।

2. *Keep on*
Keep it on.
इसे जारी रखो।

3. *To keep promise*
You should keep your promise.
तुम्हें अपने वचन का पालन करना चाहिए।

4. *Keep back*
I keep back my important documents from my friend.
मैं अपने ज़रूरी कागजात अपने दोस्तों से छुपा कर रखता हूँ।

5. *Keep away*
Keep yourself away from this mad dog.
स्वयं को इस पागल कुत्ते से दूर रखो।

6. *Keep up*
I was kept up by a severe pain.
बहुत ज़्यादा दर्द के कारण मुझे बिस्तर में रहना पड़ा।

LOOK

1. *Look after*
She is looking after her daughter.
वह अपनी लड़की की देख भाल कर रही है।

2. *Look down upon*
You should not look down upon the weak.
तुम्हें कमज़ोरों को घृणा से नहीं देखना चाहिए।

3. *Look up (for)*
   (a) I was looking up for something.
   मैं किसी वस्तु का सहारा ढूंढ रहा था।
   (b) The prices are looking up.
   कीमतें बढ़ रही हैं।
   (c) Please look up the last train (in the Railway Time-table) to Delhi.
   कृपया दिल्ली को जाने वाली अन्तिम गाड़ी को देखें।
4. *Look into*
   The officer is looking into the matter.
   अफसर मामले की जांच कर रहा है।
5. *Look for*
   I was looking for you.
   मैं आपकी तलाश कर रहा था।
6. *Look on*
   She looks on me as her brother.
   वह मुझे अपने भाई के रूप में देखती है।
7. *Look forward*
   We are looking forward to his coming here.
   हम उसके यहां आने की प्रतीक्षा कर रहे हैं।

MAKE

1. *Make up*
   She made up her mind to go to Delhi.
   उसने दिल्ली जाने का इरादा किया था।
2. *Make out*
   It is difficult to make out what he means.
   यह समझना कठिन है कि वह क्या कहता है।
3. *Make over*
   He made over his pen to me.
   उसने मुझे अपना पैन दे दिया।

4. *Make up*
He has made up his deficiency in Hindi.
उसने हिन्दी में अपनी कमी को पूरा कर लिया है।

5. *Make after*
I made after the thief.
मैं चोर के पीछे दौड़ा।

6. *To make both ends meet*
In these days it is difficult for the common people to make both ends meet.
आजकल आम लोगों के लिये निर्वाह करना मुश्किल है।

PUT

1. *Put down*
The rebellion was put down with heavy hands.
विद्रोह को सख्ती से दबा दिया गया।

2. *Put out*
He put out the fire.
उसने आग बुझा दी।

3. *Put off*
Do not put off till tomorrow what you can do today.
आज का काम कल पर मत छोड़ो।

4. *Put on*
He put on his new pants.
उसने अपनी नई पैंट पहनी है।

5. *Put by*
Put by some money for the bad days.
बुरे दिनों के लिये कुछ पैसा बचा कर रखें।

6. *Put up*
Where are you putting up now-a-days?
आजकल आप कहां ठहरे हैं ?

7. *Put up*
(a) He has put me up in respect of my election duties.
उसने मुझे मेरे चुनाव-सम्बन्धी कर्त्तव्यों के बारे में समझा दिया है।

(b) Is it he who has put you up to this mischief?
क्या उसने तुम्हें इस शरारत के लिए उकसाया है ?

PASS

1. *Pass through*
He passed through the whole matter.
उसने सारी बात सुनी या उसने सारे मामले को समझा।
2. *Pass away*
His father passed away last night.
उसके पिता पिछली रात को स्वर्ग सिधार गये।
3. *Pass off*
The meeting passed off peacefully.
बैठक शांति से समाप्त हो गई।
4. *Pass for*
She passes for a gentle lady.
वह एक भली औरत मानी जाती है।

RUN

1. *Run Over*
The child was run over by a truck
बच्चा एक ट्रक के द्वारा कुचला गया।
2. *Run through*
It is a run-through train.
यह एक यहां न रुकने वाली गाड़ी है।
3. *Run into*
A car ran into a truck.
एक कार एक ट्रक से टकरा गई।
4. *Run out*
All his savings ran out before the end of the year.
साल खत्म होने से पहले उसकी सारी बचत खत्म हो गई।
5. *Run down*
Suddenly, the wheels of the car ran down.
अचानक कार के पहिये रुक गये।

6. *Run down*
   Due to continuous work, he felt himself much run down.
   लगातार ज़्यादा काम के कारण उसे कमजोरी महसूस होने लगी।
7. *Run short*
   He is running short of money as the year is about to slide away.
   उसके पास पैसा खत्म हो रहा है जबकि यह साल खत्म होने को है।

SEE

1. *See off*
   I am going to the bus stop to see off my friend.
   मैं बस स्टैंड पर अपने दोस्त को छोड़ने जा रहा हूँ।
2. *See into*
   You should see into the matter properly.
   तुम्हें बात अच्छी तरह से समझ लेनी चाहिए।
3. *See through*
   I saw through his game.
   मैं उसकी चालाकी को भांप गया।

Chapter 18

The Tense
(काल)

यह जान लेना अत्यंत आवश्यक है कि Tenses का ज्ञान न होने से कभी भी Correct English नहीं सीखी जा सकती। Tense वास्तव में Latin शब्द 'tempus' से बना है जिसका अर्थ होता है 'समय'। अत: Tense हमें किसी भी Action के होने के समय का ज्ञान देते हैं। ये यह भी बताते हैं कि कोई Action हो रहा है, हो चुका है या होगा।

KINDS OF TENSES

Tense तीन प्रकार के होते हैं:

(A) Present Tense (वर्तमान काल) (चल रहा समय)

(B) Past Tense (भूत काल) (बीत चुका समय)

(C) Future Tense (भविष्य काल) (आने वाला समय)

(i) I make no mistake. — Present Tense
मैं कोई गलती नहीं करता हूँ।

(ii) I made a mistake. — Past Tense
मैंने एक गलती की।

(iii) I shall not make any mistake. — Future Tense
मैं कोई गलती नहीं करूंगा।

इन तीनों दिये गये Tenses में हर एक चार प्रकार का होता है:

(A) Indefinite Tense
(B) Continuous Tense
(C) Perfect Tense
(D) Perfect Continuous Tense

इनको हम बारी-बारी से पढ़ते एवं समझते चले जायेंगे।

PRESENT TENSE

यह चार प्रकार का होता है:

(A) Present Indefinite
(B) Present Continuous
(C) Present Perfect
(D) Present Perfect Continuous

(A) Present Indefinite Tense

जो Sentences अधिकतर 'ता है', 'ती है', 'ते हैं' आदि से खत्म होते हैं, उन्हें English में Present Indefinite Tenses कहा जाता है। जैसे कि:

(i) मोहन खाना खाता है।
(ii) सोहन सोता है।

इस तरह के Present Indefinite Sentences English में बनाने का formula नीचे दिया गया है :

Subject (S) + Verb (V) की First Form + 'es' or 's' + Object (O)

Note: अगर S (Subject) Plural हो तो Verb की First Form के साथ 's' or 'es' नहीं लगता और यदि 'I' Subject हो तो भी Verb की First Form के साथ 's' या 'es' नहीं लगता।

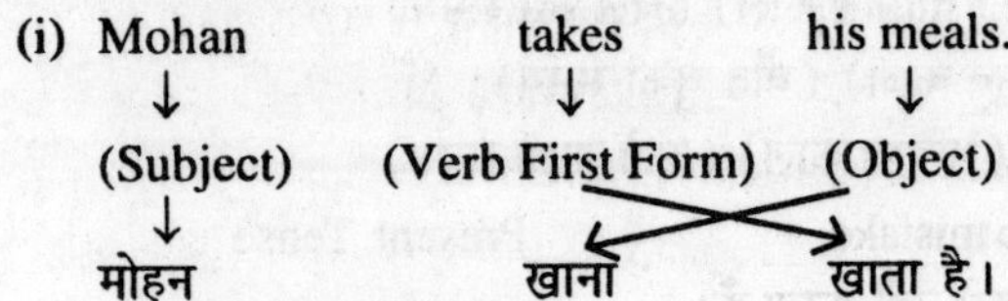

(ii) He takes bath.
वह नहाता है।

(iii) They go to school.
वे स्कूल जाते हैं।

Note: इस Sentence में 'go' के साथ 'es' नहीं लगा है क्योंकि 'They' Subject Plural है।

(iv) I make no noise in the class.
मैं कक्षा में शोर नहीं मचाता हूँ।

(v) We like mangoes.
हम आम पसन्द करते हैं।

Note: Sentences Number (iv) तथा (v) में भी Verb की First Form के साथ 's' या 'es' नहीं लगा है। ऐसे ही 'you' के साथ भी 's' या 'es' नहीं लगता)।

(vi) You do your work.
आप अपना काम करते हैं (या तुम अपना काम करते हो)।

EXERCISE 1

नीचे दिए गए खाली स्थान भरें:

1. He ...... a song.
(a) sings (b) sing.

2. She ...... me.
(a) love (b) loves

3. We ...... our duty.
(a) does (b) do

4. I never ...... a lie.
(a) tell (b) tells

5. The rabbits ...... out of their burrows.
(a) jump (b) jumps

EXERCISE 2

नीचे दिये गये वाक्यों का English में अनुवाद करें:

1. राम स्कूल जाता है।
2. हम खेलते हैं।
3. गीता गाना गाती है।
4. बन्दर नाचते हैं।
5. पक्षी चहचहाते हैं।
6. सोनू पंतग उड़ाता है।
7. पवन शरारत करता है।
8. मैं तथा सोहन पार्क में खेलते हैं।
9. रवि मोहन से लड़ता है।
10. अध्यापक विद्यार्थी को डांटता है।

Formula for Negative Sentences: Affirmative Sentences को Negative Sentences में Change करने के लिये Present Indefinite Tense में 'does not' या 'do not' का प्रयोग होता है।

Formula: S + does not/do not + 1st form of the V + O

Note: ध्यान रहे 'does not' हमेशा Third Person Singular Subject के साथ Use में लाया जाता है।

Note: Negative Sentence में कभी भी Verb की First Form के साथ 's' या 'es' का प्रयोग नहीं होता, चाहे Subject Singular ही क्यों न हो।

Examples

(a) He does not obey you.
वह आपका कहना नहीं मानता है।

(b) We do not quarrel with each other.
हम एक दूसरे से नहीं लड़ते हैं।

(c) I do not take notice of such rubbish.
मैं इस तरह की गंदी बातों पर ध्यान नहीं देता हूँ।

(d) She does not speak the truth.
वह सच नहीं बोलती है।

(e) They do not meet me on the road.
वह मुझे सड़क पर नहीं मिलते हैं।

EXERCISE 3

नीचे दिये गये खाली स्थान भरें:

1. She.....play at cards.
(a) does not (b) do not

2. The birds...... fly in the air.
(a) does not (b) do not

3. The balloon ...... burst in the cold weather
(a) does not (b) do not

4. She .... like milk.
(a) does not (b) do not

5. I .... like to play hockey.
(a) does not (b) do not

EXERCISE 4

नीचे दिये गये Sentences का English में अनुवाद करें:

1. वह नहीं खेलता है।
2. राम पतंग नहीं उड़ाता है।
3. मोहन स्कूल नहीं जाता है।
4. मैं सिगरेट नहीं पीता हूँ।
5. मेरा भाई शराब नहीं पीता है।
6. हम अण्डे नहीं खाते हैं।
7. वह रात को ठीक से नहीं सोता है।
8. दिलीप कक्षा में चुप नहीं बैठता है।
9. जगरूप चाय नहीं पीता है।
10. वे आपस में मिलजुल कर नहीं रहते हैं।

Interrogative Sentences: (1) जब हम Present Indefinite का Interrogative Sentence बनाते हैं तो Does या Do का प्रयोग Subject से पहले करते हैं।

(2) इसमें भी Verb की 1st form के साथ 's' या 'es' नहीं लगता।

Formula: Wh or how + Does or Do + S + V (1st form) + O + ?

Note: Here 'Wh' stands for 'What', 'Where', 'When', 'Why' etc.

Examples

(a) Do you know how to swim?
क्या आपको तैरना आता है ?

(b) Do you like me?
क्या आप मुझे पसन्द करते हैं।

(c) What do you think about me?
आप मेरे बारे में क्या सोचते हैं ?

(d) Where does she keep her cosmetics?
वह अपना मेकअप का सामान कहां रखती है ?

(e) When does he take his breakfast?
वह अपना नाश्ता कब लेता है?

EXERCISE 5

नीचे दिये गये खाली स्थान भरें :

1. ....he beat his brother?
(a) Does (b) Do

2. When .... you go to school?
(a) Does (b) Do

3. When....she take her bed tea?
(a) Does (b) Do

4. .... I spend my money on useless things?
(a) Does (b) Do

5. .... they sing in a sweet voice?
(a) Does (b) Do

EXERCISE 6

नीचे दिये गये Sentences का English में अनुवाद करें :

1. क्या वह आपकी बात नहीं मानता ?

2. वह कहां पर सोता है ?

3. उसे छुट्टी कब होती है ?

4. क्या वह प्रतिदिन नहाता है ?

5. क्या वह प्रतिदिन ब्रश करता है ?

6. क्या वह अपने जूते पालिश करता है ?

7. वह हर रोज़ कितना चलता है ?

8. क्या आप रोज़ सैर पर जाते हैं ?

9. क्या मैं हर वक्त हंसता रहता हूं ?

10. वह किस देश में रहता है ?

Interrogative Negative Sentences: इसका Formula लगभग Interrogative Sentences जैसा है। अन्तर केवल यह है कि इसमें 'does' या 'do' के बाद Subject

आता है और उसके बाद not लगता है।

Formula: Wh or how + does/do + S + not + V (1st form) + O + ?

Examples

(a) Does he not take interest in the deal?
क्या वह इस सौदे में रूचि नहीं लेता है?

(b) Why do you not understand me?
तुम मुझे क्यों नहीं समझते हो?

(c) Why does he not polish his shoes daily?
वह अपने जूते प्रतिदिन पालिश क्यों नहीं करता है?

(d) When do I not speak the truth?
मैं सच कब नहीं बोलता हूँ?

(e) Why do you not punish him?
तुम उसे सज़ा क्यों नहीं देते हो?

EXERCISE 7

नीचे दिये गये Sentences का English में अनुवाद करें:

1. वह तुम से हंस कर बात क्यों नहीं करता है?
2. वह तुम्हें रोकना क्यों नहीं चाहते हैं?
3. क्या वह तुम्हें पसंद नहीं करती है?
4. क्या मैं ठीक बात नहीं करता हूँ?
5. क्या वह मुझे धोख़ा नहीं देता है?
6. क्या आप मेरी बात पर विश्वास नहीं करते हैं?
7. क्या वह लड़ना नहीं चाहता है?
8. क्या आप मरना नहीं चाहते हैं?
9. क्या आप टेलीविज़न देखना पसन्द नहीं करते हैं?
10. क्या आज हवा नहीं चल रही है?

Note I: Present Indefinite Tense में कई बार 'is', 'am', 'are', 'has' या 'have' का प्रयोग हो जाता है।

Note II: Interrogative Sentences इसी Tense में कई बार 'Can', 'Dare', 'Must' आदि से शुरू हो सकते हैं।

Examples

(a) Can you do it?
क्या तुम इसे कर सकते हो?

(b) May I talk to you ?
क्या मैं आप से बात कर सकता हूँ।

(c) I have a pen.
मेरे पास एक पैन है।

(d) I am here.
मैं यहां हूं।

(B) Present Continuous Tense

जो Sentence, 'रहा है', 'रहे हैं', 'रही है' आदि से खत्म हों, उन्हें Present Continuous Tense कहा जाता है।

(i) गणेश गाना गा रहा है। (ii) लक्की पानी पी रहा है।

(iii) वे नहा रहे हैं।

Formula: इस Sentence में Verb की First Form के साथ 'ing' का प्रयोग होता है: S + is, am, are + (V-I + ing) + O.

(i) 'am' शब्द का प्रयोग केवल 'I' शब्द के Subject होने पर होता है;

(ii) 'is' शब्द का प्रयोग जब Subject Singular हो तब होता है;

(iii) तथा 'are' शब्द का प्रयोग जब Subject Plural हो तब होता है।

Examples

(a) The peon is ringing the bell.
चपरासी घण्टी बजा रहा है।

(b) The peacock is dancing.
मोर नाच रहा है।

(c) I am going to school.
मैं स्कूल जा रहा हूँ।

(d) They are laughing at the poor.
वे लोग गरीबों पर हंस रहे हैं।

(e) We are going for a great deal.
हम एक बड़ा सौदा करने जा रहे हैं।

EXERCISE 8

नीचे दिये खाली स्थान भरो:

1. She .... talking to me.
(a) is (b) am (c) are

2. I........ making fun of him.
(a) is (b) am (c) are

3. We .... telling the real thing.
(a) is (b) am (c) are

4. He........ sending a message to his friend.
(a) is (b) am (c) are

5. They........ looking for an opportunity.
(a) is (b) am (c) are

EXERCISE 9

नीचे दिये गये Sentences का English में अनुवाद करें:

1. वह नहा रही है।
2. तुम सो रहे हो।
3. मैं पढ़ रहा हूँ।
4. टोनी खेल रहा है।
5. उसके पिता जी उसे नसीहत दे रहे हैं।
6. उसकी सांस तेज़-तेज़ चल रही है।
7. घोड़ा दीवार के ऊपर से कूद रहा है।
8. चोर सेंध लगा रहा है।
9. वह कुछ सोच रहा है।
10. वह साफ-साफ बोल रहा है।

Negative Sentences: इस Tense के Negative Sentence में 'is', 'am' और 'are' के साथ 'not' Word Add हो जाता है।

Formula: S + is, am, are + not + (V-I + ing) + O.

Examples

(a) She is not writing a letter.
वह पत्र नहीं लिख रही है।

(b) They are not sleeping in their beds.
वह अपने बिस्तरों पर नहीं सो रहे हैं।

(c) He is not putting on flesh.
वह मोटा नहीं हो रहा है।

(d) I am not putting on my new shirt.
मैं अपनी नई कमीज़ नहीं डाल रहा हूँ।

(e) We are not swimming.
हम तैर नहीं रहे हैं।

EXERCISE 10

नीचे दिये गये Sentences का English में अनुवाद करें:

1. वह स्कूल नहीं जा रही है।
2. वे गुस्सा नहीं कर रहे हैं।
3. वह हंस नहीं रही है।
4. मैं खेतों में हल नहीं चल रहा हूँ।
5. माली पौधों को पानी नहीं दे रहा है।
6. पेड़ की परछाईं नीचे नहीं पड़ रही है।
7. मैं अपना वोट डालने नहीं जा रहा हूँ।
8. हम किसी से झूठ नहीं बोल रहे हैं।
9. वह एक तस्वीर नहीं बना रही है।
10. लवली अपना काम नहीं कर रही है।

Interrogative Sentences : Present Continuous Tense में Interrogative

Sentences बनाने का Formula नीचे दिया गया है:

Wh or how + is/am/are + S + (V-I + ing) + O + ?

Examples

(a) Am I disturbing you?
क्या मैं आपको परेशान कर रहा हूँ?

(b) Are you waiting for somebody?
क्या आप किसी की प्रतीक्षा कर रहे हैं?

(c) Why is she crying so hard?
वह इतनी ज़ोर से क्यों चिल्ला रही है?

(d) How are they preparing so delicious food?
वे इतना स्वादिष्ट खाना कैसे बना रहे हैं?

(e) Is he giving you something to eat?
क्या वह तुम्हें खाने के लिये कुछ दे रहा है?

EXERCISE 11

नीचे दिये गये Sentences का English में अनुवाद करें:

1. क्या वह आपकी बात पर अमल कर रहा है?
2. क्या वह आपके विरुद्ध लोगों को भड़का रहा है?
3. आप रो क्यों रहे हैं?
4. मैं बाज़ार क्यों नहीं जा रहा हूँ?
5. वह आप से क्या पूछ रहा है?
6. क्या उसका नाम बदनाम हो रहा है?
7. क्या सोना सस्ता हो रहा है?
8. मंहगाई क्यों बढ़ रही है?
9. बतासे क्यों नहीं बिक रहे हैं?
10. सभी को खाना क्यों नहीं मिल रहा है?

Hints for Translation

6. getting defamed.

Interrogative Negative Sentences: इस Tense के Interrogative Negative Sentences बनाने का Formula नीचे दिया गया है।

(Wh or how) + is/am/are + S + not + (V-I + ing) + O + ?

Examples

(a) Why is he not taking care of you?
वह आपका ध्यान क्यों नहीं रख रहा है?

(b) Am I not speaking frankly?
क्या मैं खुल कर बात नहीं कर रहा हूँ?

(c) Is she not sending a message?
क्या वह संदेश नहीं भेज रही है?

(d) Why are they not inviting you to the party.
वे आपको पार्टी पर निमन्त्रण क्यों नहीं दे रहे हैं?

(e) Why is she not helping you?
वह आपकी सहायता क्यों नहीं कर रही है?

EXERCISE 12

नीचे दिये गये Sentences का English में अनुवाद करें:

1. वह नेता भाषण क्यों नहीं दे रहा है?
2. आप ईमानदारी से काम क्यों नहीं कर रहे हैं?
3. मैं चुप क्यों नहीं बैठ रहा हूँ?
4. वह नहा क्यों नहीं रहा है?
5. वह तैयार क्यों नहीं हो रहा है?
6. क्या आप मेरी बात ध्यान से नहीं सुन रहे हैं?
7. क्यों उसको सांप डंक नहीं मार रहा है?
8. क्या वह मज़े में जिन्दगी नहीं बिता रहा है?
9. क्या वह सोच कर नहीं बोल रहा है?
10. क्या वह पैसे बैंक में नहीं डाल रहा है?

(C) Present Perfect Tense

(1) जब कोई Sentence 'चुकी है', 'चुका है', 'चुके हैं' आदि से खत्म होता है तो वह Present Perfect Tense कहलाता है।

(i) मोहन कहानी सुना चुका है। (ii) लता खाना खा चुकी है।

(2) इसमें 'has' तथा 'have' का प्रयोग होता है।

(3) 'have' तब प्रयोग में आता है जब Subject या तो 'I' हो या Plural हो।

(4) अगर Subject Singular हो तो 'has' प्रयोग में लाया जाता है।

Formula: S + has/have + V (3rd form) + O.

Examples

(a) I have done my work.
मैं अपना काम कर चुका हूँ।

(b) She has prepared the food.
वह खाना बना चुकी है।

(c) They have made up their mind.
उन्होंने अपना मन बना लिया है।

(d) The rabbit has dug a deep burrow.
खरगोश गहरा खड्डा खोद चुका है।

(e) We have plucked the flowers.
हम फूल तोड़ चुके हैं।

EXERCISE 13

नीचे दिये गये Sentences के खाली स्थान भरें:

1. He .... changed his mind.
(a) has (b) have

2. I .... made up a correct statement.
(a) has (b) have

3. The elephants .... uprooted many trees.
(a) has (b) have

4. She .... drawn a beautiful picture.
(a) has (b) have

5. We ..... made them ready to attend the meeting.
(a) has (b) have

EXERCISE 14

नीचे दिये गये Sentences का English में अनुवाद करें:

1. संदीप गाना गा चुका है।
2. रात ढल चुकी है।
3. आकाश में तारे जगमगा चुके हैं।
4. पक्षी गाना गा चुके है।
5. हम दिल्ली पहुँच चुके हैं।
6. मंत्री झूठ बोल चुका है।
7. लड़ाई शुरू हो चुकी है।
8. चोर चोरी कर चुका है।
9. सेब वृक्ष से गिर चुका है।
10. वह फसल काट चुका है।

Hints for Translation

2. is over. **7.** broken out. **8.** committed a theft. **9.** fallen. **10.** harvested.

Negative Sentences: Present Perfect को Negative Sentence बनाने का Formula नीचे दिया गया है:

Formula: S + has/have + not + V (3rd form) + O.

Examples:

(a) She has not made a noise.
उसने शोर नहीं मचाया है।

(b) They have not shown their interest in my talk.
उन्होंने मेरी बात में कोई रुचि नहीं दिखाई है।

(c) We have not taken too much drink in the party.
हमने पार्टी में ज्यादा शराब नहीं पी है।

(d) I have not settled your accounts so far.
मैंने अभी आपका हिसाब नहीं किया है।

(e) She has not still taken her meals.
उसने अभी तक भोजन नहीं किया है।

EXERCISE 15

नीचे दिये गये Sentences का English में अनुवाद करें:

1. मैंने कोई ईनाम नहीं जीता है।
2. कुलदीप कक्षा में प्रथम नहीं आया है।
3. वह सैर समाप्त नहीं कर चुका है।
4. मोहन फिल्म देखने चला गया है।
5. जगदीश अब तक नहीं खेल चुका है।
6. मैं उसे डांट नहीं चुका हूँ।
7. वह अपने पिता की बात नहीं मान चुका है।
8. वे मुझे अपनी सारी बातें नहीं बता चुके हैं।
9. पहलवान हार नहीं चुका है।
10. वह गाय का दूध नहीं दुह चुका है।

Hints for Translation
6. scolded **9.** wrestler **10.** milked

Interrogative Sentences: Present Perfect को Interrogative बनाने का Formula नीचे दिया गया है:

Formula: Wh or how + has/have + S + V (3rd form) + O + ?
Examples

(a) Have you decided?
क्या तुम फैसला कर चुके हो?

(b) Has she looked into the matter?
क्या वह विषय की अच्छी छानबीन कर चुकी है?

(c) Why have I made such an idea?
मैंने इस तरह का विचार क्यों बनाया है?

(d) How has he come to know about it?
उसे इसके बारे में कैसे पता चला है?

(e) Where has she gone?
वह कहां चली गई है ?

EXRECISE 16

नीचे दिये गये Sentences का English में अनुवाद करें:

1. वह बाहर क्यों गया है ?
2. वह जंगल में क्यों गया है ?
3. क्या हम मरुस्थल में पहुँच चुके हैं ?
4. क्या हमारी फौज आगे बढ़ चुकी है ?
5. क्या वह सब कुछ जान चुका है ?
6. क्या वे कुएं में कूद चुके हैं ?
7. क्या जानवर चारा खा चुके हैं ?
8. क्या वह आपको आगे की योजना बता चुका है ?
9. वे कहां से ये सब चीजें ला चुके हैं ?
10. क्या आप मुझे डरा चुके हैं ?

Hints for Translation
3. desert **7.** fodder **8.** frightened.

Interrogative Negative Sentences: Present Perfect के Interrogative Negative Sentences का Formula नीचे दिया गया है:

Formula: Wh or how + has/have + S + not + V (3rd form) + O + ?

Examples

(a) Why have you not got an early information?
आपको जल्दी क्यों पता नहीं चला ?

(b) Have I not attended the party?
क्या मैं पार्टी में उपस्थित नहीं हो चुका हूँ ?

(c) Why have you not got it?
तुम इसे क्यों नहीं समझ चुके हो ?

(d) Has she not drunk a cup of tea?
क्या वह चाय का एक प्याला नहीं पी चुका है ?

(e) Why have you not done so well?
आपने इतना बढ़िया काम क्यों नहीं किया है ?

EXERCISE 17

नीचे दिये गये Sentences का English में अनुवाद करें:

1. क्या आप मेरी तरफ नहीं देख चुके हैं ?

2. क्या आप खाना नहीं खा चुके हैं?
3. क्या कौवा पानी नहीं ढूंढ चुका है?
4. क्या लोमड़ी अंगूरों का स्वाद नहीं चख चुकी है?
5. क्या मैं आपकी बात पर भरोसा नहीं कर चुका हूँ?
6. क्या वह आपके कान में कुछ नहीं कह चुका है?
7. क्या अध्यापक संदीप को नहीं पीट चुका है?
8. क्या हम चुगली नहीं कर चुके हैं?
9. क्या वह दीवार के ऊपर से छलांग नहीं लगा चुका है?
10. क्या आप नई घड़ी खरीद चुके हैं?

Hints for Translation

3. searched for. **4.** tasted. **5.** believed in. **6.** whispered

(D) Present Perfect Continuous Tense

इस Tense में 'been' Word का प्रयोग होता है।

Formula: S + has/have + been + (V_1 + ing) + O + since or for + time

Note: (a) 'for' का प्रयोग Period of time के लिए होता है।

(b) 'since', का प्रयोग 'Point of time' के लिए किया जाता है।

Examples

(a) It has been raining since morning.
सुबह से वर्षा हो रही है।

(b) He has been talking meaninglessly since morning.
वह सुबह से बेतुकी बातें कर रहा है।

(c) We have been waiting for you for one hour.
हम एक घण्टे से आपका इन्तज़ार कर रहे हैं।

(d) They have been looking for you for half an hour.
वे आधे घण्टे से आपको ढूंढ रहे हैं।

(e) She has been making a doll since evening.
वह शाम से एक गुड़िया बना रही है।

EXERCISE 18

नीचे दिये गये Sentences के खाली स्थान भरें:

1. She ..... talking to me since morning.
(a) has been (b) have been

2. He ..... living in this house since 1980.
(a) has been (b) have been

3. They .... working in the fields for five hours.
(a) has been (b) have been

4. I .... trying my best since morning to learn about the real truth.
(a) has been (b) have been

5. We .... dancing in the party for the past two hours.
(a) has been (b) have been

EXERCISE 19

नीचे दिये गये Sentences का English में अनुवाद करें:

1. मैं सुबह से आपका इन्तज़ार कर रहा हूँ।
2. वह दो घण्टे से झूठ बोल रहा है।
3. पुलिस दोपहर से चोर को पीट रही है।
4. वह 1979 से इस घर में रह रहा है।
5. चपरासी काफी देर से घण्टी बजा रहा है।
6. वह एक सप्ताह से शिमला जाने की तैयारी कर रहा है।
7. मोहन सुबह से तालाब में तैर रहा है।
8. कुत्ता रात से भौंक रहा है।
9. वह पिछले साल से बीमार चल रहा है।
10. वे सुबह से लुका-छिपी खेल रहे हैं।

Negative Sentences: Present Perfect Continuous के Negative Sentences बनाने का Formula नीचे दिया गया है।

Formula: S + has/have + not + been + (V-I + ing) + O + since or for + time.

Examples

(a) They have not been proposing your name to the boss since morning.
वे प्रात: से बॉस के सामने आपका नाम नहीं दे रहे हैं।

(b) I have not been crying for a glass of water since lunch.
मैं दोपहर के खाने के बाद से पानी के एक गिलास के लिए नहीं चिल्ला रहा हूँ।

(c) She has not been attending any party without you for two months.
वह दो महीने से आपके बिना किसी पार्टी पर उपस्थित नहीं हो रही है।

(d) We have not been taking their threats seriously since January last.
हम पिछली जनवरी से उनकी धमकियों को गम्भीरता से नहीं ले रहे हैं।

(e) You have not been learning anything since 1997.
आप 1997 से कुछ नहीं सीख रहे हैं।

EXERCISE 20

नीचे दिये गये Sentences का English में अनुवाद करें:

1. मैं एक घण्टे से अपने गांव नहीं जा रहा हूँ।
2. **वह इस मकान में पन्द्रह वर्षों से नहीं रह रहा है।**
3. **आपके पिता का दांत सुबह से दर्द नहीं कर रहा है।**
4. हम पांच बजे से बाज़ार से सब्जी लेने नहीं जा रहे हैं।
5. पिछले पांच मिनट से तुम चाय नहीं पी रहे हो।
6. वह सुबह से अखबार नहीं पढ़ रहा है।
7. **वह दो घण्टे से मुझ पर गुस्सा नहीं हो रही है।**
8. **वह अपने परिणाम का इन्तज़ार दो दिनों से कर रहा है।**
9. वह पिछले बुधवार से कहीं भी दूर नहीं जा रहा है।
10. वे सुबह से हमारे साथ क्रिकेट का मैच खेल रहे हैं।

Hints for Translation

1. for **2.** for **3.** since, aching **4.** since **5.** for **9.** since

Interrogative Sentences: Present Continuous के Interrogative Sentences का Formula नीचे दिया गया है:

Formula: Wh or how + has/have + S + been + (V-I + ing) + O + since or for + time + ?

Examples

(a) Have you been asking someone for a glass of water for two minutes?
क्या आप दो मिनट से एक गिलास पानी के लिए किसी से कह रहे हैं?

(b) Has she been playing with the puppy in her room for half an hour?
क्या आधे घंटे से वह अपने कमरे में पिल्ले से खेल रही है।

(c) Where have you been going since early morning?
आप सुबह से कहां जा रहे हो?

(d) Why has he been trying to deceive us for a number of days?
वह कई दिनों से हमें धोखा देने की कोशिश क्यों कर रहा है ?

(e) Have you been doing your work seriously since Tuesday last?
क्या आप पिछले मंगलवार से अपना काम ध्यान से कर रहे हैं ?

EXERCISE 21

नीचे दिये गये Sentences का English में अनुवाद करें:

1. वह सुबह से क्या पी रही है ?
2. आप पिछले पन्द्रह मिनट से किस को खत लिख रहे हो ?
3. क्या आप एक बजे से मेरी बात ध्यान से सुन रहे हैं ?
4. आप दोपहर से मेरे साथ लड़ाई क्यों कर रहे हैं ?
5. क्या सुबह से पक्षी पेड़ पर चहचहा रहे हैं ?
6. क्या पिछले दो मिनट से गवाह अपना बयान बदल रहा है ?
7. क्या जज चार बजे से अपना फैसला सुना रहा है ?
8. क्या वह कल रात्रि से शराब पी रहे हैं ?
9. क्या कल शाम से वह गप्पें हांक रहा है ?
10. सोनू सुबह से पंतग क्यों उड़ा रहा है ?

Hints for Translation

9. indulge in gossips

Interrogative Negative Sentences: Present Perfect Continuous के Interrogative Negative Sentences बनाने का Formula नीचे दिया गया है:

Formula: Wh or how + has/have + S + not + been + (V-I + ing) + O + since or for + time + ?

Examples

(a) Why have you not been telling him the truth about his brother's behaviour for so many days?
आप उसे उसके भाई के स्वभाव के बारे में सच-सच क्यों नहीं बता रहे हैं ?

(b) Has he not been repairing the watch since morning?
क्या वह सुबह से घड़ी ठीक नहीं कर रहा है ?

(c) What have you not been changing in your life for many years?
तुम अपनी ज़िन्दगी में कई वर्षों से क्या नहीं बदल रहे हो ?

(d) Who has not been obeying you since yesterday?
आपका कहना कल से कौन नहीं मान रहा है?

(e) Why has he not been fearing anybody for the last two months?
वह पिछले दो महीनों से किसी से क्यों नहीं डर रहा है?

EXERCISE 22

नीचे दिये गये Sentences का English में अनुवाद करें:

1. वह दो बजे से शेर से क्यों नहीं डर रहा है?
2. क्या दस दिनों से वह आपकी सलाह पर अमल नहीं कर रहा है?
3. क्या वह पिछले अक्टूबर से आपसे प्यार के साथ बात नहीं कर रही है?
4. क्या वह शुक्रवार से आपसे ठीक ढंग से बात नहीं कर रहा है?
5. क्या वह पिछले छः साल से अपने माता-पिता की सेवा नहीं कर रहा है?
6. क्या 1995 से गुरु अपने शिष्यों को शिक्षा नहीं दे रहा है?
7. क्या वह एक घण्टे से आग नहीं जला रही है?
8. क्या वह दोपहर से अपनी बंदूक साफ नहीं कर रहा है?
9. क्या वह सुबह से जयपुर जाने की तैयारी नहीं कर रहा है?
10. क्या वह आधे घण्टे से आप पर हंस नहीं रहा है?

Hints for Translation

2. act upon **4.** talk properly **6.** disciples **8.** gun, cleaning **10.** laughing at.

PAST TENSE

यह चार प्रकार का होता है:

(A) Past Indefinite
(B) Past Continuous
(C) Past Perfect
(D) Past Perfect Continuous

(A) Past Indefinite Tense

Past Indefinite के Assertive (Positive) Sentences का Formula नीचे दिया गया है।

Formula: S + V-II + O

Examples

(a) He went to the shcool.
वह स्कूल गया।

(b) He played very well.
वह बहुत अच्छा खेला।

(c) Mohan started his career as a clerk.
मोहन ने अपना कैरियर क्लर्क के तौर पर शुरू किया।

(d) Satish made a hard blow on Lucky's face.
सतीश ने लक्की के मुंह पर ज़ोरदार घूंसा मारा।

(e) He motioned at me.
उसने मेरी तरह इशारा किया।

EXERCISE 23

नीचे दिये गये Sentence का English में अनुवाद करें:

1. मैं नहाने गया।
2. उसने अपने माता-पिता से आशीर्वाद लिया।
3. अध्यापक ने उसे डांटा।
4. चोर उसके घर का सारा सामान ले उड़ा।
5. हल्की सी हवा चली।
6. उसके दिमाग ने जल्दी से काम किया।
7. एक विद्रोही को मौत के घाट उतारा गया।
8. पुलिस चोर के पीछे भागी।
9. उसने रिश्वत ली।
10. जज ने उसे सजा सुनाई।

Hints for Translation

2. blessings **3.** rebuked **5.** A light breeze **7.** Rebel, executed **9.** bribe **10.** pronuounced

Negative Sentences: (a) Past Indefinite के Negative Sentences में 'did not' का प्रयोग होता है।

(b) ध्यान रखें कि 'did' के बाद Verb की First Form ही लगती है।

Formula: S + didnot (didn't) + V-I + O.

Examples

(a) He did not take tea.
उसने चाय नहीं पी।

(b) She did not sing a song.
उसने गाना नहीं गाया।

(c) They did not look worried.
वे चिन्ताजनक दिखाई नहीं दिये।

(d) I did not open the secret.
मैंने भेद नहीं खोला।

(e) We did not make out what they said.
हम वह नहीं समझे जो उन्होंने कहा।

EXERCISE 24

नीचे दिये गये Sentences का English में अनुवाद करें:

1. मैं उसे मारने नहीं गया।
2. रोहित बाजार नहीं गया।
3. पाकिस्तान शांति नहीं चाहता।
4. भारत जंग नहीं चाहता।
5. उसने चोरी नहीं की।
6. उसने मजाक नहीं किया।
7. वह झाड़ियों में नहीं छुपा।
8. म्युनिसिपल कमेटी ने शहर की सफाई की ओर ध्यान नहीं दिया।
9. वहां बम्ब नहीं फटा।
10. वह उस पार्क में नहीं गया।

Hints for Translation

3. peace **5.** commit a theft **6.** crack a joke **7.** hide **8.** pay attention to **9.** explode.

Note: Sentence No. 10 भी Past Indefinite Negative है। लेकिन यह नीचे दिये गये ढंग से लिखा जा सकता है।

(i) He did not go to that park. परन्तु एक Affirmative Sentence में used to का प्रयोग किया जा सकता है।

(ii) He used to take tea after his dinner. वह रात्रि के खाने के बाद चाय पीने का आदी था।

Remember:

(i) Affirmative Sentences में 'used to' का प्रयोग उचित है।

(ii) 'use to' का प्रयोग किसी भी प्रकार से उचित नहीं है।

Interrogative Sentences

(a) Past Indefinite के Interrogative Sentences में 'did' का प्रयोग होता है।

(b) ध्यान रहे, यहां भी 'did' के बाद Verb की First Form का ही प्रयोग होता है।

Formula: Wh or how + did + S + V-I + O + ?

Examples

(a) Did you say something?
क्या तुमने कुछ कहा ?

(b) Where did they find this round stone?
यह गोल पत्थर उन्होंने कहां पर पाया ?

(c) Why did he not understand?
वह क्यों नहीं समझ पाया?

(d) Did you make a noise?
क्या आपने शोर मचाया?

(e) When did you come?
आप कब आए?

EXERCISE 25

नीचे दिये गये Sentences का English में अनुवाद करें:

1. कल वह स्कूल क्यों गया?
2. क्या समारोह हुआ?
3. क्या आपने रेणू को फोन किया?
4. क्या मदारी ने तमाशा दिखाया?
5. क्या वर्षा हुई?
6. आपने क्यों मेरी बात मानी?
7. क्या आपने अंकल को नमस्ते की?
8. क्या आपने रवि से झगड़ा मोल लिया?
9. क्या आपने अपने नाखून काटे?
10. आपने बालों में कंघी क्यों नहीं की?

Interrogative Negative Sentences: Past Indefinite के Negative Sentences का Formula नीचे दिया गया है:

Formula: Wh or how + did + S + not + V-I + O + ?

Examples

(a) Why did he not become courageous?
वह साहसी क्यों नहीं बना?

(b) Did she not make fun of you?
क्या उसने आपका मज़ाक नहीं उड़ाया?

(c) When did they not tell you the story clearly?
उन्होंने कब तुमको कहानी साफ-साफ नहीं बताई?

(d) Why did I not help him?
मैंने उसकी सहायता क्यों नहीं की?

(e) Did Suraj not take advantage of his weakness?
क्या सूरज ने उसकी कमज़ोरी का फायदा नहीं उठाया?

EXERCISE 26

नीचे दिये गये Sentences का English में अनुवाद करें:

1. वह स्कूल क्यों नहीं गया?
2. तुम वहां क्यों नहीं जाया करते थे?

3. उसने आपसे क्या बुरा व्यवहार नहीं किया ?
4. उसने आपकी कौन सी बात नहीं मानी ?
5. वह कपड़े धोने क्यों नहीं गई ?
6. वह तैयार क्यों नहीं हुआ ?
7. वह क्यों नहीं चिल्लाया ?
8. उसने आग पर काबू क्यों नहीं पाया ?
9. वह नाची क्यों नहीं ?
10. हम हंसे क्यों नहीं ?

Hints for Translation

3. maltreat **4.** get ready **8.** overcome

(B) Past Continuous Tense

(a) जिन Sentences में हिन्दी में 'रहा था', 'रही थी', 'रहे थे' आदि का प्रयोग होता है वह प्राय: Past Continuous Tense के Sentences होते हैं।

(b) 'were' का प्रयोग तब होता है जब Subject Plural हो।

(c) अगर Subject Singular हो तो 'was' का प्रयोग किया जाता है।

Formula: S + was/were + (V-I + ing) + O.

Examples

1. She was taking her bath.
वह नहा रही थी।
2. I was singing a song.
मैं गाना गा रहा था।
3. We were making fun of him.
हम उसका मज़ाक उड़ा रहे थे।
4. They were waiting for me.
वे मेरी प्रतीक्षा कर रहे थे।
5. She was preparing coffee.
वह कॉफी बना रही थी।

EXERCISE 27

नीचे दिये Sentences के खाली स्थान भरें:

1. We ..... quarrelling with them.
(a) was (b) were

2. I ..... telling them a story.
(a) was (b) were

3. She ..... sewing her shirt.
(a) was (b) were

4. They ..... talking to each other.
(a) was (b) were

5. The monkeys ..... bouncing on their legs.
(a) was (b) were

EXERCISE 28

नीचे दिये गये Sentences का English में अनुवाद करें:

1. आप आम खा रहे थे।
2. सुनीता सो रही थी।
3. गीता नाच रही थी।
4. शेर दहाड़ रहा था।
5. हिरन भाग रहे थे।
6. बन्दर एक डाल से दूसरी डाल पर छलांगें लगा रहे थे।
7. बादल गरज रहे थे तथा बिजली चमक रही थी।
8. वह पौधों को पानी दे रहा था।
9. वह छाता लेकर बाज़ार जा रही थी।
10. हम सब सोच रहे थे।

Hints for Translation

4. roaring **5.** deer **6.** jumping **7.** lightning, flashing **9.** umbrella

Negative Sentences: Past Continuous के Nagative Sentences का Formula नीचे दिया गया है:

Formula: S + was/were + not + (V-I + ing) + O.

Examples

(a) She was not showing her anger to me.
वह अपना गुस्सा मुझे नहीं दिखा रही थी।

(b) Sohan was not looking nice in that dress.
सोहन उस पोशाक में सुन्दर नहीं लग रहा था।

(c) They were not worrying about me.
वे मेरे बारे में चिन्तित नहीं थे।

(d) The peon was not ringing the bell.
चपरासी घण्टी नहीं बजा रहा था।

(e) The children were not running behind the butterflies.
बच्चे तितलियों के पीछे नहीं दौड़ रहे थे।

EXERCISE 29

नीचे दिये गये Sentences का English में अनुवाद करें:

1. वह बहस नहीं कर रहा था।
2. वे लड़ नहीं रहे थे।
3. पक्षी उड़ नहीं रहे थे।
4. हवा तेज़ नहीं चल रही थी।
5. बाज़ार में भीड़ हो रही थी।
6. वह मेरी बात नहीं समझ रहा था।

7. सोहन व मोहन कंचे खेल रहे थे।
8. दीपू पतंग उड़ा रहा था।
9. पवन तालाब में तैर रहा था।
10. उसकी मां उसे डांट रही थी।

Hints for Translation

4. blowing hard **5.** crowd. gathering **7.** marbles **10.** scolding

Interrogative Sentences: Past Continuous Tense के Interrogative Sentences बनाने का Formula नीचे दिया गया है:

Formula: (Wh or how +) was/were + (V-I + ing) + O +?

Examples

(a) Were they trying to kill you?
क्या वे तुम्हें मारने की कोशिश कर रहे थे?

(b) Was he turning pale?
क्या उसका रंग पीला हो रहा था?

(c) Were they showing some sense of humour?
क्या वे कुछ मजाकिया दिखाई दे रहे थे?

(d) Was I composing a poem then?
क्या तब मैं एक कविता लिख रहा था?

(d) Was she loving you?
क्या वह आपसे प्यार कर रही थी?

EXERCISE 30

नीचे दिये गये Sentences का English में अनुवाद करें:

1. आप कहां जा रहे थे?
2. आप वहां क्यों जा रहे थे?
3. तुम मुझे क्या समझ रहे थे?
4. वह तुम्हें क्या समझा रहा था?
5. वह तुमसे गुस्सा क्यों हो रहा था?
6. क्या मैं सोच कर बोल रहा था?
7. क्या वह मूर्खों जैसी बातें कर रहा था?
8. क्या पार्टी में मज़ा आ रहा था?
9. आप शराब क्यों पी रहे थे?
10. आप सिगरेट क्यों पी रहे थे?

Hints for Translation

3. thinking of me or taking me for **7.** as if **10.** smoking

Interrogative Negative Sentences: Past Continuous Tense के Interrogative Negative बनाने का Formula नीचे दिया गया है:

Formula: Wh or how + was/were + S + not + (V-I + ing) + O + ?

Examples

(a) Why was he not feeling a sense of shame?
उसे शर्म क्यों नहीं आ रही थी?

(b) Why were they not taking the matter as fun?
वे बात को मज़ाक में क्यों नहीं ले रहे थे?

(c) When were you not threatening me?
तुम मुझे धमकी कब नहीं दे रहे थे?

(d) What was he not saying to you?
वह आपसे क्या नहीं कह रहा था?

(e) Why was she not caring for you?
वह आपका ख्याल क्यों नहीं रख रही थी?

EXERCISE 31

नीचे दिये गये Sentences का English में अनुवाद करें:

1. वह आपकी ओर क्यों नहीं देख रहा था?
2. वे आपसे क्यों बात नहीं कर रहे थे?
3. सुरजीत तुम्हें क्यों नहीं पीट रहा था?
4. वह आपसे डर क्यों नहीं रहा था?
5. दीपक लड़ाई में छड़ी क्यों नहीं घुमा रहा था?
6. भारत पाकिस्तान से युद्ध क्यों नहीं छेड़ रहा था?
7. लीडर ईमानदारी क्यों नहीं दिखा रहे थे?
8. थल सेना के पास हथियार क्यों नहीं पहुँच रहे थे?
9. लोग अपनी मौत के डर से सेना को उत्साहित क्यों नहीं कर रहे थे?
10. भारत अमेरिका की तरह अमीर क्यों नहीं बन रहा था?

Hints for Translation

1. looking at **5.** stick **6.** starting war **8.** weapon, infantry

(C) Past Perfect Tense

जो Sentence हिन्दी में अधिकतर 'चुकी थी', 'चुका था', 'चुके थे' आदि से खत्म हों, उनको हम Past Perfect Tense कह सकते हैं।

(i) राधा गांव पहुँच चुकी थी। (ii) बिल्ली दूध पी चुकी थी।

Past Perfect के Affirmative Sentences का Formula नीचे दिया गया है:

Formula: S + had + V-III + O.

Examples

(a) Radha had reached the village.
राधा गांव पहुँच चुकी थी।

(b) The cat had drunk the milk.
बिल्ली दूध पी चुकी थी।

(c) The match had started.
मैच शुरू हो चुका था।

(d) They had killed the bird.
वह पक्षी को मार चुके थे।

(e) I had opened the door.
मैं दरवाज़ा खोल चुका था।

EXERCISE 32

नीचे दिये गये Sentences का English में अनुवाद करें:

1. चोर जा चुका था।
2. वह रो चुकी थी।
3. मन्त्री अपना देश छोड़कर भाग चुका था।
4. देश की सबसे बड़ी गुप्तचर संस्था फेल हो चुकी थी।
5. शेयरों का घोटाला हो चुका था।
6. कानून अपने हाथ खड़े कर चुका था।
7. वह फल तोड़ चुका था।
8. वह अपने हाथ का मुक्का बना चुका था।
9. तारे निकल चुके थे।
10. धूल उड़ चुकी थी।

Hints for Translation

3. fled **4.** intelligence agency **5.** shares scam **10.** dust

Negative Sentences: Past Perfect Tense के Negative Sentences का Formula नीचे दिया गया है–

Formula: S + had + not (hadn't) + V-III + O.

Examples

(a) He had not told him the real thing.
उसने उसे सच्ची बात नहीं बताई थी।

(b) I had not made a mistake.
मैंने गलती नहीं की थी।

(c) We had not joined the meeting.
हम सभा में उपस्थित नहीं हुए थे।

(d) They had not taken us seriously.
उन्होंने हमें गम्भीरता से नहीं लिया था।

(e) He had not cut the wings of the birds.
वह पक्षी के पंख नहीं काट चुका था।

EXERCISE 33

नीचे दिये गये Sentences का English में अनुवाद करें:

1. वह खाना नहीं खा चुका था।
2. वह किसी को भी अपनी बात नहीं बता चुका था।
3. वह गरीब पर नहीं हंस चुका था।
4. उसकी कार खराब नहीं हो चुकी थी।
5. वह सोनू को चाकू नहीं मार चुका था।
6. वे क़त्ल कर चुके थे।
7. हम सैर पर नहीं जा चुके थे।
8. वह अंधेरे में नहीं पढ़ चुकी थी।
9. हम टी० वी० नहीं देख चुके थे।
10. बच्चा कुल्फी नहीं खा चुका था।

Hints for Translation

4. gone out of order **6.** Committed a murder **9.** watch or view **10.** ice-cream.

Interrogative Sentences: Past Perfect के Interrogative Sentences का Formula नीचे दिया गया है:

Formula: Wh or how + had + S + V-III + O + ?

Examples

(a) When had he dropped this idea?
वह इस विचार का त्याग कब कर चुका था?

(b) Why had you taken the matter in your hand?
तुम यह बात अपने हाथ में क्यों ले चुके थे?

(c) Why had he dug up so deep?
वह इतनी गहराई तक क्यों खोद चुका था?

(d) Had she changed her dress?
क्या वह अपनी ड्रेस बदल चुकी थी?

(e) Had you looked into the matter?
क्या आप मामला देख चुके थे?

EXERCISE 34

नीचे दिये गये Sentences का English में अनुवाद करें:

1. आपको दाल में काला कब दिखाई दे चुका था?
2. आपको मेरी बात पर विश्वास क्यों नहीं हो चुका था?

3. आप उसको भला-बुरा क्यों कह चुके थे?
4. क्या आप झूठ बोल चुके थे?
5. क्या जज सही फैसला दे चुका था?
6. क्या तुम मन्दिर जा चुके थे?
7. क्या भगवान उनकी बात सुन चुका था?
8. क्या जंग शुरू हो चुकी थी?
9. आपको क्या समझ नहीं आ चुका था?
10. आपको यह क्यों समझ नहीं आ चुका था?

Hints for Translation
1. smelt a rat **8.** broken out.

Interrogative Negative Sentences: Past Perfect के Interrogative Negative Sentences बनाने का Formula नीचे दिया गया है:

Formula: Wh or how + had + S + not + V-III + O + ?

Examples

(a) Had you not visited the Taj Mahal?
क्या तुम ताजमहल नहीं देख चुके थे?

(b) Why had this camel not walked well across the desert?
यह ऊँट मरुस्थल में ठीक से क्यों नहीं चल चुका था।

(c) Had you not made your maiden speech?
क्या आप अपना पहला भाषण नहीं दे चुके थे?

(d) Why had he not listened to you?
वह आपकी बात क्यों नहीं सुन चुका था?

(e) **Had she not kissed her son?**
क्या वह अपने बेटे को नहीं चूम चुकी थी?

EXERCISE 35

नीचे दिये गये Sentences का English में अनुवाद करें:

1. वह बुरी संगत क्यों नहीं छोड़ चुका था?
2. वह मेक-अप क्यों नहीं कर चुकी थी?
3. वह पार्टी पर क्यों नहीं आ चुका था?
4. क्या हम आप पर हंस नहीं चुके थे?
5. क्या हम ताश नहीं खेल चुके थे?
6. क्या वह गाने के मुताबिक नाच नहीं कर चुकी थी?
7. वह घर छोड़कर क्यों नहीं जा चुका था?

8. मेंढ़क कुएं में छलांग क्यों नहीं लगा चुका था?
9. उसका रक्तचाप ठीक क्यों नहीं हो चुका था?
10. उसे बीमारियों से छुटकारा क्यों नहीं मिल चुका था?

Hints for Translation

1. given up **2.** make up **5.** played at cards **6.** song **8.** frog

(D) Past Perfect Continuous Tense

Past Perfect Continuous Tense के Affirmative Sentences बनाने का Formula नीचे दिया गया है:

Formula: S + had + been + (V-I + ing) + O + since or for + time.

Examples

(a) He had been working in the fields since morning.
वह सुबह से खेतों में काम कर रहा था।

(b) She had been singing a song for two hours.
वह दो घण्टे से गाना गा रही थी।

(c) It had been raining for one hour.
एक घण्टे से वर्षा हो रही थी।

(d) She had been arranging flowers in the room since afternoon.
वह दोपहर से कमरे में फूल लगा रही थी।

(e) I had been praying to God for the last twenty minutes
मैं पिछले बीस मिनट से भगवान से प्रार्थना कर रहा था।

EXERCISE 36

नीचे दिये गये Sentences का English में अनुवाद करें:

1. वह कल से नाश्ता नहीं कर रहा था।
2. वह कई महीनों से रात को चोरों की तरह घर में घुस रहा था।
3. वह कई वर्षों से मूर्तियां बनाने का धन्धा कर रहा था।
4. पुलिस कल सुबह से चोर को ढूँढ रही थी।
5. मन्त्री पिछले दो घण्टे से भाषण दे रहा था।
6. वह बच्चों को दो दिन से वही कहानी सुना रहा था।
7. पिछले दस मिनट से वह मेरी बात नहीं सुन रहा था।
8. वह दस सालों से झूठ बोल रही थी।

9. सतीश सुबह से नदी में तैर रहा था।

10. पवन सुबह से ही अपने काम में मग्न था।

Hints for Translation

1. breakfast **2.** like thieves **3.** idols **10.** busy

Note: Perfect Continuous Tense में कई बार Present Participle के स्थान पर किसी Adjective का प्रयोग होता है (जैसे कि ऊपर Sentences No. 10).

Negative Sentences: Past Perfect Continuous Tense के Negative Sentences बनाने का Formula नीचे दिया गया है:

Formula: S + had + not + been + (V-I + ing) + O + since or for + time.

Examples

(a) She had not been watering the plants for two hours.
वह दो घण्टे से पौधों को पानी नहीं दे रही थी।

(b) He had not been discussing the topic with me since morning.
वह सुबह से मेरे साथ इस विषय पर बहस नहीं कर रहा था।

(c) I had not been working in this office since 1980.
मैं 1980 से इस दफ्तर में काम नहीं कर रहा था।

(d) He had not been bathing in the rain since evening.
वह शाम से वर्षा में नहीं नहा रहा था।

(e) My mother had not been working in the kitchen since morning.
मेरी माताजी सुबह से रसोई में काम नहीं कर रही थीं।

EXERCISE 37

नीचे दिये गये Sentence का English में अनुवाद करें:

1. मैं दो घण्टे से नींद में बातें नहीं कर रहा था।
2. वह पांच घण्टे से जुआ नहीं खेल रहा था।
3. वे सुबह से शराब नहीं पी रहे थे।
4. मैं कल शाम से आपको नहीं ढूँढ रहा था।
5. कल देर रात्रि में चोर उसके घर चोरी नहीं कर रहे थे।
6. वह पिछले आधे घण्टे से मेरी बातों का बुरा नहीं मान रहा था।
7. वह किसी से भी पिछले पांच घण्टे से नहीं झगड़ रहा था।

8. **वे दो घण्टे से आपको कुछ नहीं कह रहे थे।**

9. **वह पिछले तीन घण्टे से सभी को गालियां नहीं दे रहा था।**

10. **वह आपको देख कर नहीं मुस्कुरा रहा था।**

Hints for Translaiton

2. gambling **10.** smiling

Interrogative Sentences: Past Perfect Continuous के Interrogative Sentences बनाने का Formula नीचे दिया गया है:

Formula: Wh or how + had + S + been + (V-I + ing) + O + since or for + time +?

Examples

(a) Had he been asking you anything?
क्या वह आपसे कुछ पूछ रहा था?

(b) Had she been telling you her pathetic story?
क्या वह आपको अपनी दुख भरी दास्तान सुना रही थी।

(c) Since when, had he been staying in that house?
वह उस घर में कब से रह रहा था?

(d) Since which day, had she been telling you this lie?
वह आपको किस दिन से यह झूठ बता रही थी?

(e) Had they been running behind the train?
क्या वे गाड़ी के पीछे दौड़ रहे थे?

EXERCISE 38

नीचे दिये गये Sentence का English में अनुवाद करें:

1. क्या वह पिछले साल से आपसे मित्रता निभा रहा था?
2. क्या आप मेरी बातों की ओर ध्यान नहीं दे रहे थे?
3. क्या चूहा बिल्ली के गले में घण्टी डाल रहा था?
4. वह आपको बहुत देर से पसन्द क्यों नहीं कर रही थी?
5. वह कौन सी चीज़ आपको तीन घण्टे से दिखा रहा था?
6. वह पिछले साल से हमसे नफरत क्यों कर रहा था?
7. रामू दो साल से गांव में बदमाशी क्यों कर रहा था?
8. आप मेरी बात पर काफी देर से यकीन क्यों नहीं कर रहे थे?

9. मैं आपको काफी देर से क्यों नहीं देख रहा था?

10. वह दो हफ्तों से अपनी परीक्षा की तैयारी क्यों कर रहा था?

Hints for Translation

1. keeping up friendship **3.** belling **6.** despising

Interrogative Negative Sentences: Past Perfect Continuous के Interrogative Negative Sentences बनाने का Formula नीचे दिया गया है:

Formula: Wh or how + had + S + not + been + (V-I + ing) + O + since or for + true + ?

Examples

(a) Had he not been obeying you?
क्या वह आपकी आज्ञा का पालन नहीं कर रहा था?

(b) Why had they not been taking care of their children since morning?
वे सुबह से अपने बच्चों का ध्यान क्यों नहीं रख रहे थे?

(c) Why had you not been throwing the trash in the dustbin?
आप गन्दी चीजें कूड़ेदान में क्यों नहीं फेंक रहे थे?

(d) Had they not been playing cards since afternoon?
क्या वे दोपहर से ताश नहीं खेल रहे थे?

(e) Had she not been tossing up in her bed due to pain?
क्या वह दर्द के मारे अपने बिस्तर में तड़प नहीं रही थी?

EXERCISE 39

नीचे दिये गये Sentences का English में अनुवाद करें:

1. आपको कौन सी बात पांच घण्टे से समझ नहीं आ रही थी?
2. इतनी देर से दरवाजा कौन नहीं खटखटा रहा था?
3. आप कल से घर में क्या नहीं कर रहे थे?
4. वह आपकी बातों पर काफी देर से विश्वास क्यों नहीं कर रहा था?
5. शेर दो दिन से गुफा से बाहर क्यों नहीं आ रहा था?
6. मोर बादल आने पर भी नाच क्यों नहीं रहे थे?
7. वह दो घण्टे से आपसे क्यों नहीं झगड़ रहा था?
8. उसकी कहानी तीन घण्टे से कौन नहीं सुन रहा था?

9. वह हमसे नाराज़ क्यों नहीं हो रहा था?

10. कल से उसकेअच्छे गुण कौन नहीं सीख रहा था?

Hints for Translation

2. knocking **5.** cave **6.** cloud **7.** quarrelling **9.** getting angry **10.** virtues

FUTURE TENSE

यह चार प्रकार का होता है:

(A) Future Indefinite
(B) Future Continuous
(C) Future Perfect
(D) Future Perfect Continuous

हम पहले Future Indefinite Tense का अध्ययन करेंगे।

(A) Future Indefinite Tense

(a) जो Sentence हिन्दी में 'जायेगा', 'जायेगी', 'जायेंगे' आदि से समाप्त होते हैं उनको Future Indefinite Tense कहा जा सकता है:

(i) राजू स्कूल जायेगा।
(ii) रीटा स्कूल जायेगी।
(iii) हम स्कूल जायेंगे।

(b) Future Indefinite Tense में 'shall' व 'will' का प्रयोग होता है।

(c) अगर Subject 'I' या 'we' (First Person Singular या Plural) हो तो 'shall' का प्रयोग होता है।

(d) बाकी सभी जगह, अधिकतर 'will' का प्रयोग होता है।

Future Indefinite Tense का formula नीचे दिया गया है:

Formula: S + shall/will + V-I + O.

Examples

(a) He will go to bazaar.
वह बाजार जायेगा।

(b) We shall beat you.
हम तुम्हें मारेंगे (या हरा देंगे)।

(c) You will open the lock.
तुम ताला खोलोगे।

(d) The train will come.
गाड़ी आयेगी।

(e) The bus will go.
बस जायेगी।

EXERCISE 40

नीचे दिये गये Sentences के खाली स्थान भरें:

1. I .... draw a picture
(a) shall (b) will

2. They ....give you good advice.
(a) shall (b) will

3. She .... obey you.
(a) shall (b) will

4. We .... take tea.
(a) shall (b) will

You .... swim in the canal.
(a) shall (b) will

EXERCISE 41

नीचे दिये गये Sentence का English में अनुवाद करें:

1. वह आज नहायेगा।
2. हम आज बाज़ार जायेंगे।
3. वह आपकी बात सुनेगा।
4. वह मुझसे नाराज़ हो जायेगा।
5. वह गुड़िया बनायेगी।
6. वह गाय का दूध दुहेगा।
7. वह स्टेशन पर जायेगा।
8. डाकिया आयेगा।
9. सोनू शोर करेगा।
10. मैं सभी को बताऊँगा।

Hints for Translation

1. bathe **2.** bazaar **3.** listen to **6.** milk **8.** postman

Negative Sentences: Future Indefinite Tense के Negative Sentences बनाने का Formula नीचे दिया गया है:

Formula: S + shall/will + not + V-I + O.

Examples

(a) She will not get angry with you.
वह आपसे गुस्सा नहीं होगी।

(b) I shall not show you my pocket.
मैं आपको अपनी जेब नहीं दिखाऊंगा।

(c) They will not visit the zoo.
वे चिड़ियाघर नहीं जायेंगे।

(d) During summer holidays, I shall go to Shimla.
गर्मियों की छुट्टियों में मैं शिमला जाऊंगा।

(e) They will not give donation to the school.
वे स्कूल को चन्दा नहीं देंगे।

EXERCISE 42

नीचे दिये गये Sentence का English में अनुवाद करें:

1. मैं संदीप से नहीं लड़ूंगा।
2. मैं तुम्हें नहीं छोड़ूँगा।
3. वह स्कूटर को ठीक नहीं करवायेगा।
4. वह आपको कोई बात ठीक से नहीं बतायेगी।
5. हम सब देश से गद्दारी नहीं करेंगे।
6. वह दिल के दौरे से नहीं मरेगा।
7. वे उसे चाकू नहीं मार देंगे।
8. सुनीता सब्ज़ी नहीं काटेगी।
9. मंजू चाय नहीं बनायेगी।
10. वह चाय नहीं पीयेगा।

Hints for Translation

2. leave **3.** get...repaired **4.** correct **5.** betray **9.** vegetable.

Interrogative Sentences: Future Indefinite Tense के Interrogative Sentences बनाने का Formula नीचे दिया गया है:

Formula: Wh or how + shall/will + S + V-I + O + ?

Examples

(a) Will he speak the truth?
क्या वह सच बोलेगा ?

(b) Shall I believe (in) you.
क्या मैं आप पर विश्वास करूंगा ?

(c) Will they punish you?
क्या वे आपको सज़ा देंगे ?

(d) Will you take them otherwise?
क्या आप उनकी बातों का बुरा मानेंगे ?

(e) Shall we light a cigarette?
क्या हम सिगरेट जलायेंगे ?

EXERCISE 43

नीचे दिये गये Sentences का English में अनुवाद करें:

1. क्या तूफान आयेगा ?
2. क्या मछुआरे मछली पकड़ने जायेंगे ?
3. क्या तुम पेड़ पर चढ़ जाओगे ?
4. क्या आप पतंग खरीदेंगे ?
5. क्या वे अच्छे अंक प्राप्त करेंगे ?
6. क्या मैं परीक्षा में नकल करूंगा ?
7. क्या वह दीवार पर इश्तहार लगायेगा ?
8. क्या वह किसी की बात नहीं सुनेगी ?
9. हम बाज़ार क्यों नहीं जायेंगे ?
10. पुलिस समय पर क्यों नहीं पहुँचेगी ?

Hints for Translation

1. storm **2.** fishermen **5.** good marks **6.** copy **7.** stick bills

Interrogative Negative Sentences: Future Indefinite Tense के Interrogative Negative Sentences बनाने का Formula नीचे दिया गया है:

Formula: Wh or how + shall/will + S + not + V-I + O + ?

Examples

(a) Will he not take a chance again?
क्या वह दोबारा कोशिश नहीं करेगा?

(b) Why shall I not ask him any question?
मैं उससे कोई सवाल क्यों नहीं करूंगा?

(c) When will he not listen to you?
वह आपकी बात कब नहीं सुनेगा?

(d) Will you not show me your hands?
क्या तुम मुझे अपने हाथ नहीं दिखाओगे?

(e) Will she not pare her nails?
क्या वह अपने नाखून नहीं काटेगी?

EXERCISE 44

नीचे दिये गये Sentences का English में अनुवाद करें:

1. क्या वह आप पर ज़रा भी विश्वास नहीं करेगी?
2. क्या आप पार्टी में नहीं नाचेंगे?
3. आप मेरी सहायता क्यों नहीं करेंगे?
4. क्या मैं पेड़ को नहीं काटूँगा?
5. क्या वह कपड़े नहीं धोयेगी?
6. क्या आप कपड़ों पर स्त्री नहीं करेंगे?
7. क्या आज का मैच भारत नहीं जीतेगा?
8. क्या आप बात को हंसी में नहीं टालेंगे?
9. क्या मैं बंदूक साफ नहीं करूंगा?
10. क्या नाई आपके बाल नहीं काटेगा?

Hints for Translation

5. wash **6.** iron **10.** barber, cut your hair.

(B) Future Continuous Tense

(a) जो शब्द हिन्दी में 'रहे होंगे', 'रही होगी', 'रहा होगा' आदि से समाप्त होते हैं, वह अधिकतर Future Continuous Tense के वाक्य होते हैं।

(b) इनमें 'be' शब्द का प्रयोग होता है। इस Tense को बनाने का Formula नीचे दिया गया है:

Formula: S + shall/will + be + (V-I + ing) + O.

Examples

(a) He will be preparing for the forthcoming examinations.
वह आने वाली परीक्षा की तैयारी कर रहा होगा।

(b) She will be arranging a nice dress for herself.
वह अपने लिये अच्छी पोशाक का प्रबन्ध कर रही होगी।

(c) The storm will be blowing over.
तूफान ढल रहा होगा।

(d) The stars will be twinkling.
तारे चमक रहे होंगे।

(e) **I shall be keeping myself fit with light exercise.**
मैं हल्की कसरत से अपने आपको ठीक रख रहा होऊँगा।

EXERCISE 45

नीचे दिये गये Sentence का English में अनुवाद करें:

1. वह तुम्हारी शिकायत कर रही होगी।

2. बच्चा चाकलेट खा रहा होगा।

3. मेरी बेटी ठंडा पेय पीने के लिए जिद्द कर रही होगी।

4. वे हिरण को पकड़ने की कोशिश कर रहे होंगे।

5. वह घर का सारा काम खत्म कर रही होगी।

6. वह अपनी नई साइकिल पर जा रहा होगा।

7. वह पानी की लहरों से बातें कर रही होगी।

8. वह पानी में अपनी परछाईं देख रहा होगा।

9. जुगनू रात को चमक रहा होगा।

10. उसका कारखाना ठीक चल रहा होगा।

Hints for Translation

1. complaining **2.** chocolate **4.** deer **7.** waves **8.** shadow **9.** glow-worm **10.** running smoothly.

Negative Sentences: Future Continuous Tense के Negative Sentences बनाने का Formula नीचे दिया गया है:

Formula: S + shall/will + not + be + (V-I + ing) + O.

Examples

(a) He will not be getting involved in any case.
वह किसी भी केस में नहीं फंस रहा होगा।

(b) She will not be praising her son.
वह अपने लड़के की तारीफ नहीं कर रही होगी।

(c) I shall not be advancing forward without your advice.
मैं आपकी सलाह के बिना आगे नहीं बढ़ रहा होऊँगा।

(d) I shall not be shutting the window.
मैं खिड़की को बन्द नहीं कर रहा होऊँगा।

(e) They will not be wandering on the mountain peakes.
वे पहाड़ों की चोटियों पर नहीं घूम रहे होंगे।

EXERCISE 46

नीचे दिये गये Sentences का English में अनुवाद करें:

1. वह ठीक से सांस नहीं ले रहा होगा।
2. वह खांसी नहीं कर रही होगी।
3. वह अपनी बीमारी से घबरा नहीं रहा होगा।
4. वे दर्द से कराह नहीं रहे होंगे।
5. वह आपसे कुछ भी नया नहीं सीख रहा होगा।
6. आज वह कहीं भी नहीं जा रहा होगा।
7. आज वह नाश्ते में अण्डा नहीं ले रहा होगा।
8. वह कांच के टुकड़ों को इकट्ठा नहीं कर रहा होगा।
9. वह आपको गाना नहीं सुना रही होगी।
10. मैं किसी की भी बात पर विश्वास नहीं कर रहा होऊँगा।

Hints for Translation

1. breathing properly **2.** coughing **4.** crying with pain **8.** pieces of glass.

Interrogative Sentences: Future Continuous Tense के Interrogative Sentences बनाने का Formula नीचे दिया गया है:

Formula: Wh or how + will/shall + S + be + V-I + O + ?

Examples

(a) Why will he be talking to you secretly?
वह तुम्हारे साथ चोरी-छिपे क्यों बात कर रहा होगा।

(b) **Shall I be making an excuse?**
क्या मैं एक बहाना बना रहा होऊँगा?

(c) **When will they be exchanging strong words with each other?**
वे एक दूसरे से कब सख्त शब्द बोल रहे होंगे?

(d) **Why will they be ringing up the police?**
वे पुलिस को फोन क्यों कर रहे होंगे?

(e) **What shall I be doing for you?**
मैं आपके लिए क्या कर रहा होऊँगा?

EXERCISE 47

नीचे दिये गये Sentences का English में अनुवाद करें:

1. क्या वह नहाने जा रहा होगा?
2. क्या आप मुझसे बात करने आ रहे होंगे?
3. आप उसके बारे में क्या पता लगा रहे होंगे?
4. मैं आपसे क्या बात छुपा रहा हूँगा?
5. कौन-सा सिपाही लड़ाई पर जा रहा होगा?
6. क्या मन्त्री झूठ बोल रहा होगा?
7. कौन सा मन्त्री रिश्वत ले रहा होगा?
8. आप बिजली की चोरी क्यों कर रहे होंगे?
9. कौन सा दुकानदार वस्तुओं में मिलावट कर रहा होगा?
10. कैमीकल दूध कौन बना रहा होगा?

Hints for Translation

4. concealing from you **5.** soldier **8.** stealing, electricity **9.** adulterating **10.** chemical, milk.

Interrogative Negative Sentences: Future Continuous Tense के Interrogative Negative Sentence बनाने का Formula नीचे दिया गया है:

Formula: Wh or how + will/shall + S + not + be + (V-I + ing) + O + ?

Examples

(a) Who will not be taking chemical milk in a few years?

कुछ ही सालों में कौन कैमीकल दूध नहीं पी रहा होगा?

(b) Why shall we not be eating only adulterated food in a few years?
कुछ ही सालों में हम मिलावट वाली ही वस्तुएं क्यों नहीं खा रहे होंगे?

(c) Will you not be looking forward?
क्या आप आगे नहीं देख रहे होंगे?

(d) Shall I not be standing in a queue before the ration depot?
क्या मैं राशन डिपो के सामने लाइन में खड़ा नहीं हो रहा होऊँगा?

(e) Who will not be looting this country in the coming days?
आने वाले दिनों में इस देश को कौन नहीं लूट रहा होगा?

EXERCISE 48

नीचे दिये गए Sentence का English में अनुवाद करें:

1. क्या आप मुझे धमकी दे रहे होंगे?
2. क्या आप अफसर की मिन्नत कर रहे होंगे?
3. हमारे देश से अफसरशाही राज्य कौन खत्म कर रहा होगा?
4. कुछ ही सालों में कौन ईमानदारी से सभी प्रकार के टैक्स दे रहा होगा?
5. क्या मैं आपकी इ़ज्ज़त नहीं कर रहा होऊँगा?
6. क्या आप रेल पर बिना टिकट यात्रा नहीं कर रहे होंगे?
7. क्या यह गरीब देश सदा दूसरे देशों से सहायता मांगता रहेगा।
8. आप किस बात के लिए जिम्मेदार नहीं ठहराये जा रहे होंगे?
9. आकाश में बादल क्यों नहीं उड़ रहे होंगे?
10. मौसम अचानक क्यों बदल रहा होगा?

Hints for Translation

1. threatening **2.** making a request to **3.** bureaucracy **7.** beginning **8.** held responsible **10.** changing suddenly.

(C) Futlure Perfect Tense

(a) इस Tense में have का प्रयोग होता है।

Note: ध्यान रहे, चाहे Subject Singular हो अथवा Plural, इसमें 'have' का ही प्रयोग होता है।

(b) जो Sentences हिन्दी में 'चुका होगा', 'चुके होंगे', 'चुकी होगी' आदि से खत्म

होते हैं, प्राय: उनको Future Perfect Tenses कहा जाता है।

(c) इस Tense के Affirmative Sentences बनाने का Formula नीचे दिया गया है।

Formula: S + shall/will + have + V-III + O.

Examples

(a) She will have changed her mind.
वह अपना इरादा बदल चुकी होगी।

(b) I Shall have trapped him in my sweet words.
मैं उसे अपनी मीठी बातों में फंसा चुका होऊँगा।

(c) They will have taken their final decision.
वे अपना अन्तिम फैसला कर चुके होंगे।

(d) You will have fallen down from the horse.
तुम घोड़े से नीचे गिर चुके होंगे।

(e) We shall have moved across the line of control.
हम नियंत्रण रेखा पार कर चुके होंगे।

EXERCISE 49

नीचे दिये गये Sentences को English में अनुवाद करें:

1. मैं उसके कान खींच चुका होऊँगा।
2. वह ठीक हो चुका होगा।
3. आप मेरी बात मान चुके होंगे।
4. वह बांसुरी बजा चुका होगा।
5. तुम मुझ पर गुस्सा कर चुके होगे।
6. वह हमसे सब कुछ पूछ चुकी होगी।
7. उसका हृदय जोर से धड़क चुका होगा।
8. वह फिल्म देख चुका होगा।
9. हम पूरी स्कीम बना चुके होंगे।
10. वह आपकी बात पर अमल कर चुका होगा।

Hints for Translation

1. pulled **2.** recovered **4.** played on the flute **7.** beaten loudly.

Negative Sentences: Future Perfect Tense के Negative Sentences बनाने का Formula नीचे दिया गया है:

Formula: S + shall/will + not + have + V-III + O.

Examples

(a) She will not have told everything.
वह सब कुछ नहीं बता चुकी होगी।

(b) They will not have drawn the correct map.
वह ठीक नक्शा नहीं खींच चुके होंगे।

(c) He will not have found the lost coin.
वह गुमशुदा सिक्के को ढूंढ नहीं चुका होगा।

(d) I shall not have booked him for his mistake.
मैं उसकी गलती के लिए उसे नहीं पकड़ चुका होऊँगा।

(e) We shall not have killed the mad dog.
हम पागल कुत्ते को नहीं मार चुके होंगे।

EXERCISE 50

नीचे दिये गए Sentences का English में अनुवाद करें:

1. वह आपकी दुःख भरी दास्तान नहीं सुन चुका होगा।
2. आप बाजार नहीं जा चुके होंगे।
3. मैं अपने हाथ और मुँह नहीं धो चुका होऊँगा।
4. वह फैन्सी ड्रेस में नहीं जा चुकी होगी।
5. मैं उसे आपकी समस्या के बारे में नहीं बता चुका होऊँगा।
6. वह जल्दी सैर नहीं कर चुका होगा।
7. वह कड़वी दवाई नहीं खा चुका होगा।
8. हम सब मिठाई नहीं खा चुके होंगे।
9. मैं क्लब में जुआ नहीं खेल चुका होऊँगा।
10. बूढ़ा आदमी अपनी लाठी नहीं फेंक चुका होगा।

Hints for Translation

3. washed **4.** fancy dress **5.** problem **7.** better medicine **9.** club **10.** stick

Interrogative Sentences: Future Perfect Tense के Interrogative Sentences का Formula नीचे दिया गया है:

Formula: Wh or how + will/shall + S + have + V-III + O + ?

Examples

(a) Why will you have knocked at the door?
आपने दरवाज़ा क्यों खटखटाया होगा ?

(b) Shall I have put on my new clothes?
क्या मैं अपने नये कपड़े पहन चुका होऊँगा?

(c) Why will they have put out the light ?
वह लाईट क्यों बुझा चुके होंगे ?

(d) What shall we have told you?
हम आपको कौन सी बात बता चुके होंगे ?

(e) When will you have taken your dinner ?
आप रात्रि को कब भोजन कर चुके होंगे।

EXCERISE 51

नीचे दिये गये Sentences का English में अनुवाद करें:

1. आपका क्या नुकसान हो चुका होगा ?
2. वह दिल्ली क्यों पहुँच चुका होगा ?
3. गाड़ी स्टेशन पर क्यों रुक चुकी होगी ?
4. आपको कौन सी बात तकलीफ दे चुकी होगी ?
5. क्या मैं सुन्दर नहीं लग चुका होऊँगा ?
6. वह आपसे क्यों लड़ चुका होगा ?
7. जानवर क्यों घास चर चुके होंगे ?
8. वह फर्श को साफ क्यों कर चुकी होगी ?
9. वह जुकाम से परेशान क्यों हो चुका होगा ?
10. वह किसके सहारे जी चुकी होगी ?

Hints for Translation

1. loss. **2.** reached **3.** stopped **4.** troubled **7.** grazed **8.** swept the floor **9.** troubled due to sneezing **10.** help

Interrogative Negative Sentences: Future Perfect Tense के Interrogative Negative Sentences बनाने का Formula नीचे दिया गया है।

Formula: Wh or how + will/shall + S + not + have + V-III + O + ?

Examples

(a) **Shall I not have caught your words?**
क्या मैं आपकी बात नहीं समझ चुका होऊँगा ?

(b) Will they not have got surprised?
क्या उन्हें हैरानगी नहीं हो चुकी होगी ?

(c) Why will they not have hinted at this matter?
वह इस बात की ओर इशारा क्यों नहीं कर चुके होंगे ?

(d) Will you not have checked out all the accounts of the company?
क्या आप कम्पनी के सारे खातों की जांच–पड़ताल नहीं कर चुके होंगे ?

(e) When shall we not have kept the thing in order?
हम कब चीज़ें ठीक जगह पर नहीं रख चुके होंगे?

EXERCISE 52

नीचे दिये गये Sentences का English में अनुवाद करें:

1. वह आपकी क्या मदद नहीं कर चुका होगा?
2. वह मेरी कौन सी बात पर खुश नहीं हो चुका होगा?
3. क्या आपकी पहुँच दूर तक नहीं हो चुकी होगी?
4. क्या मन्त्री ईनाम नहीं बाँट चुका होगा?
5. मैं आपकी बातों का गलत अर्थ क्यों नहीं निकाल चुका होऊँगा।
6. वह तलवार से आप पर वार क्यों नहीं कर चुका होगा?
7. वह शोर क्यों नहीं मचा चुका होगा?
8. क्या वे आपका वेतन नहीं बढ़ा चुके होंगे?
9. क्या बच्चे बूढ़े बाबा पर पत्थर नहीं फेंक चुके होंगे?
10. क्या तुम दीवारों पर पेंट नहीं करवा चुके होगे?

Hints for Translation

3. access **4.** given away **6.** made an attempt **8.** salary, increased.

(D) Future Perfect Continuous Tense

Future Perfect Continuous Tense के Affirmative Sentences बनाने का Formula नीचे दिया गया है:

Formula: S + will/shall + have + been + (V-I + ing) + O + since/for + time

Examples

(a) She will have been waiting for you since morning.
वह सुबह से आपका इन्तजार कर रही होगी।

(b) It will have been raining since morning.
सुबह से बारिश हो रही होगी।

(c) I shall have been working in my office before the sunset.
मैं सूर्य डूबने से पहले अपने दफ्तर में काम कर रहा होऊँगा।

(d) They will have been singing for two hours.
वे दो घण्टे से गाना गा रहे होंगे।

(e) I shall have been riding my horse for one hour.
मैं एक घण्टे से अपने घोड़े की सवारी कर रहा होऊँगा।

EXERCISE 53

नीचे दिये गये Sentences का English में अनुवाद करें:

1. वह सुबह से भगवान को याद कर रही होगी।
2. मेरी बूढ़ी दादी मां तीन घंटे से माला जप रही होगी।
3. वह मेरे पहुँचने से पहले आपकी बातों का खण्डन कर चुकी होगी।
4. वह कल रात से डरावना उपन्यास पढ़ रहा होगा।
5. वह पिछले हफ्ते से आपको कोस रहा होगा।
6. वह कल से यात्रा कर रहा होगा।
7. वह कल से गहरी नींद में सो रहा होगा।
8. वह इस फैक्टरी में 1977 से काम कर रहा होगा।
9. चपरासी सुबह से घण्टी बजा रहा होगा।
10. वह तीन घण्टे से भाषण दे रहा होगा।
11. वे कई वर्षों से आपको मूर्ख बना रहे होंगे।

Hints for Translation

2. telling the beads **4.** horror fiction (or novel) **5.** cursing **10.** making fool of

Negative Sentences: Future Perfect Continuous Tense के Negative Sentences बनाने का Formula नीचे दिया गया है:

Formula: S + will/shall + have + not + been + (V-I + ing) + since, for + O + time.

Note: S + shall/will + not + have.... भी ठीक माना जायेगा।

Examples

(a) They will have not been playing in the garden since morning.
वे सुबह से बाग में नहीं खेल रहे होंगे।

(b) She will have not been asking you any question regarding this incident for two hours.
वह दो घण्टे से आपसे इस घटना के बारे में नहीं पूछ रही होगी।

(c) I shall have not been getting the exact information about you for one hour.
मैं एक घण्टे से आपके बारे में पूरी जानकारी नहीं प्राप्त कर रहा होऊँगा।

(d) We shall have not been telling him the story of fairies since last night.
हम पिछली रात से उसे परियों की कहानी नहीं सुना रहे होंगे।

(e) She will have not been attending the meeting due to a personal reason.
वह किसी निजी कारणवश बैठक में उपस्थित नहीं हो रही होगी।

EXERCISE 54

नीचे दिए गये Sentences का English में अनुवाद करें:

1. मैं आपकी बात पर भरोसा नहीं कर रहा होऊँगा।

2. वह चार दिनों से आपको नहीं खोज रहा होगा।

3. तीन घण्टे से इधर से कोई भी नहीं गुजर रहा होगा।

4. मुर्गी सुबह से दाना नहीं खा रही होगी।

5. वह आप पर दो घण्टे से जादू नहीं चला रहा होगा।

6. सभी लोग आपकी तरफ दो घण्टे से नहीं देख रहे होंगे।

7. वे अपनी गलती पर दो दिनों से पछता नहीं रहे होंगे।

8. बन्दर उसकी टोपी उठा कर दो घण्टे से दौड़ नहीं रहा होगा।

9. आकाश में बिजली कल रात से नहीं चमक रही होगी।

10. आप सुबह से इन्द्रधनुष आकाश में नहीं देख रहे होंगे।

Hints for Translation
2. searching for **3.** passing **4.** cock, corn **5.** magic **7.** repenting

Interrogative Sentences: Future Perfect Continuous Tense के Interrogative Sentences बनाने का Formula नीचे दिया गया है:

Formula: Wh or how + will/shall + S + have + been + (V-I + ing) + O + since, or for + time +?

Examples

(a) Why will you have been brooming the floor since morning?
आप सुबह से फर्श साफ क्यों कर रहे होंगे?

(b) Shall I have been watching him through my red eyes for fi minutes?
क्या मैं पांच मिनट से उसको अपनी लाल आंखों से देख रहा होऊँगा।

(c) Who will have been making a fool of you for three days?
कौन तुम्हें तीन दिनों से मूर्ख बना रहा होगा?

(d) Will you have been digging deep into your heart for a month for searching the Almighty?
क्या तुम एक मास से अपने दिल की गहराई में भगवान को खोज रहे होगे?

(e) Will your grand-father have been dying by inches since 1999?
क्या 1999 से आपके दादा जी एड़ियां रगड़-रगड़ कर मर रहे होंगे?

EXERCISE 55

नीचे दिये गये Sentences का English में अनुवाद करें :

1. मैं आपके लिये चार घण्टे से क्या कर रहा होऊँगा?
2. कौन कल से आपसे टकराने की कोशिश कर रहा होगा?
3. कौन भगवान को पाने के लिए दो साल से बकरे की भेंट दे रहा होगा?
4. क्या वर्षा चार घण्टे से हो रही होगी?
5. वह आपकी बात पर कब से विचार कर रहा होगा?
6. क्या वह अपने बेटे को दो घण्टे से पीट रहा होगा?
7. क्या वह जीवन भर अपने धर्म का पालन कर रहा होगा?
8. क्या वह पिछले कई वर्षों से मछली का व्यापार कर रहा होगा?
9. वह आपकी बातों पर विश्वास क्यों नहीं कर रहा होगा?
10. क्या बढ़ई सुबह से खिड़कियां व दरवाज़े बना रहा होगा?

Hints for Translation

1. To do for **2.** to come into conflict with **3.** making an offering of goats. **8.** deal in **10.** carpenter

Interrogative Negative Sentences: Future Perfect Continuous Tense के Interrogative Negative Sentences बनाने का Formula नीचे दिया गया है:

Formula: Wh or how + will/shall + S + have + not + been + (V-I + ing) + O + since or for + time + ?

Examples

(a) Will she have not been preparing food for us since morning?
क्या वह सुबह से हमारे लिए खाना नहीं बना रही होगी?

(b) Shall we have not been looking for the real culprit for two hours?
क्या दो घण्टे से हम वास्तविक दोषी को नहीं ढूँढ रहे होंगे?

(c) Why shall I have not been ploughing the fields since morning?
मैं सुबह से खेतों में हल क्यों नहीं चला रहा होऊँगा?

(d) Shall I have not been talking to him in an honest manner for five days?
क्या मैं पांच दिनों से उससे ईमानदारी से बात नहीं कर रहा होऊँगा।

(e) Will they have not been calling you for fifteen minutes?
क्या वे पन्द्रह मिनट से आपको नहीं पुकार रहे होंगे?

EXERCISE 56

नीचे दिये गये Sentences का English में अनुवाद करें :

1. क्या वह बछड़े को तीन घण्टे से नहीं नहला रहा होगा?
2. क्या वह सुबह से पतंग नहीं उड़ा रहा होगा?
3. आप कब मेरी बात का बुरा नहीं मान रहे होंगे?
4. आप कौन सी चीज मुझसे दो घण्टे के लिए नहीं छिपा रहे होंगे?
5. आप शाम से दर्पण के पास खड़े होकर क्यों नहीं तैयार हो रहे होंगे?
6. वह कल से ब्यूटी पार्लर क्यों नहीं जा रही होगी?
7. आप अपने से बड़ों का आदर दो घण्टे से क्यों नहीं कर रहे होंगे?
8. वह आपसे दो महीने से दूर क्यों रह रहा होगा?
9. वह आपके साथ तीन वर्षों से विदेश क्यों नहीं जा रहा होगा?
10. बच्चे क्लास में तीन दिनों से शोर क्यों मचा रहे होंगे?

Hints for Translation

1. bathing the calf **3.** to take an offence at **5.** mirror **6.** beauty parlour.

Chapter 19

Change of Tenses

(एक Tense को दूसरे Tense में परिवर्तित करना)

हम एक Tense को दूसरे Tense में परिवर्तित कर सकते हैं। लेकिन इसके लिए सभी Tenses के Formulae का ज्ञान होना बेहद ज़रूरी है।

PRESENT, PAST AND FUTURE INDEFINITE TENSES

Change of Present Indefinite Tense into Past Indefinite Tense

(i) राम जाता है।
↓ ↓

Ram goes.

अगर हम इस Sentence को ध्यान से पढ़ें, तो उसका Formula यह बनेगा।

Formula: S + (V-I+s/es)

इसमें Object नहीं है।

यह Formula Present Indefinite Tense का है। अगर हमको इसे Past Indefinite Tense में Change करना हो, तो यह नीचे दिये गये ढंग से Change होगा।

Formula of Past Indefinite Tense

S + V-II + O

Ram went.

राम गया।

(ii) सीता गाना गाती है।
↓

Sita sings a song.
↓ ↓ ↓

S + V (1st Form) + O

Change into Past Indefinite Tense:

Formula:

S + V-II + O

Sita sang a song.

सीता ने गाना गाया।

Change of Past Indefinite into Present Indefinite Tense

(i) 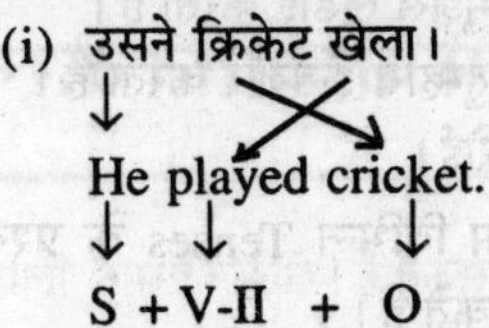

Change it into Present Indefinite Tense:

Formula:

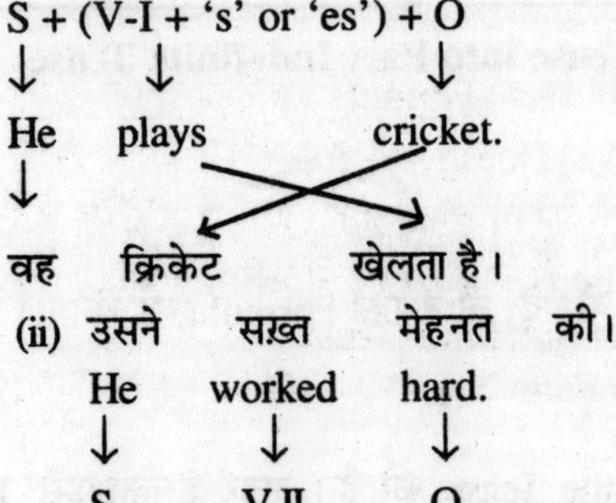

(ii) उसने सख़्त मेहनत की।

He worked hard.

↓ ↓ ↓

S V-II O

Change it into Present Indefinite Tense:

Formula:

S + (V-I + 's' or 'es') + O

↓ ↓ ↓

He + works + Hard

He works hard.

वह सख्त मेहनत करता है।

EXERCISE 1

नीचे दिये गये वाक्यों का पहले अंग्रेज़ी में अनुवाद करें तथा बाद में जो वाक्य Present Indefinite के हैं, उन्हें Past Indefinite में परिवर्तित करें:

1. सतीश खेलता है।
2. सीमा नाची।
3. वे सभी उसकी मूर्खता पर हँसे।
4. उसने काफी ऊँचे स्वर में गाना गाया।
5. वह आपसे कुछ कहती है।
6. बच्चा हँसता है।
7. वह आपको देख कर मुस्कराई।
8. वह मुझसे लड़ाई करता है।
9. वह तुम्हारा इन्तज़ार करता है।
10. वह रोई।

Interrogative Sentences (प्रश्नवाचक): हम विभिन्न Tenses के प्रश्न-वाचकों को भी एक दूसरे के Tenses में परिवर्तित कर सकते हैं।

Examples

(a) क्या वह आपसे प्यार करती है।

Does she love you?

अगर हम इस वाक्य को ध्यान से पढ़ें तो इसका Formula इस तरह बनता है:

Formula: (Wh or how अगर हो तो +) Does/Do + S + V-I + O ?

यह Formula Present Indefinite के प्रश्नवाचक का है। इसका अर्थ यह है कि अब हम इस Sentence को Past Indefinite के प्रश्न वाचक में परिवर्तित करेंगे।

Formula of Interrogative of Past Indefinite Tense

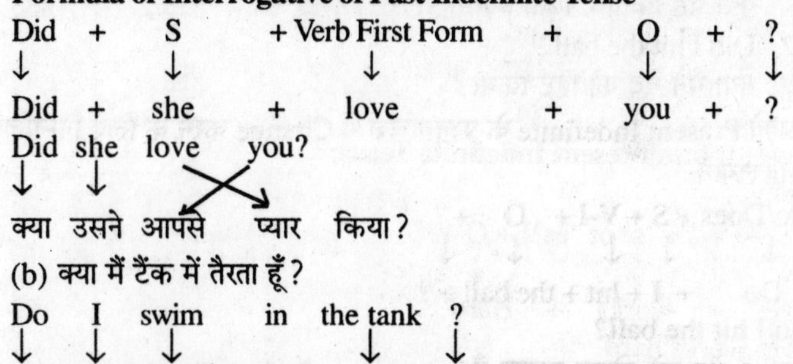

Do + S + Verb First Form + O + ?

Change it into Past Indefinite Tense

यहां पर Interrogative Past Indefinite का Formula लगाएं।

(Wh or how अगर हो तो) + Did + S + V-I + O + ?
↓ ↓ ↓ ↓ ↓
Did + I + swim + in the tank + ?

Did I swim in the tank? क्या मैं टैंक में तैरा ?

अगर Sentence Past Indefinite प्रश्नवाचक हो तो यह निम्नलिखित ढंग से Present Indefinite प्रश्नवाचक में परिवर्तित किया जा सकता है।

1. Did he read the book?
क्या उसने किताब पढ़ी ?

अब उसको Present Indefinite के प्रश्नवाचक में परिवर्तित करने के लिए निम्नलिखित Formula लगाएं।

Formula: (Wh or how अगर हो तो +) Do/Does + S + V-I + O + ?

Note: 'do' शब्द का प्रयोग तब होता है अगर कर्ता (Noun) Plural हो और 'I' के रूप में सामने आये। अन्यथा 'Does' का ही प्रयोग होता है।

यहाँ पर Wh or how नहीं है, तो Formula लगाएं

Do/Does + S + V-I + O + ?
↓ ↓ ↓ ↓ ↓
Does + he + read + the book + ?
Does he read the book?
क्या वह किताब पढ़ता है ?

2. Did I hit the ball?
क्या मैंने गेंद को हिट किया ?

इसको Present Indefinite के प्रश्नवाचक में Change करने के लिए निम्नलिखित Formula लगायें:

Do/Does + S + V-I + O + ?
↓ ↓ ↓ ↓ ↓
Do + I + hit + the ball + ?

Do I hit the ball?

क्या मैं गेंद को ठोकर मारता हूँ?

EXERCISE 2

नीचे दिये गये Sentences का पहले अंग्रेज़ी में अनुवाद करें तथा बाद में जो Sentences Past Indefinite के प्रश्नवाचक हैं, उन्हें Present Indefinite के

प्रश्नवाचक में परिवर्तित करें। इसी तरह, जो Present Indefinite प्रश्नवाचक Sentences के हैं, उन्हें Past Indefinite प्रश्नवाचक में परिवर्तित करें।

1. क्या वह रोता है?	**6.** वह क्यों रोया?
2. क्या वह गिर गई?	**7.** वह स्कूल क्यों नहीं जाता है?
3. वह कहाँ गया?	**8.** हमने साहस क्यों नहीं दिखाया?
4. क्या वह खुश दिखाई देती है?	**9.** वे यहाँ क्यों नहीं आया करते?
5. गुरमीत क्यों नहीं बोला?	**10.** क्या वह खूबसूरत लगता है?

PRESENT, PAST AND FUTURE (CONTINUOUS) TENSES

निम्नलिखित Sentences को पढ़िये:

(i) मैं जा रहा हूँ। (ii) मैं जा रहा था। (iii) मैं जा रहा होऊँगा।

I am going. I was going. I will be going.

अगर हम तीनों Sentences को ध्यान से पढ़ें तो हम देखेंगे कि वाक्य—

No. (i) Present Continuous Tense में;

No. (ii) Past Continuous Tense में; तथा

No. (iii) Future Continuous Tense में है।

इस प्रकार, किसी भी Sentence का Tense एक से दूसरे में परिवर्तित कर सकते हैं।

Change of Present Continuous into Past and Future Continuous Tenses

(i) She is going to the school.

वह स्कूल जा रही है।

पहले हम यह पता लगाते हैं कि यह Present Continuous Tense किस प्रकार के हैं। यहां पर इस Tense का Formula लगायें।

Formula: S + is/am/are + (V-I + ing) + O.

Note : 'am' शब्द का प्रयोग अगर Subject 'I' हो तब होता है; 'are' का प्रयोग अगर Subject Plural हो तब होता है; अगर Subject Singular हो तो 'is' का प्रयोग किया जाता है।

She is going to school.

↓ ↓ ↓ ↓

S + is + (V-I + ing) + O

Change it into Past Continuous Tense:

Formula: S + was/were + (V-I + ing) + O.
↓ ↓ ↓ ↓
She + was + going + to school.

She was going to school.

वह स्कूल जा रही थी।

Note: 'were' का प्रयोग केवल तब होता है जब Subject Plural हो, अगर Subject Singular हो तब 'was' का ही प्रयोग होता है।

Change it into Future Continuous Tense

Formula: S + will/shall + be + (V-I + ing) + O.

She + will + be + going + to school.

She will be going to school.

वह स्कूल जा रही होगी।

Change of Past Continuous into Present and Future Continuous Tense

अगर Sentence Past Continuous Tense में दिया गया हो तो हम इसे Future व Present के Continuous में भी Change कर सकते हैं।

1. I was taking tea.
   मैं चाय पी रहा था।

Change it into Present Continuous Tense

Formula: S + is/am/are + (V-I + ing) + O.
↓ ↓ ↓ ↓
I + am + taking + tea.

I am taking tea.

मैं चाय पी रहा हूँ।

Change it into Future Continuous Tense.

Formula: S + will/shall + be + (V-I + ing) + O
↓ ↓ ↓ ↓ ↓
I + shall + be + taking + tea.
I shall be taking tea.
↓
मैं चाय पी रहा हूँगा।

Note: साधारणतया 'I' तथा 'We' के साथ 'shall' लगता है तथा बाकी सभी Subjects के साथ 'will' लगाया जाता है।

Change of Future Continuous into Present and Past Continuous Tense

1. They will be singing a song.

वे गाना गा रहे होंगे।

Change it into Present Continuous Tense

Formula: S + is/am/are + (V-I + ing) + O

↓ ↓ ↓ ↓

They + are + singing + a song.

They are singing a song.

↓

वह गाना गा रही है।

Change it into Past Continuous Tense

Formula: S + was/were + (V-I+ ing) + O.

↓ ↓ ↓ ↓

They + were + singing a song.

They were singing a song.

↓

वे गाना गा रहे थे।

EXCERISE 3

नीचे दिये गये Sentences का पहले अंग्रेजी में अनुवाद करें फिर Present Continuous Tense के वाक्यों को Past व Future Continuous Tense में परिवर्तित करें। फिर Past Continuous Tense के वाक्यों को Present व Future Continuous Tense में परिवर्तित करें। इसी तरह, Future Continuous Tense के वाक्यों को Past व Present Continuous Tense में परिवर्तित करें।

1. वे गाना गा रहे होंगे।

2. मैं खाना खा रहा होऊँगा।

3. तुम खेल रहे थे।

4. वह हँस रही थी।

5. हम सो रहे होंगे।

6. वह नाच रही थी।

7. तुम झूठ बोल रहे थे।

8. पक्षी चहचहा रहे होंगे।

9. आकाश में काले-काले बादल छा रहे होंगे।

10. बच्चा मुस्कुरा रहा था।

PRESENT, PAST AND FUTURE PERFECT TENSES

(i) वह पेड़ पर चढ़ चुकी है।

She has climbed up the tree.

↓ ↓ ↓ ↓

S + has + VIIIrd Form + O.

Formula: S + has/have + V-III + O

यह Formula Present Perfect Tense का है।

Note: 'Have' शब्द का प्रयोग तब होता है जब Subject Plural हो या 'I' शब्द Subject के रूप में प्रयुक्त किया जाये।

Change it into Past Perfect Tense

Formula: S + had + V-III + O

↓ ↓ ↓ ↓

She + had + climbed up + the tree.

She had climbed up the tree.

↓

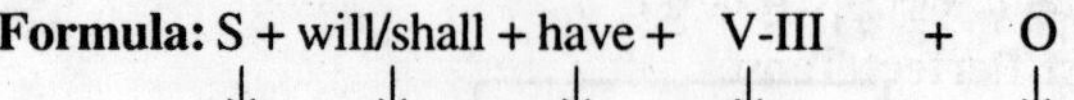

वह पेड़ पर चढ़ चुकी थी।

Change it into Future Perfect Tense

Formula: S + will/shall + have + V-III + O

↓ ↓ ↓ ↓ ↓

She + will + have + climbed up + the tree

She will have climbed up the tree.

↓

वह पेड़ पर चढ़ चुकी होगी।

Change of Past Perfect into Present and Future Perfect Tenses

(i) They had killed the cat.

वे बिल्ली को मार चुके थे।

Change it into Present Perfect Tense

Formula: S + has/have + V-III + O

↓ ↓ ↓ ↓

They + have + killed + the cat.

They have killed the cat.

↓

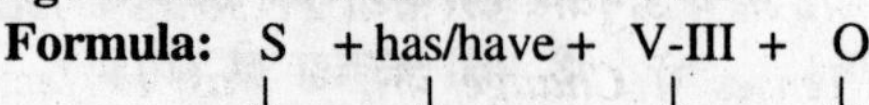

वे बिल्ली को मार चुके हैं।

Change it into Future Perfect Tense

Formula: S + will/shall + have + V-III + O

↓ ↓ ↓ ↓ ↓

They + will + have + killed + the cat

They will have killed the cat.

↓

वे बिल्ली को मार चुके होंगे।

Change of Future Perfect into Present and Future Perfect Tenses

(i) I shall have done my work.

↓

मैं अपना काम कर चुका हूँगा।

Change into Present Perfect Tense

Formula: S + has/have + V-III + O

↓ ↓ ↓ ↓

I + have + done + my work.

I have done my work.

↓

मैं अपना काम कर चुका हूँ।

Change into Past Perfect Tense

Formula : S + had + V-III + O

↓ ↓ ↓ ↓

I + had + done + my work.

I had done my work.

↓

मैं अपना काम कर चुका था।

EXERCISE 4

नीचे दिये गये वाक्यों का अंग्रेजी में अनुवाद करें तथा Present Perfect को Past व Future के Perfect Tenses में Change करें, व Past Perfect को Future के व Persent के Perfect Tense में परिवर्तित करें। इसी तरह Future Perfect को Persent व Past के Perfect Tenses में परिवर्तित करें।

1. वह हँस चुका होगा।

2. वह नहीं जा चुकी थी।

3. वह खाना खा चुका है।

4. बादल आकाश में गरज चुके थे।

5. वर्षा हो चुकी होगी।
6. वे मूर्ख बन चुके होंगे।
7. वह पागल हो चुका था।
8. शेर मर चुका था।
9. बन्दर पेड़ पर चढ़ चुका था।
10. हम मैच जीत चुके थे।

PRESENT, PAST AND FUTURE PERFECT CONTINUOUS TENSES

Change of Present Perfect Continuous into Past and Future Perfect Continuous Tenses

1. It has been raining since morning.
   सुबह से वर्षा हो रही है।

Change it into Past Perfect Continuous Tense

Formula: S + had + been + (V-I+ ing) + O + since for + time.

↓ ↓ ↓ ↓ ↓ ↓

It had been raining since morning.

It had been raining since morning.

सुबह से वर्षा हो रही थी।

Change it into Future Perfect Continuous Tense

Formula: S + will/shall + have + been + (V-I + ing) + O + since for + time.

↓ ↓ ↓ ↓ ↓ ↓ ↓

It + will + have + been + raining + since + morning.

It will have been raining since morning.

सुबह से वर्षा हो रही होगी।

Change of Past Perfect Continuous into Present and Future Perfect Continuous Tenses

1. She had been preparing food for two hours.
   वह दो घण्टे से भोजन बना रही थी।

Change it into Persent Perfect Continuous Tense

Formula: S + have + been +(V-I + ing) + O + since for + time.

↓ ↓ ↓ ↓ ↓ ↓ ↓

She + has + been + preparing + food + for + two + hours

She has been preparing food for two hours.

वह दो घण्टे से भोजन बना रही है।

Change it into Future Perfect Continuous Tense

Formula: S + will/shall + have + been + (V-I + ing) + O + since for + time.

↓ ↓ ↓ ↓ ↓ ↓ ↓ ↓

She + will + have + been + preparing + food + for + two hours

She will have been preparing food for two hours.

वह दो घण्टे से खाना बना रही होगी।

Change of Future Perfect Continuous into Present and Past Perfect Continuous Tense

(i) I shall have been telling a story for one hour.

मैं एक घण्टे से कहानी सुना रहा हूँगा।

Change it into Present Perfect Continuous Tense

Formula: S + have + been + (V-I + ing) + O + since/for + time

↓ ↓ ↓ ↓ ↓ ↓ ↓

I + have + been + telling + a story + for + one hour.

I have been telling a story for one hour.

मैं एक घण्टे से कहानी सुना रहा हूँ।

Change it into Past Perfect Continuous Tense

Formula: S + had + been + (V-I + ing) + O + since/for + time

↓ ↓ ↓ ↓ ↓ ↓ ↓

I + had + been + telling + a story + for + one hour.

I had been telling a story for one hour.

मैं एक घण्टे से कहानी सुना रहा था।

EXERCISE 5

नीचे दिये गये वाक्यों का अंग्रेजी में अनुवाद करें तथा Present Perfect Continuous के वाक्यों को Past व Future Continuous में परिवर्तित करें। इसी प्रकार Past Perfect Continuous के वाक्यों को Present व Future Perfect Continuous में परिवर्तित करें तथा Future Perfect Continuous के वाक्यों को Present व Past Perfect Continuous में परिवर्तित करें।

1. वह सुबह पांच बजे से सैर कर रहा है।
2. तुम दो साल से कुछ नहीं कर रहे होगे।
3. वह तीन दिनों से भूखी सो रही थी।
4. हम पांच घण्टे से शोर मचा रहे थे।
5. वह दो दिन से कुछ भी नहीं खा-पी रहा था।
6. सुबह छः बजे से वर्षा हो रही होगी।
7. वे दो सप्ताह से मुझसे कोई बात नहीं

कर रहे थे।

8. हम दोपहर से आपका इन्तजार कर रहे हैं।

9. वह पिछले बीस मिनट से नहीं आ रहा है।

10. वह 1951 से इस शहर में रह रही थी।

EXERCISE 6

नीचे दिये गये वाक्यों का अंग्रेज़ी में अनुवाद करें और उसके पश्चात् उन अनुवादित वाक्यों को उसी प्रकार के दूसरे दो Tenses के वाक्यों में परिवर्तित करें। प्रत्येक प्रकार के वाक्य के अन्त में कोष्ठक में Tense का नाम भी लिखें:

1. मैंने अपने कर्त्तव्य का पालन किया है।
2. वह अभी तक नहीं लौटा।
3. वह आपकी बात मान चुका होगा
4. सूर्य अस्त हो चुका होगा।
5. हमने किसी को निमन्त्रण नहीं दिया।
6. उसने आपके साथ उचित व्यवहार नहीं किया।
7. मैंने उसे खूब पीटा।
8. यह आपको मंहगा पड़ेगा।
9. आप वहां क्या कर रहे है?
10. वह क्या चाहता है।
11. मैं उसके साथ जाना नहीं चाहता।
12. इसमें मेरा कोई दोष नहीं।
13. वह कल तक लौटेगा।
14. क्या उसने आपको बहुत तंग किया?
15. क्या आप कभी अमेरिका गये हैं?
16. आप इतने उदास क्यों हैं?
17. दो दिन से जोरदार वर्षा हो रही होगी।
18. मैंने कभी ताजमहल नहीं देखा था।
19. मैं आपकी प्रतीक्षा कर रहा हूँगा।
20. मैं प्रातः से बहुत व्यस्त हूँ।
21. मैं अपने कर्तव्य का पालन भली-भांति कर रहा हूँ।
22. वह उस कार्य को नहीं कर सका।
23. आपको वहां अवश्य जाना चाहिए।
24. मैं उस पर विश्वास नहीं कर सका।
25. आप कब से तालाब में स्नान कर रहे थे?
26. मैं आपकी सहायता करूँगा।
27. उसके भाई ने उसे चाँटा मारा।
28. हम सदा अपने अध्यापकों का सम्मान करते हैं।
29. हमारी सेनाओं ने शत्रु को पाठ पढ़ा दिया।
30. मैं कुछ भी नहीं कर रहा हूँ।
31. हम अपनी मंज़िल पर पहुँच चुके होंगे।
32. आपको कोई कठिनाई नहीं होगी।
33. उसने किसी को धोखा नहीं दिया।
34. यह पुस्तिका ज्ञान का एक बड़ा भंडार है।
35. क्या आप कई वर्षों से बहुत सी कठिनाइयाँ सहन कर रहे होंगे?

Hints for Translation

1. duty **4.** set **8.** cost you dearly **12.** fault **14.** teased **20.** busy **21.** well **23.** must **24.** believe in **27.** slapped **29.** taught a lesson **31.** destination **33.** deceived **34.** treasure-house **35.** facing.

Chapter 20

Modals
(सहायक और रूप विषयक)

Modals and Auxiliaries एक प्रकार से Verb के सहायक होते हैं एवं वाक्य को ठीक ढंग से बनाने के लिये प्रयोग में लाये जाते हैं।

KINDS OF MODALS

Modal दो प्रकार के होते हैं:

(A) Primary Auxiliaries of Modals.

(B) Modal Auxiliaries.

(A) Primary Auxiliaries of Modals

ये तीन प्रकार के होते हैं:

(a) Be = be, is, am, are, was, were, being, been.

(b) Do = do, did, done, does, doing.

(c) Have = have, has, had, having.

लेकिन कई बार 'have', 'be', तथा 'do' का प्रयोग Full Verb के तौर पर भी किया जाता है।

Examples

(a) I have a book.
मेरे पास एक किताब है।

(b) He did his work quite well.
उसने अपना काम बिल्कुल ठीक किया।

(c) She does not do her job properly.
वह अपना काम ठीक प्रकार से नहीं करती है।

नीचे दिये गये Sentences में 'do,' 'be' तथा 'have' Primary Auxiliaries के तौर पर प्रयोग में लाये गये हैं।

DO

1. I do not kill the birds.
   मैं पक्षियों को नहीं मारता हूँ।
2. I do not go for a walk.
   मैं सैर को नहीं जाता हूँ।
3. She does not make a mistake.
   वह गलती नहीं करती है।
4. He does not come out of what is in his mind.
   वह नहीं बताता है कि उसके मन में क्या है।

HAVE

यह Perfect Tense के वाक्यों को बनाने का काम करता है।

1. They have played extremely well.
   वे बहुत अच्छी तरह खेले हैं।
2. We have made up our mind to go to Delhi.
   हम दिल्ली जाने का मन बना चुके हैं।
3. He has lost his courage.
   उसका हौसला पस्त हो गया है।

BE

यह Continuous Sentences में Use किया जाता है तथा Indefinite Tense के Passive Voice में भी प्रयुक्त होता है।

1. The peon is ringing the bell.
   चपरासी घण्टी बजा रहा है।
2. I am going to school.
   मैं स्कूल जा रहा हूँ।
3. They were dancing on the floor.
   वे फर्श पर नाच रहे थे।

USED IN PASSIVE VOICE

1. I was scolded for my mistake.
   मैं अपनी गलती के लिए डांटा गया।

2. She was given a lot of money.
उसे बहुत सा पैसा दिया गया।

3. I was awaken by a loud noise.
मुझे तीव्र शोर ने जगा दिया।

EXERCISE 1

नीचे दिये गये वाक्यों का अंग्रेजी में अनुवाद करें:

1. वह सो रहा है।
2. वह बाजार जा चुकी है।
3. क्या आप उसे जानते हैं ?
4. वह पत्र नहीं लिखती है।
5. वह मुझसे कुछ कह रहा था।
6. हम ताश खेल रहे हैं।
7. वे तुमसे ठीक ढंग से बात नहीं करते हैं।
8. उसके पिता द्वारा उसे ईनाम दिया गया।
9. वह चिड़ियाघर देखने जा रहा है।
10. वह रास्ते में खड़ा हँस रहा था।
11. तुम्हे ज़ोर से भूख क्यों नहीं लगती ?
12. वे झूठ नहीं बोलते हैं।
13. सोहन अपने पिता द्वारा पीटा गया है।
14. वह ठीक से सांस नहीं ले रहा है।
15. वे मन्दिर जा रहे हैं।

(B) Modal Auxiliaries

इनको Helping Verb भी कहा जाता है क्योंकि ये दूसरे Verbs के साथ मिलकर Sentences को पूरा क़रने का कार्य करते हैं। ये नीचे दिये गये हैं:

1. Shall
2. Will
3. Should
4. Would
5. Can
6. Could
7. May
8. Might
9. Must
10. Ought to
11. Dare
12. Used to
13. Mustn't
14. Daren't
15. Need
16. Needn't

WILL

(A) 'will' Word का प्रयोग Second Person तथा Third Person के Simple Future Tense में होता है जिसमें Second Person या Third Person Predication

करता है:

(i) She will go with me.
वह मेरे साथ जायेगी।

(ii) He will tell everything to my father.
वह मेरे पिताजी को सब बता देगा।

B. जब will की Form में Request की जाए:

(i) Will you lend me your book please?
क्या आप कृपया मुझे अपनी पुस्तक उधार देंगे?

(ii) Will you please listen to me for a moment?
क्या आप कृपया एक क्षण के लिए मेरी बात सुनेंगे?

C. जब Universal Truth या General Truth के बारे में बात होती है:

(i) The clouds will rush across the sky.
बादल आकाश में भागेंगे।

(ii) The stars will twinkle in the sky.
तारे आकाश में टिमटिमायेंगे।

Note: इस प्रकार के वाक्यों को Geographical Phenomenon (अर्थात् भौगोलिक दृश्य) भी कह सकते हैं।

D. जब कोई विशेष habit बतानी हो:

(i) Mohan will never speak the truth in such circumstances.
मोहन इस तरह के हालात में कभी सच नहीं बोलेगा।

(ii) She will always take tea after her lunch.
वह दोपहर के खाने के बाद हमेशा चाय पीयेगी।

E. जब कोई दृढ़ निश्चय किया जाये:

(i) I shall die but never obey you.
मैं मर जाऊंगा पर तुम्हारी बात कभी नहीं मानूँगा।

(ii) She will die of hunger but will never do anything illegal.
वह भूख से मर जायेगी पर कोई गैरकानूनी काम नहीं करेगी।

F. जब कोई आशा प्रकट की जाये:

(i) It will be a good day for you.
यह तुम्हारे लिये एक अच्छा दिन होगा।

(ii) It will rain today.
आज वर्षा होगी।

G. जब कोई इच्छा प्रकट करता है:

(i) Who will give me a five-rupee note?
कौन मुझे पांच रुपये का नोट देगा?

(ii) Who will give me a gift?
कौन मुझे तोहफा देगा?

H. जब कोई धमकी दी जाए:

(i) Will you show me your note-book or do I have to come to your seat?
क्या तुम मुझे अपनी कापी दिखाओगे या मुझे ही तुम्हारी सीट पर आना होगा?

(ii) Will you believe in peace or do I have to adopt some other way?
क्या तुम शान्ति में विश्वास करोगे या फिर मुझे कोई दूसरा रास्ता अपनाना पड़ेगा?

I. जब किसी को Invitation दी जाये:

(i) Will you join us at dinner in my residence today?
क्या आप हमारे साथ मेरे घर में रात्रि के भोजन के लिए आयेंगे?

(ii) Will you like to have a meeting with me here?
क्या आप मेरे साथ यहां मुलाकात करना पसंद करेंगे?

J. जब किसी से कोई Promise किया जाता है।

(i) I shall bring justice to you.
मैं आपको न्याय दिलाऊँगा।

(ii) She will certainly not make fun of you.
वह निश्चित तौर पर आपका मज़ाक नहीं उड़ायेगी।

Note: 'fun' Uncountable Noun है। इसलिए इसके साथ Article नहीं लगेगा परन्तु यह वाक्य ठीक है—What is the fun? अथवा What fun?

K. जब किसी को धमकी दी जाये:

(i) I will not let him go as a winner.
मैं उसे जीत कर नहीं जाने दूँगा।

(ii) Do not worry! I shall be there to take care of them.
घबराने की बात नहीं। मैं वहाँ पर रहूँगा उनकी खबर लेने के लिए।

L. जब किसी बात से इन्कार किया जाये:

(i) I shall not move a muscle.
मैं बिल्कुल भी नही हिलूँगा।

(ii) I will not like it if he comes to the party.
मैं उसका पार्टी में आना पसन्द नहीं करूंगा।

M. जब किसी पर विश्वास किया जाये:

(i) I know that you will believe me.
मैं जानता हूँ तुम मुझ पर विश्वास करोगे।

(ii) I am sure that you will take care of my son.
मुझे विश्वास है कि तुम मेरे बेटे का ध्यान रखोगे।

SHALL

Shall अधिकांशत: Future Tense में First Person के साथ Use में लाया जाता है।

A. Simple Future Tense में इसका प्रयोग इस प्रकार होगा:

(i) I shall go there.
मैं वहां जाऊँगा।

(ii) I shall talk to him.
मैं उससे बात करूँगा।

B. जब किसी की अनुमति लेनी हो:

(i) Shall I sing a song?
क्या मैं गाना गाऊँ?

(ii) Shall I bring a pizza for you?
क्या मैं तुम्हारे लिए एक पिज्ज़ा लाऊँ?

C. जब किसी को सलाह देनी हो:

(i) Shall I give you some good advice that you can become a good hero.
क्या मैं तुम्हें एक अच्छी सलाह दूँ कि आप एक अच्छे हीरो बन सकते हैं?

(ii) Shall I make it clear that you should be there in the hour of need?
क्या मैं एक बात साफ तौर पर कह दूँ कि जरूरत पड़ने पर तुम्हारा वहाँ होना ज़रूरी है?

Note: 'Shall' शब्द का प्रयोग Second या Third Person के साथ भी हो सकता है अगर वहां बात:

(a) एक Promise हो;
(b) एक Command हो;

(c) एक Threat हो; (d) एक दृढ़ निश्चय हो;

(e) या एक प्रबल इच्छा हो; (f) एक Prohibition हो; अथवा

(g) एक Legal Injunction हो।

(a) यदि एक Promise हो:

(i) You shall be rewarded for such a courageous task.
तुम्हें इतने हौंसले वाले काम करने के लिए जरूर इनाम मिलेगा।

(ii) You shall be saluted by all for such a great work.
तुम्हें तुम्हारे इस महान कार्य के लिए सभी सलाम करेंगे।

(b) यदि एक Command हो:

(i) You shall not move a bone until my next order.
तुम मेरे अगले हुक्म तक बिलकुल नहीं हिलोगे।

(ii) You shall not make a noise as long as I am here.
जब तक मैं यहाँ हूँ, आप शोर नहीं करेंगे।

(c) यदि एक Threat हो:

(i) You shall be taken to the boss for doing these types of deeds.
इस तरह के काम करने के कारण तुम्हें बॉस के पास ले जाना होगा।

(d & e) यदि एक Determination अथवा will की Declaration हो:

(i) You shall have to speak the truth.
तुम्हें सच बोलना होगा।

(ii) You shall have to keep some money for the future.
तुम्हें भविष्य के लिए कुछ पैसा रखना होगा।

(iii) You shall have to declare your assets.
तुम्हें अपनी सम्पत्ति की घोषणा करनी होगी।

(f) यदि एक Prohibiton हो:

(i) You shall not drink here.
तुम्हें यहां शराब पीने की इजाजत नहीं है।

(ii) You shall not smoke here.
तुम्हें यहां सिगरेट पीने की इजाजत नहीं है।

(g) यदि एक Legal Injunction अथवा Obligation हो:

(i) You shall have to fill up your Income Tax Return by the end of this month.
तुम्हें इस महीने के अन्त तक अपने आयकर की रिटर्न भरनी होगी।

(ii) You shall have to obey the court.
तुम्हें कोर्ट का आदेश मानना होगा।

WOULD

Would शब्द नीचे दिये गये ढंगों में Use होता है:

A. यदि Past Tense में 'will' की जगह Indirect Speech हो—
He told me that he would give me a surprise
उसने मुझसे कहा कि वह मुझे आश्चर्य चकित कर देगा।

Other Types of Usage:

Would का प्रयोग किसी भी Tense में इस प्रकार हो सकता है:

(A) To make a polite request.
(B) To express a habit or attitude.
(C) To express preference for one out of two options.
(D) To express polite invitation.
(E) To express a wish.
(F) To express probability.
(G) To express an unreal condition.
(H) To express determination.

A. To make a polite request (विनम्र विनती):

(i) Would you please come with me?
क्या कृपया आप मेरे साथ आयेंगे?

(ii) Would you please give me a pen?
क्या कृपया आप मुझे एक पैन देंगे?

B. To express a habit or an attitude (आदत अथवा आचार-व्यवहार):

(i) She would have a little prayer before the breakfast.
वह नाश्ता करने से पहले भगवान का थोड़ी देर के लिए नाम लेती थी (या लेगी)।

(ii) They would make a fun of the poor.
वे गरीबों का मजाक उड़ाते थे (या उड़ायेंगे)।

C. To express the preference for one out of two options:

(i) They would rather die than be thieves.
वे चोर बनने से मरना अच्छा समझते हैं (या समझेंगे)।

(ii) They would rather be poor than be robbers.
वे लुटेरा बनने से गरीब बनना अधिक पसन्द करेंगे (या करते हैं)।

D. To express polite invitation:

(i) Would you please join us at dinner in my house?
क्या आप रात्रि भोजन के लिए हमारे घर आयेंगे?

(ii) Would you like to share lunch with me?
क्या आप दोपहर का खाना मेरे साथ खायेंगे?

E. To express willingness or intention:

(i) I would go there if you wish so or so wish.
अगर तुम चाहते हो तो मैं वहाँ जाऊँगा।

(ii) I would help him if you say so.
अगर आप कहते हैं तो मैं उसकी सहायता करूंगा।

F. To express a wish:

(i) I wish I were rich by God's blessings.
काश! भगवान के आशीर्वाद से मैं अमीर होता।

(ii) I would take a cup of tea.
मैं एक कप चाय पीऊँगा।

G. To express probability (अंदाजा लगाना):

(i) Mohan would have arrived in the ground when we reach there.
जब हम वहाँ पहुँचेंगे, मोहन मैदान में पहुँच चुका होगा।

(ii) She would have prepared or cooked the food.
वह भोजन बना चुकी होगी।

H. To express an unreal condition:

(i) Had you spoken the truth, the case would not have got complicated.
अगर आपने सच बोला होता तो केस इतना पेचीदा न हो गया होता।

(ii) Had you told me about it in the beginning, the matter would not have become so knotty.
अगर आपने मुझे शुरू में ही इस विषय के बारे में बता दिया होता तो बात इतनी उलझनदार नहीं होती।

I. To express determination (निश्चय):

(i) He would try to do it till his last breath.
वह इसे अपनी अन्तिम सांस तक करने की कोशिश करेगा।

(ii) He would join the army at the earliest.
वह जल्दी-से-जल्दी फौज में भर्ती हो जायेगा।

CAN

Can का प्रयोग नीचे दिये गये ढंगों से होता है:

A. To express capacity and ability to do something;
B. To make a request;
C. To express an impossibility;
D. To give permission;
E. To convey a derogatory sense; and
F. General usage.

A. To express capacity and ability to do something:

(i) I can solve this question without consulting anybody.
मैं यह सवाल बिना किसी की सलाह से हल कर सकता हूँ।

(ii) I can get this mango down on my hand without shaking the branch.
मैं बिना टहनी हिलाये यह आम अपने हाथ में ला सकता हूँ।

B. To make request (विनती)

(i) Can I take your bag for a minute?
क्या मैं एक मिनट के लिए आपका बैग ले सकता हूँ?

(ii) Can I go through this newspaper?
क्या मैं यह अखबार पढ़ सकता हूँ?

C. To express impossibility (अनहोनी):

(i) Can a child survive in such an environment?
क्या एक बच्चा इस तरह के माहौल में जिन्दा रह सकता है?

(ii) Can a man do this?
क्या कोई आदमी इस तरह कर सकता है?

D. To express permission (इजाज़त):

(i) You can go out only after doing your work.
तुम बाहर केवल अपना काम खत्म करने के बाद ही जा सकते हो।

(ii) You can come out with your ideas only when I permit you to do so.
तुम अपने विचार तब दे सकते हो जब मैं तुम्हें ऐसा करने की आज्ञा दूँ।

E. To convey a derogatory sense:

(i) To get himself rich, he can commit any crime.
धनी बनने के लिए वह कोई भी अपराध कर सकता है।

(ii) To get the matter clear, we can wait for a couple of days more.
बात को साफ-साफ समझने के लिए हम दो दिन और इन्तज़ार कर सकते हैं।

F. General Usage (साधारण):

(i) He can talk.
वह बोल सकता है (या बात कर सकता है)।

(ii) You can walk.
आप चल सकते हैं।

(iii) They can laugh.
वे हंस सकते हैं।

COULD

'Could' शब्द का प्रयोग नीचे दिये गये प्रकार से होता है:

Past Tense में 'can' की जगह जब वाक्य Indirect Speech में हो।

(i) He said that he could tell me the story.
उसने मुझे कहा कि वह कहानी सुना सकता था।

(ii) They said that they could do what they liked.
उन्होंने कहा कि वे जो चाहते थे, वही कर सकते थे।

Other Types of Usage

(A) To express past ability.
(B) To make a polite request.
(C) To get permission from others.
(D) General usage.

(A) To express past ability (पुरानी क्षमता):

(a). I could bring him down in my youth.
अपने जवानी के दिनों में मैं उसको हरा सकता था।

(b) I could catch a live snake if I had not lost my hands.
अगर मेरे हाथ न कटे होते तो मैं एक ज़िन्दा सांप पकड़ सकता था।

(B) To make a polite request (विनती):

(i) Could I take your bicycle for a moment?
क्या एक क्षण के लिए मैं आपकी साइकिल ले सकता हूँ ?

(ii) Could you come to my residence in the evening?
क्या आप सायं को मेरे घर पर आ सकते हो ?

(C) To get permission (आज्ञा लेना):

ये वाक्य काफी हद तक Request के वाक्यों जैसे ही होते हैं।

(i) Could I talk to you?
क्या मैं आपसे बात कर सकता हूँ ?

(ii) Could we go together?
क्या हम इकट्ठे जा सकते हैं ?

(D) General Usage (साधारण प्रयोग):

(i) I could realise your problem.
मैं आपकी तकलीफ को महसूस कर सकता हूँ।

(ii) I could feel your disagreement.
मैं आपकी असहमति को महसूस कर सकता हूँ।

MIGHT

'Might' Word 'may' शब्द को Past Tense में प्रकट करता है:

(i) He asked me if he might bring something to eat for me.
उसने मुझसे पूछा कि क्या वह मेरे लिए खाने को कुछ लाया है।

(ii) He told me that he might listen to me (on) some other day.
उसने मुझसे कहा कि वह मेरी बात किसी और दिन सुन सकेगा।

Other Types of Usage (इज़ाजत देना या लेना)

(A) To give or seek permission.
(B) To express a remote possibility.

(A) To give or seek permission:

(i) Might I come in, sir?
क्या मैं अन्दर आ सकता हूँ, श्रीमान् ?

(ii) You might go to the bazaar.
तुम बाजार जा सकते हो।

(B) To express a remote possibility:

(i) It might be a hot day today.
आज गर्म दिन हो सकता है।

(ii) You might quarrel with me.
तुम मेरे साथ लड़ सकते हो।

MAY

'May' Word का प्रयोग निम्नलिखित ढंगों से होता है:

(A) To seek permission.
(B) To give permission.
(C) To express a purpose.
(D) To write declarative sentences.
(E) To express a curse.
(F) To express a possibility.
(G) To express a wish or a prayer.
(H) To offer help, service etc.

(A) To seek permission:

(i) May I come in sir?
क्या मैं अन्दर आ सकता हूँ, श्रीमान्?

(ii) May I go for lunch?
क्या मैं दोपहर के भोजन के लिए जा सकता हूँ?

(B) To give permission:

(i) You may come in.
तुम अन्दर आ सकते हो।

(ii) You may go for lunch.
तुम दोपहर के खाने के लिए जा सकते हो।

(C) To express a purpose:

(i) Move fast so that you may be able to attend the meeting.
तेज़ चलो ताकि सभा में पहुँच सको।

(ii) He is laughing loudly so that he may hide his own fear.
वह ज़ोर से हंस रहा है ताकि अपना डर छिपा सके।

(D) In declarative sentences:

(i) It may snow to night.
आज रात हिमपात हो सकता है (अथवा, हिमपात होगा)।

(ii) They may kill him.
वे उसे मार सकते हैं (अथवा, हो सकता है कि वे उसे मार दें)।

Note: इस प्रकार के वाक्यों में Traditional Writers प्राय: 'become' या 'get' का प्रयोग करते थे। आधुनिक, लेखक 'go' का अधिक प्रयोग करते हैं।

(E) To express a curse (कोसना):

(i) May you die on the spot!
भगवान करे तुम अभी मर जाओ!

(ii) May you become poor at the earliest.
भगवान करे तुम जल्दी से गरीब हो जाओ।

(F) To offer help, service etc. (मदद देने के उद्देश्य से):

(i) May I fetch a glass of water for you?
क्या मैं आपके लिए एक गिलास पानी ले आऊँ?

(ii) May I lead you (or guide you)?
क्या मैं आपको रास्ता दिखाऊँ?

(G) To express a wish or prayer:

(i) May God help you !
भगवान तुम्हारी सहायता करे !

(ii) May you become rich !
भगवान करे तुम अमीर हो जाओ!

(H) To express possibility (सम्भावना):

(i) He may ask you about your health.
वह तुम्हें तुम्हारी सेहत के बारे में पूछ सकता है।

(ii) She may ask you about your financial position?
वह तुम्हें तुम्हारी आर्थिक हालत के बारे में पूछ सकती है।

MUST

Must शब्द का प्रयोग निम्नलिखित प्रकार से होता है:

(A) To express duty.

(B) To express a necessity.
(C) To give an advice.
(D) To express some possibility.
(E) To express a determination.
(G) To express a compulsion.
(G) To express an obligation.

(A) To express duty:

(i) You must take charge of this task.
तुम्हें इस कार्य का भार ज़रूर उठाना चाहिए।

(ii) You must be ready for sacrificing your life for your country.
तुम्हें अपने देश पर अपने प्राण न्यौछावर करने के लिए तैयार रहना चाहिए।

(B) To express a necessity:

(i) You must go for a morning walk.
तुम्हें सुबह अवश्य टहलना चाहिए।

(ii) You must go to school daily in order to be a gentleman.
एक भद्रपुरुष बनने के लिए तुम्हें हर रोज़ स्कूल जाना चाहिए।

(C) To give an advice:

(i) You must have an extra pair of shoes.
तुम्हारे पास एक जोड़े जूते अतिरिक्त होने चाहिए।

(ii) You must obey your parents.
तुम्हें अपने माता-पिता की आज्ञा का पालन करना चाहिए।

(D) To express some possibility (सम्भावना):

(i) She must have prepared or cooked the dinner.
वह रात का खाना बना चुकी होगी।

(ii) He must have drunk a full bottle.
वह एक पूरी बोतल पी गया होगा।

Note: 'must have' Past Tense में घटी घटना की ओर संकेत करता है। Future Tense दर्शाने के लिए 'must be able to' का प्रयोग होता है।

(E) To express a determination:

(i) We must sing well.
हमें जरूर ठीक प्रकार से गाना चाहिए।

(ii) We must beat him.
हमें उसे ज़रूर मारना (अथवा हराना) चाहिए।

(F) To express an obligation:

(i) You must love the poor.
तुम्हें गरीबों से अवश्य प्यार करना चाहिए।

(ii) **You must obey your parents.**
तुम्हें अपने माता-पिता की आज्ञा का पालन अवश्य करना चाहिए

MUSTN'T (MUST NOT)

Mustn't का प्रयोग केवल Compulsion व Obligation में होता है:

(i) **You mustn't play with him.**
तुम्हें उसके साथ नहीं खेलना चाहिए।

(ii) You mustn't talk to him.
तुम्हें उससे बात नहीं करनी चाहिए।

SHOULD

'Should' का प्रयोग Past Tense की Indirect Speech में 'shall' के स्थान पर होता है:

(i) He told me that I should do my work carefully.
उसने मुझसे कहा कि मुझे अपना काम ध्यानपूर्वक करना चाहिए।

(ii) She told me that she should work quickly.
उसने मुझसे कहा कि उसे अपना काम जल्दी करना चाहिए।

Other Types of Usage

(A) To express duty or moral obligation.
(B) To express an advice.
(C) To express guess.
(D) To express a condition.
(E) To express a probability.
(F) To express caution.

(A) To express duty or moral obligation:

(i) You should help the little ones.
तुम्हें छोटों की सहायता करनी चाहिए।

(ii) You should do something remarkable for your country.
तुम्हें अपने देश के लिए कोई महत्त्वपूर्ण कार्य करना चाहिए।

(B) To express an advice:

(i) You should not tell a lie.
तुम्हें झूठ नहीं बोलना चाहिए।

(ii) You should not lose your temper.
तुम्हें नाराज़ नहीं होना चाहिए।

(C) To express a guess:

(i) It should be thundering tonight.
आज रात बादल गरजना चाहिए।

(ii) She should be at home now.
उसे अब घर पर होना चाहिए।

(D) To express a condition:

(i) Should I do something for you?
क्या मैं आपके लिए कुछ करूँ?

(ii) Should you need something, call out for me.
अगर तुम्हें कुछ चाहिए हो तो मेरा नाम पुकार लेना।

(E) To express a probability:

(i) We should be there during the early hours of the morning.
सुबह–सुबह हमें वहां होना चाहिए।

(ii) You should be able to do your work in time.
तुम्हें अपना काम ठीक समय पर कर लेने योग्य होना चाहिए (अथवा, तुम अपना काम सही समय पर कर लोगे)।

(F) To express caution:

(i) Be a wise boy, lest you should be labelled a fool.
एक समझदार लड़का बनो; कहीं ऐसा न हो कि तुम्हें मूर्ख कहा जाये।

Note: Translation करते समय विद्यार्थी प्रायः Literal Translation की ओर ही ध्यान देते हैं। उन्हें विभिन्न प्रकार के हिन्दी के वाक्यों को Idiomatic English में बदलने का ढंग भी सीखना चाहिए।

(ii) Do something courageous, lest you should be declared a coward.
कोई साहसपूर्ण काम करो, नहीं तो तुम्हें डरपोक करार दिया जायेगा (अर्थात्, ऐसा न हो कि तुम्हें डरपोक करार दे दिया जाये)।

OUGHT TO

'Ought to' नीचे दिये गये तरीकों से Use में आता है:

(A) To express duty
(B) To express advice
(C) To express an obligation

(A) To express duty:

(i) You ought to love birds.
तुम्हें पक्षियों से प्यार करना चाहिए।

(ii) You ought to do your work honestly.
तुम्हें अपना काम ईमानदारी से करना चाहिए।

(B) To express an advice:

(i) You ought to obey your elders.
तुम्हें अपने से बड़ों की आज्ञा का पालन करना चाहिए।

(ii) You ought to go for a little walk in the morning.
तुम्हें सुबह सैर के लिए जाना चहिए।

(C) To express an obligation:

(i) You ought to obey the laws of the land.
तुम्हें देश के कानूनों का पालन करना चाहिए।

(ii) We ought to be ready to die for our country.
हमें अपने देश के लिए मरने को तैयार रहना चाहिए।

DARE

'Dare' Word का प्रयोग साहस सम्बंधी बातों में किया जाता है।

(i) How dare you touch my hand?
तुमने मेरा हाथ छूने की हिम्मत कैसे की?

(ii) How dare you talk to me?
तुमने मुझसे बात करने की हिम्मत कैसे की?

(iii) How dare he call you names?
उसकी क्या मजाल कि वह तुम्हें गालियां दें?

DAREN'T (DARE NOT)

(i) He daren't kick you.
उसमें तुम्हें पैर मारने की हिम्मत नहीं है।

(ii) She daren't make an excuse.
उसमें बहाना बनाने की हिम्मत नहीं है।

(iii) He dare not come here.
उसकी यहां आने की मजाल नहीं है।

USED TO

'Used to' शब्द नीचे दिये गये तरीकों से प्रयोग में लाया जाता है।

A. To express some habit of the past.
B. To show existence of something in the past.

A. To express some habit of the past:

(i) I used to go for a morning walk daily in my young age.
मैं अपनी जवानी के दिनों में रोज़ सुबह टहलने जाया करता था।

(ii) She used to sing a song at night.
वह रात को गाना गाया करती थी।

B. To show existence of something in the past:

(i) At this spot, there used to be a multi-storyed building.
इस जगह पर एक बहु-मंज़िला इमारत हुआ करती थी।

(ii) There used to be my own home in this street.
इस गली में मेरा अपना घर हुआ करता था।

NEED

'Need' शब्द का प्रयोग Obligation के तौर पर होता है।

(i) Need I ask you again?
क्या मुझे आपको दुबारा कहना पड़ेगा?

(ii) Need you eat more?
क्या तुम्हें और खाने की जरूरत है?

NEEDN'T (NEED NOT)

'Need not' का प्रयोग Obligation के तौर पर होता है। यह Negative Message Convey करता है।

(i) You needn't say anything.
तुम्हें कुछ भी कहने की ज़रूरत नहीं।

(ii) You need not tell another false story.
तुम्हें और झूठी कहानी सुनाने की ज़रूरत नहीं है।

EXERCISE 2

नीचे दिये गये वाक्यों का अंग्रेजी में अनुवाद करें:

1. वह खाना खा रहा था।
2. **किसान हल चला रहा था।**
3. **हमें अच्छा इन्सान बनना चाहिए।**
4. वह रोज़ मन्दिर जाया करता था।
5. हम दोनों इकट्ठे खाना खाया करते थे।
6. तुम्हें जाना ही होगा।
7. तुम्हे यहाँ शोर करने की इज़ाजत नहीं है।
8. भगवान तुम्हें लम्बी आयु दे।
9. चुप हो जाओ।
10. वह स्कूल नहीं जाता है।
11. आज शायद बारिश हो।
12. तुम्हे बच्चों से प्यार करना चाहिए।
13. **तुम्हें किसी से भला-बुरा नहीं कहना चाहिए।**
14. क्या मैं आपके लिए एक गिलास दूध लाऊँ?
15. क्या मैं आपकी पुस्तक उधार ले सकता हूँ?
16. वह हंस रहा था।
17. वह क्यों रो रही थी।
18. तुम्हें अपने से बड़ों की आज्ञा का पालन करना चाहिए।
19. तुम्हें ज़रूर नहाना चाहिए।
20. तुम्हें ज़रूर मेरे साथ चलना चाहिए।

EXERCISE 3

1. क्या मैं आपकी कार दो **दिनों के** लिए उधार ले सकता हूँ।
2. तुम कहां खो गये थे?
3. श्याम अच्छी किताबें पढ़ता था।
4. तुम ज़रूर प्रथम आओगे।
5. वह जरूर हार जायेगा।
6. तुम्हें क्या **लगता** है?
7. तुम्हें सरकार के सारे कर देने ही होंगे।
8. तुम्हें जज का फैसला मानना ही होगा।

9. दीवार पर इश्तहार लगाना माना है।

10. कृपया मेरी बात ध्यान से सुनें।

11. आपका क्या ख्याल है कि खाना बन चुका होगा?

12. भगवान तुम्हें सदा सुखी रखे!

13. मुझे तुम पर पूरा भरोसा है।

14. मैं उसे बुरी तरह पीट सकता था अगर मेरे पांव न दर्द कर रहे होते।

15. वह सदा सच क्यों नहीं बोलता?

16. वह हमारे साथ कॉलेज जायेगा।

17. उसने मुझसे कहा अगर मैं उसके लिए कुछ अच्छा कर सकता।

18. कल रात वर्षा होगी।

19. खबरदार! जो मुझसे जुबान लड़ाई।

20. अगर तुम मेरी बात नहीं मानोगे तो तुम्हें दण्ड दिया जायेगा।

Hints for Translation

Exercise (2)—2. plough **3.** human beings **7.** will have to (or shall)

Exercise (3)—5. lose **7.** taxes **8.** judgement **9.** bill-sticking, prohibited **13.** faith **14.** aching **20.** obey, be punished.

Chapter 21

Voice

(वाच्य)

KINDS OF VOICE

English में दो प्रकार के वाच्य होते हैं—कर्तृवाच्य और कर्मवाच्य।

कर्तृवाच्य (Active Voice) को हम कर्मवाच्य (Passive Voice) में Change कर सकते हैं।

(A) Active Voice में कर्ता (Subject) पहले तथा Object बाद में आता है।

(i) Ram writes a letter.
राम एक पत्र लिखता है।

यह वाक्य एक Active Voice है। किसी भी वाक्य को हम तब Active Voice कहते हैं जब इसका Subject कोई Action सीधे तौर पर करता है, अन्यथा इसे Passive Voice कहा जाता है।

अब ऊपर दिया गया Sentence साफ तौर पर प्रकट करता है कि राम लिखने का कार्य करता है। अत: यह Sentence एक Active Voice है।

(ii) A letter is written by Ram.
एक पत्र राम के द्वारा लिखा जाता है।

Sentence (ii) में राम को सीधे तौर पर लिखते हुए नहीं बताया गया। अत: यह Sentence Passive Voice है।

(B) Passive Voice बनाते समय वाक्य में पहले वाक्य का (Active Voice) का Object, Passive Voice का Subject बन जाता है। इसी प्रकार Active Voice का Subject, Passive Voice का Object बन जाता है।

वह शोर मचाता है।

He makes a noise. (Active Voice)
↓ ↓ ↓
S V O

A noise is made by him (Passive Voice)
↓ ↓ ↓
S V O

उसके द्वारा शोर मचाया जाता है।

Passive Voice में प्राय: 'by' शब्द का प्रयोग होता है।

(C) लेकिन कुछ ऐसे भी वाक्य हैं जिनमें 'by' प्रयोग में नहीं लाया जाता बल्कि उसकी जगह 'to' 'at' 'with' 'in' etc. प्रयोग में लाये जाते हैं।

Examples

(a) I know him. (Active Voice)
मैं उसे जानता हूँ।
He is known to me. (Passive Voice)
वह मेरे द्वारा जाना जाता है।

(b) Her conduct makes me angry.
उसके व्यवहार से मुझे गुस्सा आता है।
I am made angry at her conduct.
मैं उसके व्यवहार से गुस्सा हो जाता हूँ।

(c) They annoy me very much.
वे मुझे बहुत नाराज़ करते हैं।
I am annoyed with them very much.
मैं उनसे बहुत नाराज़ रहता हूँ।

(D) जो Sentences 'it is time' से शुरू होते हैं, वे Passive Voice में 'it is time for' से शुरू होते हैं।

(i) It is time to have a cup of tea.
एक कप चाय पीने का समय हो गया है।
It is time for a cup of tea to be had.
यह समय एक कप चाय पीने का है।

(E) कुछ वाक्यों में जहां Verb पहले आने वाले Noun की Quality के अनुसार

प्रयुक्त होता है, वहां Passive Voice में 'When + V-III' or 'When it is + V-III' का प्रयोग होता है।

Examples

(a) Sugar tastes sweet. (Active Voice)
चीनी चखने में मीठी होती है।
Sugar is sweet when tasted. (Passive Voice)
चीनी मीठी होती है जब चखी जाती है।
Sugar is sweet when it is tasted.(Passive Voice)
चीनी मीठी होती है जब यह चखी जाती है।

(b) An acid tastes sour. (Active Voice)
तेज़ाब चखने में खट्टा होता है।
An acid is sour when tasted. (Passive Voice)
तेज़ाब खट्टा होता है जब चखा जाता है।
An acid is sour when it is tasted. (Passive Voice)
तेजाब खट्टा होता है जब यह चखा जाता है।

(F) कई बार 'by' शब्द का प्रयोग किया ही नहीं जाता।

Examples

(a) He has stolen my pen. (Active Voice)
उसने मेरा पैन चुरा लिया है।
My pen has been stolen. (Passive Voice)
मेरा पैन चुराया गया है।

(b) He has stolen my pencil. (Active Voice)
उसने मेरी पैन्सिल चुरा ली है।
My pencil has been stolen. (Passive Voice)
मेरी पैन्सिल चुरा ली गई है।

Note: इस प्रकार के वाक्यों में हमारा ध्यान कर्ता (व्यक्ति) से हट कर कर्म (वस्तु) की स्थिति-परिवर्तन की ओर अधिक जाता है।

(G) कुछ वाक्य जिनमें "may, might, can, could, should, ought" etc. का प्रयोग होता है, उनके Passive Voice में 'be' शब्द का प्रयोग होता है।

Examples

(a) We should not make a noise.
हमें शोर नहीं करना चाहिए।

A noise should not be made (by us).

शोर (हमारे द्वारा) नहीं किया जाना चाहिए।

(B) You can do it.

तुम इसे कर सकते हो।

It can be done (by you).

यह (तुम्हारे द्वारा) किया जा सकता है।

(H) Imperative Sentences नीचे दिये गये ढंग से Passive Voice में परिवर्तित किये जाते हैं।

Examples

(a) Stop now.

अब रुको।

You are ordered to stop now.

तुम्हें अब रुकने का हुकम दिया जाता है।

(b) Attack, comrades !

साथियो ! हमला करो।

You are commanded to attack.

तुम्हें हमला करने का आदेश दिया जाता है।

(c) Help the poor.

गरीबों की मदद करो।

You are advised to help the poor.

तुम्हें गरीबों की मदद करने की सलाह दी जाती है।

(I) जिन Sentences में दो Object होते हैं, वे दो ढंगों से Passive Voice में Change होते हैं।

(i) She gave me this bag.

उसने मुझे यह बैग दिया।

This bag was given to me by her.

यह बैग मुझे उसके द्वारा दिया गया।

I was given this bag by her.

मुझे यह बैग उसके द्वारा दिया गया।

EXERCISE 1

नीचे दिये गये Sentences का अंग्रेजी में अनुवाद करें:

1. मुझे उसके द्वारा पैन्सिल दी गई।
2. गुलाब का फूल, जब सूंघा जाये, तो मधुर होता है।
3. तुम्हें उसके द्वारा धोखा दिया गया।
4. वह तुम्हारे द्वारा जानी जाती है।
5. तुम्हें आगे बढ़ने का हुक्म दिया जाता है।
6. उसे चाकू मार दिया गया।
7. यहाँ पर शोर नहीं किया जाना चाहिए।
8. तुम्हें छोटों से प्यार करने की सलाह दी जाती है।
9. पौधों को हवा द्वारा हिलाया जाता है।
10. उसकी कापी आपके द्वारा चुराई गई।
11. झूठ आपके द्वारा बोला गया।
12. वह इस कार्य को भली-भांति कर सकता है।
13. आपको उसकी बात मान लेनी चाहिए।
14. वह स्कूल बस द्वारा जाता है।
15. तुम्हारे द्वारा उसको पीटा गया।
16. यह कार्य उसके द्वारा भली-भांति किया जा सकता है।
17. उसकी बात आपके द्वारा मानी जानी चाहिए।
18. हमें अपने देश के कानूनों पर पाबन्द रहना चाहिए।

Hints for Translation

2. when tasted. **6.** knifed. **9.** are shaken. **14.** by bus. **18.** abide by.

Note: Sentences No (14) और (18) में Active Voice में 'by' के प्रयोग से हमें यह नहीं समझ लेना चाहिए कि केवल 'by' के प्रयोग से ही Sentence Passive Voice में परिवर्तित किया जाता है।

Chapter 22

Change of Voice

(वाच्य-परिवर्तन)

TENSEWISE

Abbreviations

S = Subject
O = Object
V = Verb
cS = Object changed into subject
cO = Subject changed into object

इस Chapter में हम Tense के हिसाब से होने वाले परिवर्तनों का अध्ययन करेंगे।

(A) Present Indefinite Tense: Present Indefinite Tense के Affirmative Sentences को Passive Voice में परिवर्तित करने का Formula नीचे दिया गया है।

Active Voice: S + (V-I + s/es) + O.

Passive Voice: Changed Subject (cS) + is/am /are (be) + V-III + by + changed Object (cO)

(a) 'am' वहां पर प्रयोग में लाया जायेगा जहां Subject 'I' हो।
(b) 'is' वहां पर प्रयोग में लाया जायेगा जहां Subject Third Person व Singular हो।
(c) 'are' वहां पर प्रयोग में लाया जायेगा जहां Subject Plural हो।

Examples

(a) He sings a song.
वह गाना गाता है।
A song is sung by him.
उसके द्वारा गाना गाया जाता है।

(b) I love my country.
मैं अपने देश से प्यार करता हूँ।
My country is loved by me.
मेरे देश को मेरे द्वारा प्यार किया जाता है।

EXERCISE 1

नीचे दिये गये Sentences को Passive Voice में Change करें:

1. She loves her home.
वह अपने घर से प्यार करती है।

2. He writes a letter.
वह एक पत्र लिखता है।

3. They leave their bed early.
वे लोग अपने बिस्तर जल्दी छोड़ देते हैं।

4. He steals my book.
वह मेरी किताब चुराता है।

5. We play cards.
हम ताश खेलते हैं।

Interrogative Sentences (प्रश्नवाचक वाक्य): प्रश्नवाचक वाक्यों को Passive Voice में परिवर्तित करने का Formula नीचे दिया गया है:

Active Voice: Wh or how + do/ does + S + V-I + O + ?

Passive Voice: Wh or how + is/am/are + cS + V-III + by + cO + ?

Examples

(a) Do you like her?
क्या आप उसे पसन्द करते हैं?
Is she liked by you?
क्या वह आपके द्वारा पसन्द की जाती है?

(b) Does she hit the ball?
क्या वह गेंद को ठोकर मारती है?
Is the ball hit by her?
क्या गेंद को उसके द्वारा ठोकर मारी जाती है?

EXERCISE 2

नीचे दिये वाक्यों को Passive Voice में परिवर्तित करें:

1. Do you love your brother?
क्या आप अपने भाई से प्यार करते हैं।

2. Does he sing a song?
क्या वह गाना गाता है?

3. Do they dance with music?
क्या वे संगीत के साथ नृत्य करते हैं?

4. Do we take tea?
क्या हम चाय पीते हैं?

5. Does she make a doll?
क्या वह एक गुड़िया बनाती है ?

(B) Present Continuous Tense: Persent Continuous के Affirmative Sentences का Passive Voice नीचे दिये गये ढंग से बनता है:

Active Voice: S + is/am/are + (V-I + ing) + O.
Passive Voice: cS + is/am/ are/ + being + V-III + by + cO.

Examples

(a) She is ringing the bell.
वह घण्टी बजा रही है।
The bell is being rung by her.
घण्टी उसके द्वारा बजाई जा रही है।

(b) They are taking their meals.
वे अपना भोजन खा रहे हैं।
Their meals are being taken by them.
उनका भोजन उनके द्वारा खाया जा रहा है।

EXERCISE 3

नीचे दिये गये Sentences के Passive Voice बनायें:

1. She is playing cricket.
वह क्रिकेट खेल रही है।
2. We are helping the flood victims.
हम बाढ़ पीड़ितों की सहायता कर रहे हैं।
3. **Mukesh is writing on the** blackboard.
मुकेश श्यामपट पर लिख रहा है।
4. They are making fun of you.
वे आपका मज़ाक उड़ा रहे हैं।
5. **He is catching the ball.**
वह गेंद को पकड़ रहा है।

Interrogative Sentences (प्रश्नवाचक वाक्य): Present Continuous Tense के प्रश्नवाचक को अगर Passive Voice में परिवर्तित करना हो तो उसका Formula नीचे दिया गया है:

Active Voice: (Wh or how) + is/ am/ are + S + (V-I + ing) + O + ?
Passive Voice: (Wh or how) + is/am/are cS + being + V-III + by + cO+?

Examples

(a) Why are you telling a lie?
आप झूठ क्यों बोल रहे हैं ?
Why is a lie being told by you ?
तुम्हारे द्वारा झूठ क्यों बोला जा रहा है ?

(b) What are you doing?
आप क्या कर रहे हैं ?
What is being done by you?
तुम्हारे द्वारा क्या किया जा रहा है ?

EXERCISE 4

नीचे दिये गये Sentences को Passive Voice में परिवर्तित करें:

1. Is he making an excuse?
क्या वह कोई बहाना बना रहा है ?
2. Are you sending him a message?
क्या तुम उसे संदेश भेज रहे हो ?
3. Am I going to kill a lion?
क्या मैं एक शेर को मारने जा रहा हूँ ?
4. Is she slapping across your face?
क्या वह तुम्हारे मुंह पर थप्पड़ मार रही है ?
5. Are we breaking the chairs?
क्या हम कुर्सियां तोड़ रहे हैं ?

Note: Sentence No. 3 में Passive Voice में 'to kill', 'to be killed' में परिवर्तित हो जायेगा।

(C) Present Perfect Tense: Present Perfect Tense के Affirmative Sentences को Passive Voice में परिवर्तित करने का Formula नीचे दिया गया है:

Active Voice: S + has/have + V-III + O.
Passive Voice: cS + has/have + been + V-III + by + cO.

Examples

(a) She has stolen a bag.
उसने एक बैग चुराया है।
A bag has been stolen by her.
एक बैग उसके द्वारा चुरा लिया गया है।

(b) They have beaten the enemy.
वे दुश्मन को पीट चुके हैं।

The enemy has been beaten by them.
दुश्मन उनके द्वारा पीटा जा चुका है।

EXERCISE 5

नीचे दिये गये वाक्यों को Passive Voice में परिवर्तित करें:

1. The thief has broken into the house.
चोर घर में सेंध लगा चुका है।
2. She has made a loud cry.
वह एक ज़ोरदार चीख मार चुकी है।
3. He has taken the charge.
वह चार्ज ले चुका है।
4. They have thrown him down with a rod.
वे उसे एक डंडे से मारकर नीचे गिरा चुके हैं।
5. She has broken the glass.
वह गिलास तोड़ चुकी है।

Interrogative Sentences (प्रश्नवाचक वाक्य): Present Perfect के प्रश्नवाचक वाक्यों को Passive Voice में परिवर्तित करने का Formula नीचे दिया गया है।

Active Voice: (Wh or how) + has/have + S + V-III + O + ?

Passive Voice: (Wh or how) + has/have + cS + been + V-III + by + cO + ?

Examples

(a) Who has made a noise?
किसने शोर मचाया है?
By whom has a noise been made?
किसके द्वारा शोर मचाया गया है?

(b) Have you broken the door?
क्या आप दरवाजा तोड़ चुके हैं?
Has the door been broken by you?
क्या दरवाज़ा आपके द्वारा तोड़ा गया है?

EXERCISE 6

नीचे दिये गये वाक्यों को Passive Voice में परिवर्तित करें:

1. Who has killed the bird?
पक्षी को कौन मार चुका है?
2. Have you listened to me?
क्या आप मेरी बात सुन चुके हैं?

3. Has he jumped over the wall?
क्या वह दीवार के ऊपर से कूद चुका है?

4. Why have you scattered the papers?
आप कागजातों को क्यों बिखेर चुके हैं?

5. What have you said?
आप क्या कह चुके हैं?

(D) Present Perfect Continuous Tense: Present Perfect Continuous Tense का Passive Voice नहीं होता।

(E) Past Indefinite Tense: Past Indefinite Tense के Affirmative वाक्यों के Passive Voice बनाने का Formula नीचे दिया गया है:

Active Voice: S + V-II + O.

Passive Voice: cS + was/were + V-III + by + cO.

Examples

(a) My father gave me a watch.
मेरे पिताजी ने मुझे एक घड़ी दी।

A watch was given to me by my father.
मेरे पिता द्वारा मुझे एक घड़ी दी गई।

(b) Dinesh bought a bicycle.
दिनेश ने एक साइकिल खरीदी।

A bicycle was bought by Dinesh.
दिनेश द्वारा एक साईकिल खरीदी गई।

EXERCISE 7

नीचे दिये गये वाक्यों का Passive Voice बनायें:

1. The hen laid an egg.
मुर्गी ने एक अण्डा दिया ।

2. The horse threw him down.
घोड़े ने उसे नीचे फेंका (अथवा गिरा दिया)।

3. He climbed up the tree.
वह पेड़ पर चढ़ गया।

4. He kissed me.
उसने मेरा चुम्बन लिया (या चूमा)।

5. He wove a new story.
उसने एक नई कहानी बनाई।

Interrogative Sentences (प्रश्नवाचक वाक्य): Past Indefinite Tense के प्रश्नवाचक वाक्यों को Passive Voice बनाने का Formula नीचे दिया गया है।

Active Voice: (Wh or how) + did + S + V-I + O + ?
Passive Voice: (Wh or how) + was/were + cS + V-III + by + cO + ?

Examples

(a) Why did he kick you?
उसने तुम्हें पैर क्यों मारा?
Why were you kicked by him?
तुम उसके द्वारा पैर क्यों मारे गये?

(b) Did you know her?
क्या आप उसे जानते थे?
Was she known to you?
क्या वह आपके द्वारा जानी जाती थी?

EXERCISE 8

1. Did you love her?
   क्या आपने उसे प्यार किया?
2. Why did he shout at you?
   वह आप पर क्यों चिल्लाया?
3. What did they bring for you?
   वे आपके लिए क्या लाये?
4. Did she do her task quite well?
   क्या उसने अपना काम ठीक ढंग से किया?
5. Did we buy a medicine for him?
   क्या हम उसके लिए एक दवा खरीद कर लाये?

(F) Past Continuous Tense: Past Continuous Tense के Affirmative Sentences के Passive Voice बनाने का Formula नीचे दिया गया है।

Active Voice: S + was/were + (V-I + ing) + O.
Passive Voice: cS + was/were + being + V-III + by + cO.

Examples

(a) She was speaking the truth.
वह सच बोल रही थी।
The truth was being spoken by her.
उसके द्वारा सच बोला जा रहा था।

(b) They were runing a factory.
वे एक कारखाना चला रहे थे।

A factory was being run by them.
एक फैक्टरी उनके द्वारा चलाई जा रही थी।

EXERCISE 9

नीचे दिये गये वाक्यों को Passive Voice में परिवर्तित करें:

1. They were following an old tradition.
वे एक पुरानी रस्म को मान रहे थे।
2. She was sewing a skirt.
वह एक स्कर्ट सी रही थी।
3. We were looking at them.
हम उनको देख रहे थे।
4. I was giving instructions to him.
मैं उसे हिदायतें दे रहा था।
5. They were celebrating a festival.
वह एक त्योहार मना रहे थे।

Interrogative Sentence (प्रश्नवाचक वाक्य): Past Continuous Tense के प्रश्नवाचक वाक्यों को Passive Voice में परिवर्तित करने का Formula नीचे दिया गया है:

Active Voice: (Wh or how) + was/were + S + (V-I + ing) + O + ?

Passive Voice: (Wh or how) + was/were + cS + being + V-III + by + cO + ?

Examples

(a) Was she writing on the paper?
क्या वह कागज़ पर लिख रही थी?
Was the paper being written on by her?
क्या उसके द्वारा कागज़ पर लिखा जा रहा था?

(b) Were they sending their messengers?
क्या वह अपने संदेशवाहक को भेज रहे थे?
Were their messengers being sent by them?
क्या संदेशवाहक उनके द्वारा भेजे जा रहे थे?

EXERCISE 10

नीचे दिये गये वाक्यों को Passive Voice में परिवर्तित करें:

1. Was she fighting with you?
क्या वह आपसे लड़ रही थी?
2. Were we laughing at the poor?
क्या हम गरीबों पर हंस रहे थे?

3. Were they travelling by bus?
क्या वे बस से सफर कर रहे थे?
4. Was he gambling?
क्या वह जुआ खेल रहा था?
5. Was I crying at you ?
क्या मैं आप पर चिल्ला रहा था?

(G) Past Perfect Tense: Past Perfect Tense के Affirmative Sentences को Passive Voice में परिवर्तित करने का Formula नीचे दिया गया है:

Active Voice: S + had + V-III + O.

Passive Voice: cS + had + been + V-III + cO.

Examples

(a) She had attended the meeting.
वह सभा में उपस्थित हो चुकी थी।
The meeting had been attended by her.
उसके द्वारा सभा में उपस्थिति दी जा चुकी थी।

(b) They had drunk a bottle of liquor.
वे शराब की एक बोतल पी चुके थे।
A bottle of liquor had been drunk by them.
शराब की एक बोतल उनके द्वारा पी जा चुकी थी।

EXERCISE 11

नीचे दिये गये वाक्यों को Passive Voice में परिवर्तित करें:

1. They had broken the window pane.
वे खिड़की का शीशा तोड़ चुके थे।
2. She had made a sweet dish.
वह एक मीठा पकवान बना चुकी थी।
3. The horse had broken loose from the stable.
घोड़ा तबेले से रस्सी तुड़ा कर भाग चुका था।
4. We had made great strides.
हम तेज़ी से उन्नति कर चुके थे।
5. They had cut the cloth.
वह कपड़े को काट चुके थे।

(H) Past Perfect Continuous Tense. इस Tense का Passive Voice नहीं होता।

(I) Future Indefinite Tense. Future Indefinite Tense के Affirmative वाक्यों को Passive Voice में **परिवर्तित करने का** Formula नीचे दिया गया है:

Active Voice: **S + will/shall + V-I + O.**

Passive Voice: cS + will/shall + be + V-III + by + cO.

Examples

(a) **I shall take care of you.**
मैं आपका ध्यान रखूँगा।
You will be taken care of by me.
मेरे द्वारा तुम्हारा ध्यान रखा जाएगा।

(b) **We will praise you.**
हमलोग आपकी तारीफ करेंगे।
You will be praised by us.
आप हमारे द्वारा सराहे जायेंगे।

EXERCISE 12

नीचे दिये गये वाक्यों को Passive Voice में परिवर्तित करें:

1. They will throw the plate.
वे प्लेट को फेंकेंगे।

2. I shall look into the matter.
मैं मामले की जांच करूंगा।

3. We shall play against you.
हम आपके विरुद्ध खेलेंगे।

4. He will change the topic.
वह विषय को बदल देगा।

5. She will ring the police.
वह पुलिस को फोन करेगी।

Interrogative Sentence (प्रश्नवाचक वाक्य): Future Indefinite Tense के Affirmative के प्रश्नवाचक वाक्यों को Passive Voice में परिवर्तित करने का Formula नीचे दिया गया है:

Active Voice: (Wh or how) + will/shall + S + V-I + O + ?

Passive Voice: (Wh or how) + will/shall + cS + be + V-III + by + cO +?

Note: इस Tense में 'who,' 'which' आदि वाले वाक्यों में Formula में थोड़ा सा अन्तर है।

(i) Who will bell the cat ?
(ii) Which book will you select?

Who, which etc के Passive Voice इस प्रकार के होंगे।

(i) By whom will the cat be belled?
(ii) Which book will be selected by you?

Other Examples

(a) Will you pull the car?
क्या आप कार को खींचेंगे?
Will the car be pulled by you?
क्या कार आपके द्वारा खींची जायेगी?

(b) **Shall I bet you one hundred rupees?**
क्या मैं आपसे एक सौ रुपये की शर्त लगाऊँगा?
Will you be bet one hundred rupees by me?
क्या मेरे द्वारा आपसे एक सौ रुपये की शर्त लगाई जायेगी?

EXERCISE 13

नीचे दिये गये वाक्यों को Passive Voice में परिवर्तित करें:

1. Shall we scold you?
   क्या हम आपको डांटेंगे?
2. Will they come here in time?
   क्या वे यहां ठीक समय पर आयेंगे?
3. Will Sohan drink a lot of water?
   क्या सोहन बहुत सा पानी पीयेगा?
4. Will Jagdish play a trick?
   क्या जगदीश चालाकी करेगा?
5. Will they sing a song?
   क्या वे गाना गायेंगे?

(J) Future Continuous Tense. Future Continuous Tense का Passive Voice नहीं बनता।

(K) Future Perfect Tense: Future Perfect Tense के Affirmative वाक्यों को Passive Voice बनाने में नीचे लिखा Formula प्रयुक्त होता है:

Active Voice: S + will/shall + have + V-III + O.
Passive Voice: cS + will/shall + have + been + V-III + by + cO.

Examples

(a) **She will have told you the whole story.**
वह तुम्हें सारी कहानी सुना चुकी होगी।
(b) **The whole story will have been told to you by her.**
तुम्हें सारी कहानी उसके द्वारा बताई (या सुनाई) जा चुकी होगी।
(c) **I shall have cut the fruit.**
मैं फल को काट चुका होऊँगा।
(d) **The fruit will have been cut by me.**
फल मेरे द्वारा काटा जा चुका होगा।

EXERCISE 14

नीचे दिये गये वाक्यों को Passive Voice में लिखें:

1. I Shall have measured the length of the wall.
मैं दीवार की लम्बाई नाप चुका हूँगा।
2. He will have dropped it on the way.
वह इसे रास्ते में गिरा चुका होगा।
3. They will have cut your throat.
वे आपका गला काट चुके होंगे।
4. You will have thrown your arms up in the sky with joy.
तुम खुशी से अपनी बाहें आकाश में ऊपर कर चुके होगे।
5. You will have filled bottle with oil.
तुम बोतल तेल से भर चुके होगे।

Interrogative Sentences (प्रश्नवाचक वाक्य): Future Perfect Tense के प्रश्ववाचक वाक्यों को Passive Voice में परिवर्तित करने का Formula नीचे दिया गया है:

Active Voice: (Wh or how) + will/shall + S + have + V-III + O + ?

Passive Voice: (Wh or how) + will/shall + cS + have + been + V-III + by + cO +?

Examples

(a) Why will you have committed such a blunder?
आप इतनी बड़ी गलती क्यों कर चुके होंगे?
Why such a blunder will have been committed by you?
इतनी बड़ी गलती आपसे कैसे हो चुकी होगी?

(b) Shall I have disturbed you?
क्या मैं आपके काम में ख़लल डाल चुका हूँगा?
Will you have been distrubed by me?
क्या मेरे द्वारा आपके काम में ख़लल डाला जा चुका होगा?

EXERCISE 15

नीचे दिये गये वाक्यों को Passive Voice में परिवर्तित करें:

1. Will you have registered their name?
क्या आप उनके नाम का पंजीकरण कर चुके हैं?

2. Will you have closed the ration depot?
क्या आप राशन डिपो बन्द कर चुके होंगे?

3. Shall I have done something wrong?
क्या मैं कोई गलत काम कर चुका हूँगा?

4. Why shall we have not obeyed you?
हम आपकी आज्ञा का पालन क्यों नहीं कर चुके होंगे?

5. Will she have prepared her maiden speech?
क्या वह अपना पहला भाषण तैयार कर चुकी होगी?

(L) Future Perfect Continuous Tense: इस Tense का Passive Voice नहीं होता।

EXERCISE 16

नीचे दिये गये वाक्यों का अंग्रेजी में अनुवाद करें, तथा जिन वाक्यों की Voice Change हो सकती है, उनकी Voice बदलें:

1. वह तुम्हारी तरफ क्यों नहीं देख रहा?
2. वह स्कूल में चोरी करता हुआ रंगे हाथों पकड़ा गया।
3. **उन्होंने मेरी बात की ओर कोई ध्यान नहीं दिया।**
4. वे खोई हुई साइकिल की खोज कर रहे हैं।
5. वह रमेश द्वारा बुरी तरह से पीटा गया।
6. उसके द्वारा बीस रोटियां खाई गईं।
7. रवि अध्यापक द्वारा डांटा जा रहा था।
8. उसके द्वारा खाना खाया जायेगा।
9. हम गाड़ी द्वारा चेन्नई जायेंगे।
10. वह इन्द्रधनुष को देख कर खुश हुए।
11. गणेश ने बच्चों के लिए मिठाई खरीदी।
12. वह मेले में खेलता हुआ गुम हो गया।
13. **भगत सिंह मुस्कुराते हुए फाँसी पर चढ़ गया।**
14. तुम किसके बारे में सोच रहे थे?
15. वह आपसे क्या कह चुका था?
16. उसके द्वारा गुड़िया बनाई जा चुकी है।
17. वह तेज़ाब से जल चुका था।
18. उसे क्या हो गया था?
19. आप किसके द्वारा नौकरी पर रखे गये हैं?
20. वह पानी में कैसे तैरा?

Hints for Translation

2. caught red-handed **3.** paid no heed, **4.** lost bicycle, searching for, **5.** black and blue **7.** scolded **9.** by train **10.** rainbow **11.** sweets **12.** fair **13.** smilingly, kissed the noose **16.** doll **17.** acid **18.** What had gone wrong with him? **19.** appointed to **20.** swim in water.

Chapter 23

The Adverb

(क्रिया-विशेषण)

एक Adverb निम्नलिखित Parts of Speech को Qualify करता है:

1. An Adjective
2. A Verb
3. Another Adverb

इसके विषय में निम्नलिखित बातें याद रखें:

1. Before an Adjective: Adverb प्राय: Adjective से पहले आता है।

Examples

(a) He is a *very* intelligent boy.
वह बहुत बुद्धिमान लड़का है।

(b) She is an *exceedingly* weak girl.
वह अत्यधिक मंद बुद्धि वाली लड़की है।

2. Before an Adverb: यह प्राय:किसी और Adverb से पहले आता है।

Examples

(a) He walks *very* slowly.
वह बहुत धीरे चलता है।

(b) The horse runs *very* fast.
घोड़ा बहुत तेज़ भागता है।

3. After a Verb: यह प्राय: Verb के बाद आता है।

Examples

(a) The horse runs *fast.*
घोड़ा तेज भागता है।

(b) They sat *merrily* in the park.
वे पार्क में प्रसन्नता से बैठे थे।

4. Between the Modal and the Main Verb: Adverb प्राय: Modal और मुख्य Verb के बीच प्रयुक्त होता है।

Examples

(a) You have *always* helped me.
आपने सदा मेरी सहायता की है।

(b) She has *never* complained against you.
उसने आपके विरुद्ध कभी शिकायत नहीं की।

5. Use of Enough: 'enough' का प्रयोग प्राय: Qualified Adjective के बाद होता है।

Examples

(a) He was kind *enough* to help me.
वह इतना दयालु था कि उसने मेरी सहायता की।

(b) He is not good *enough* to listen to you.
वह इतना अच्छा नहीं है कि आपकी बात सुने।

6. Adverb as an emphasiser: कई बार adverb का प्रयोग एक emphasiser के रूप में होता है।

Examples

(a) *Never* mind what he says.
परवाह न करो (या बुरा न मनाओ) वह क्या कहता है।

(b) *Always* keep to the left.
सदा बाईं ओर चलो।

(c) *Fortunately,* we have reached our destination before sunset.
सौभाग्यवश, सूर्य अस्त होने से पहले हम अपनी मंजिल पर पहुँच चुके हैं।

(d) *Here* comes Rajesh.
लो, राजेश आ गया।

इस प्रकार से Adverb प्राय: Sentence के आरम्भ में प्रयोग होता है।

7. The Use of 'only' नीचे लिखे वाक्यों में 'only' के प्रयोग को ध्यान से पढ़ें:

(i) ***Only*** **I have five rupees.**
केवल मेरे ही पास पांच रुपये हैं (अर्थात् और किसी के पास नहीं)।

(ii) **I have *only* five rupees.**
मेरे पास केवल पांच रुपये हैं (अर्थात् मेरे पास और कुछ भी नहीं)।

(iii) I have five rupees *only.*

मेरे पास केवल पांच रुपये हैं (अर्थात् धन केवल इतना है। हो सकता है मेरे पास पांच रुपये के अतिरिक्त और वस्तुए हों)।

EXERCISE 1

नीचे लिखे वाक्यों का अंग्रेजी में अनुवाद करें और उन अनुवादित वाक्यों में Adverb को underline करें:

1. क्या वह ऊँची आवाज़ में चिल्लाया?
2. क्या आप प्रतिदिन स्कूल जाते हैं?
3. उसने पत्र बहुत सुन्दर ढंग से लिखा।
4. उसने क्रोध में आकर पुस्तक को नीचे फेंक दिया।
5. वह कभी-कभी यहां आता है।
6. हम प्राय: प्रात: सैर करने जाते हैं।
7. क्या आप वहां देर से पहुँचे?
8. इस कपड़े का रंग बड़ा चमकीला है।
9. वह धीरे-धीरे सब सीख जायेगा।
10. वह सदा कोई न कोई नया विचार लेकर आता है।

Hints for Translation

1. loudly **2.** daily **3.** very, beautifully **4.** angrily **5.** occasionally **6.** offen **7.** there, late **8.** very **9.** by and by **10.** even (or always), some.

Formation of Adverbs

Word	*Meaning*	*Adverb*
Agree	सहमत होना	Agreeably
Angry	क्रुद्ध	Angrily
Attend	हाज़िर होना	Attentively
Awful	भयानक	Awfully
Calm	शांत	Calmly
Candid	स्पष्ट	Candidly
Capable	योग्य, क्षमता वाला	Capably
Careful	ध्यान रखने वाला	Carefully
Ceremony	शिष्टाचार	Ceremoniously
Certain	निश्चित	Certainly

Word	*Meaning*	*Adverb*
Charming	मोहित करने वाला	Charmingly
Cheap	सस्ता	Cheaply
Cheerful	प्रसन्नचित्त	Cheerfully
Chief	मुख्य	Chiefly
Clear	साफ	Clearly
Coherent	युक्ति-युक्त	Coherently
Cold	(अधिक) ठंडा	Coldly
Conclusive	निर्णयात्मक	Conclusively
Confident	विश्वास वाला (युक्त)	Confidently
Conscious	सूझ, होश	Consciously
Continual	लगातार	Continually
Continuous	लगातार	Continuously
Cool	ठंडा	Coolly
Correct	ठीक	Correctly
Courageous	हौसले वाला	Courageously
Cozy	आराम वाला	Cozily
Create	पैदा करना	Creatively
Crime	जुर्म	Criminally
Criticise	आलोचना करना	Critically
Curious	जिज्ञासु	Curiously
Curt	संक्षिप्त	Curtly
Doubt	शंका	Doubtfully, doubtlessly
Fear	भय	Fearfully
Feeble	कमज़ोर	Feebly
Happy	प्रसन्न	Happily
Nature	प्रकृति	Naturally
Satisfy	संतुष्ट करना	Satisfactorily
Scene	दृश्य	Scenically

Word	Meaning	Adverb
Secret	**भेद**	**Secretly**
Side	**ओर**	**Beside, aside**
Simple	साधारण	Simply
Sincere	सच्चा	Sincerely
Single	अकेला	Singly, singularly
Slave	दास	Slavishly
Sleep	सोना	Sleepily
Slight	थोड़ा-सा	Slightly
Slow	धीमा	Slowly
Soft	नर्म	Softly
Soften	नर्म करना	Softly
Steal	चुराना	Stealthily
Strong	मजबूत	Strongly
Stupid	मूर्ख	Stupidly
Stylish	**सजीला, फैशनेबल**	**Stylishly**
Successful	**सफल**	**Successfully**
Sudden	**अचानक**	**Suddenly**
Sufficient	**पर्याप्त**	**Sufficiently**
Superstitious	**अंधविश्वासी**	**Superstitiously**
Sure	निश्चित	Surely
Surprising	आश्चर्यजनक	Surprisingly
Swift	तेज	Swiftly
Sympathetic	हमदर्द	Sympathetically
Sympathise	हमदर्दी रखना	Symphathetically
System	प्रणाली	Systematically
Systematic	पद्धति के अनुसार	Systematically
Terrible	भयानक	Terribly
Wise	बुद्धिमान	Wisely

Chapter 24

The Conjunction
(संयोजक)

संयोजक वह शब्द हैं जो दो छोटे-छोटे वाक्यों को या दो शब्दों अथवा Phrases इत्यादि को आपस में जोड़ते हैं।

(i) Madhu *and* Sudha are fast friends.
मधु व सुधा पक्की सहेलियां हैं।

इस वाक्य में 'and' शब्द ने दो संज्ञाओं—मधु व सुधा को आपस में एक ही वाक्य में ठीक से संयोजित किया है।

(ii) Kulwant is *not only* gentle, *but also* intelligent.
कुलवंत केवल भद्रपुरुष ही नहीं बल्कि बुद्धिमान भी है।

इस वाक्य में 'not only.... but also' संयोजक है।

(iii) I can speak English *or* Punjabi.
मैं अंग्रेजी या पंजाबी बोल सकता हूँ।

इस वाक्य में 'or' संयोजक है।

प्रयोग में आने वाले अन्य संयोजक निम्नलिखित हैं:

1. And और
2. But परन्तु
3. Whether क्या
4. Because क्योंकि
5. If यदि
6. Otherwise नहीं तो, अन्यथा
7. As क्योंकि, जैसा कि
8. Since क्योंकि, (इतने) समय से (point of time)

9. Either..... or यह..... या यह (of two)
10. Neither..... nor न यह..... न यह (of two)

KINDS OF CONJUNCTIONS

There are two kinds of conjunctions as follows:
(A) Coordinative Conjunctions
(B) Subordinative Conjunctions

(A) Coordinative Conjunctions: Coordinative Conjunctions वे होते हैं जो किन्हीं दो Words, Phrases या Clauses को आपस में जोड़ते हैं। यह Coordinate Clauses बनाते हैं और Compound Sentences में इनका प्रयोग होता है; *e.g.,* and, but, also, or, not only, but also etc.

यह चार प्रकार के होते हैं:
(A1) Additive Conjunctions
(A2) Adversative Conjunctions
(A3) Illative Conjunctions
(A4) Alternative Conjunctions

(A1) Additive Conjunctions: ये वे शब्द हैं जो प्राय: दो Coordinative Clauses को जोड़ते हैं; *e.g.,* and, also, now, well, as well as etc.

Example

(a) He come to me and sat for a long time in my room.
वह मेरे पास आया और काफी देर तक मेरे कमरे में बैठा रहा।

(A2) Adversative Conjunctions: ये Conjunctions दो Statements के बीच Contrast का बोध करवाते हैं, *e.g.,* still, but, yet, however, only etc.

Examples

(a) He is a strong boy but not a wise one.
वह लड़का ताकतवर है लेकिन अकलमंद नहीं।

(b) He is weak, still he can walk.
वह कमज़ोर है, फिर भी चल सकता है।

EXERCISE 1

नीचे दिये गये वाक्यों का अंग्रेजी में अनुवाद करें:

1. वह बुरा आदमी है पर झूठा नहीं।
2. माना कि तुम अकलमंद हो, फिर भी दूसरों की बात सुनना ज़रूरी है।
3. वह गुस्से में था फिर भी मेरी बात ध्यान से सुन रहा था।
4. वह एक अन्धा आदमी है लेकिन दूसरों की बात पर वह कम विश्वास करता है।
5. वह लंगड़ा है पर तेज़ दौड़ता है।

(A3) Illative Conjunctions: ये वो शब्द हैं जो कि पहले आई हुई व्याख्या का सार अभिव्यक्त करते हैं; *e.g.*, for, therefore, so, then, etc.

Examples

(a) No one is there, so, you can sing a song for me alone.
वहाँ पर कोई नहीं, इसलिए तुम मेरे अकेले के लिए गाना गा सकते हो।

(b) You always speak the truth, so, your appearance (or presence) makes the people happy.
आप सदा सत्य बोलते हैं, इसलिए आपकी उपस्थिति से लोग प्रसन्न होते हैं।

(c) You talk too much and so, people take a bad impression about you.
तुम ज़्यादा बोलते हो, इसलिए लोग तुम्हें बुरा समझते हैं।

(d) He could not come, for, he was ill.
वह नहीं आ सका, क्योंकि वह बीमार था।

(e) He was ill, therefore, he didn't come.
वह बीमार था, इसलिए वह नहीं आया।

EXERCISE 2

1. यहां पर कोई भी नहीं, तो तुम किसके लिए भाषण तैयार कर रहे हो?
2. तुम ज़्यादा गुस्से में रहते हो, इसलिए तुम्हारा रक्तचाप बढ़ जाता है।
3. यहां पर कोई भी नहीं, तो आप अपनी कविता किसके लिए पढ़ेंगे।
4. तुम्हें कोई काम धन्धा करना चाहिए, तभी तुम्हें पैसे मिलेंगे।
5. तुम किसी का बुरा नहीं सोचते, इसलिए समाज में अच्छे माने जाते हो।

(A4) Alternative Conjunctions: ये वे शब्द होते हैं जो दो बातों में से एक

चुनने का मौका देते हैं। *e.g.*, otherwise, else, either.... or etc.

Examples

(a) Talk slowly otherwise you will be heard by some of our enemies.
धीरे बात करो नहीं तो हमारा कोई दुश्मन तुम्हारी बात सुन लेगा।

(b) Neither he himself does the work nor he lets anybody else do it.
न तो वह खुद काम करता है न किसी और को करने देता है।

EXERCISE 3

नीचे दिये गये वाक्यों का अंग्रेजी में अनुवाद करें:

1. न तो वह अपनी बात करता है न किसी और की सुनता है।
2. ध्यान से चलो नहीं तो गिर जाओगे।
3. खूब मेहनत करो नहीं तो फेल हो जाओगे।
4. न वह खुद खाना खाता है न किसी अन्य को खाने देता है।
5. न वह खेलता है न ही पढ़ता है।

(B) Subordinative Conjunctions: ये एक Clause को दूसरे Clause से जोड़ते हैं जो नीचे दिये गये तरीकों से समझे जा सकते हैं।

Note: यह Subordinate Clause बनाते हैं और Complex Sentences में प्रयुक्त होते हैं।

(B1) **Time:** before, since, after, while, until, till, so long etc.
(B2) **Cause:** as, because, since.
(B3) **Purpose:** that, in order to, so that etc.
(B4) **Place:** where, whenever etc.
(B5) **Condition:** as if, unless, supposing etc.
(B6) **Result or effect:** so that.
(B7) **Manner:** as if, as, so, far as etc.
(B8) **Contrast or concession:** although, though, however, whichever etc.
(B9) **Comparison:** as much as, than, less than etc.

Time

(i) He made his way for home after the Sun had risen.
वह अपने घर की तरफ तब गया जब सूर्य निकल चुका था।

(ii) Since how long have you been staying in Delhi?
आप दिल्ली में कब से रह रहे हो?

(iii) Do not move until we tell you to do so.
हिलना मत जब तक हम हिलने के लिए नहीं कहते।

Cause

(i) He was punished because he told a lie.
उसे सज़ा मिली क्योंकि उसने झूठ बोला था।

(ii) She will be taken to the doctor because she is ill.
उसे डॉक्टर के पास ले जाया जायेगा क्योंकि वह बीमार है।

Purpose

(i) We will go to the school daily so that we may learn something good in life.
हम रोज़ स्कूल जायेंगे ताकि हम जीवन में कुछ अच्छा सीख सकें।

(ii) I will talk to him so that he may not beat you in the days to come.
मैं उससे बात करूंगा ताकि वह तुम्हें आने वाले दिनों में न मार सके।

Place

(i) I will be there where you go.
मैं वहीं मिलूंगा (होऊँगा) तुम जहां जाओगे।

(ii) Do not go there where nobody likes you.
वहां मत जाओ जहां तुम्हें कोई पसन्द नहीं करता।

Condition

(i) If you hate me, do not come here to meet me.
अगर तुम मुझसे घृणा करते हो तो मुझसे मिलने यहां मत आओ।

(ii) You may eat if you are hungry.
तुम खा सकते हो अगर तुम्हें भूख लगी है।

Result or Effect

(i) He is so poor that he cannot arrange two meals a day.
वह इतना गरीब है कि दो वक्त का खाना भी एक दिन में नहीं जुटा सकता।

(ii) He is so foolish that he does not respect his elders.
वह इतना मूर्ख है कि अपनों से बड़ों की इज़्ज़त नहीं करता।

Manner

(i) He did as he was told.
उसने वैसा ही किया जैसा उसे कहा गया था।

(ii) As the wind blows over the snowy mountain peaks, it will mak the weather cold.
चूँकि हवा बर्फ से ढंके पहाड़ों की चोटियों से गुजरती है, यह मौसम को ठण्ड करेगी।

Contrast or Concession

(i) Although he looks smart, yet he is a fool.
यद्यपि वह चालाक लगता है, फिर भी वह मूर्ख है।

(ii) Although he looks fat, yet he does not have much strength i his limbs.
यद्यपि वह मोटा दिखाई पड़ता है, फिर भी उसमें ज़्यादा ताकत नहीं है।

Comparison

(i) He is as dull as his brother (is).
वह उतना ही बुद्धू है जितना कि उसका भाई।

(ii) She is as wise as her mother (is).
वह उतनी ही बुद्धिमान है जितनी की उसकी माताजी।

Compound Conjunctions: जो Phrases Conjunctions के तौर पर प्रयोग में लाए जाते हैं, उनको Compound Conjunctions कहा जाता है। जैसे—As well as, as if, in order that etc.

Examples

(a) She talks *as if* she were a queen.
वह ऐसे बात करती है कि जैसे कि कोई रानी हो।

(b) He *as well as* Tony makes a noise in the classroom.
वह तथा टोनी कक्षा में शोर मचाते हैं।

EXERCISE 4

नीचे दिये गये वाक्यों का अंग्रेजी में अनुवाद करें:

1. आप कब से मेरी बात नहीं सुन रहे हैं?
2. रेणु उतनी ही सुन्दर है जितनी कि उसकी बहन।
3. तुम्हें अपना काम खुद करना चाहिए ताकि तुम्हें कुछ करना आये।
4. सूर्य निकलते ही चारों तरफ रोशनी फैल जाती है।
5. मैं इतना थक चुका था कि चल भी नहीं सकता था।
6. बहती गंगा में हाथ धो लो।
7. वह सोने को भी पसन्द करता है व चांदी को भी।
8. वह गरीब है पर खुश है।
9. वह गरीब है पर सच बोलता है।
10. जब मैं बड़ा हुआ तब मुझे समझ आ गई।
11. वह उतना ही बातूनी है जितना कि उसका चाचा।
12. क्योंकि उसने मेरी बात नहीं मानी, मैंने उसे बहुत पीटा।
13. मैं जैसे ही कमरे में गया बिजली चली गई।
14. सच बोलोगे तो डर नहीं लगेगा।
15. जल्दी चलो नहीं तो देरी हो जायेगी।
16. चाहे तुम बहुत सोचते हो, फिर भी काम को ठीक ढंग से नहीं कर पाते।
17. धीरे बोलो, कोई सुन लेगा।
18. थैला भारी था, उसके हाथ से छूटकर नीचे फर्श पर गिर गया।
19. उसने पूरी कोशिश की पर जीत न सका।
20. उसने झूठ बोला पर पकड़ा गया।

EXERCISE 5

नीचे दिये गये वाक्यों का अंग्रेजी में अनुवाद करें:

1. वह तेज़ भागा पर मुझे नहीं पकड़ सका।
2. मैं तथा वह कल फिल्म देखने गये थे।
3. न मैं, न मेरा भाई किसी की बात पर जल्दी विश्वास करते हैं।
4. कुछ पैसा बचाओ जो भविष्य में काम आ सके।

5. सोचो तथा कुछ करो।
6. क्योंकि वह कल दिल्ली चला गया था, मैंने संदेश उसके भाई को दे दिया।
7. या तो सो जाओ या फिर पढ़ो।
8. वह हाकी ही नहीं, बल्कि क्रिकेट भी अच्छी तरह खेलता है।
9. तुम इतनी देर से कहां थे?
10. मैंने तुम्हें ऐसा क्या कह दिया जो तुम रोने लगे?
11. वह इतना अकलमंद नहीं जितना तुम उसे समझते हो।
12. वह अमीर है पर कन्जूस है।
13. कुर्सी को बढ़ई के पास ले जाना पड़ेगा क्योंकि इसकी एक टांग टूट गई है।
14. वह हंसता था तो उसके दांत चमकते थे।
15. जैसे ही रात हुई, ओस गिरने लगी।
16. वह भाग गया क्योंकि वह तुमसे नाराज़ था।
17. तुम्हारी जरूरत पड़ेगी तो तुम्हें बुला लूँगा।
18. रोओ मत, तुम्हारा पैन अभी मिल जायेगा।
19. संदीप उतना ही अच्छा गाता है जितना कि गणेश।
20. तुम्हें तब तक घर पहुँच जाना चाहिए।
21. वहां कभी झगड़ा मोल मत लो जहां आसपास आपको कोई न जानता हो।
22. वह सुन्दर है पर शराब पीता है।
23. उठो तथा काम पर लग जाओ ताकि एक अच्छे आदमी बन सको।
24. वह जितना भी भाग ले, गाड़ी नहीं पकड़ सकता।

Chapter 25

The Preposition

(सम्बन्धसूचक अव्यय)

Preposition वह शब्द होता है जो एक Noun या एक Pronoun का दूसरे शब्दों से सम्बन्ध बताता है और इस प्रकार उनको उन शब्दों से जोड़ता है।

Examples

(a) The cat jumped *over* the wall.
बिल्ली दीवार के ऊपर से कूद गई।

Note: इस Sentence में 'over' शब्द ने बिल्ली के कूद वाले प्रभाव या कार्य को दीवार से जोड़ दिया है।

KINDS OF PREPOSITIONS

यह मुख्य रूप से तीन प्रकार की होती है:

(A) Preposition used for place (स्थान के लिए)

(B) Preposition used for time (समय के लिए)

(C) Preposition used with nouns, adjectives and verbs

1. Prepositions Used for Place

(A) छोटे शहरों व गांव या कस्बों के लिए 'at' का प्रयोग किया जाता है। यदि वाक्य में दो स्थानों का वर्णन हो तो छोटे स्थान के साथ 'at' जबकि बड़े शहर या देश के साथ 'in' शब्द का प्रयोग किया जाता है।

Examples

(a) I live at Rampur.
मैं रामपुर में रहता हूँ।

(b) I live at Rampur in India.
मैं रामपुर में रहता हूँ जो कि भारत में है।

(B) बड़े शहरों, द्वीपों, देशों आदि के साथ 'in' शब्द का प्रयोग होता है।

Examples

(a) I live in Mumbai.
मैं मुम्बई में रहता हूँ।

(b) She lives in London in England.
वह लन्दन में रहती है जो कि इंगलैण्ड में है।

(C) सैक्टरों, मार्किटों और गलियां से पहले भी 'in' का प्रयोग होता है।

Examples

(a) I live in Sadhu Colony.
मैं साधू कालोनी में रहता हूँ।

(b) I live in Sector no 5.
मैं पांच नम्बर सैक्टर में रहता हूँ।

(c) My shop is situated in Abdul Market.
मेरी दुकान अब्दुल मार्किट में स्थित है।

(D) किसी मकान का पता बताने पर भी 'at' लगता है।

He lives at 300, Parker Lane, Delhi.
वह मकान न० 300 में पार्कर लेन जो कि दिल्ली में है, रहता है।

Note: यहां मकान का नम्बर बताने के कारण 'at' लगा है। यदि केवल गली का नाम बताया जाता तो 'in' लगता।

(E) किसी निश्चित या विशेष स्थान के बारे में बताने के लिए भी 'at' का ही प्रयोग होता है।

Examples

(a) She met me at the airport.
वह मुझे हवाई अड्डे पर मिली।

(b) I will see you again at the bus-stop.
मैं तुम्हें बस स्टॉप पर फिर मिलूंगा।

(F) स्थान की नज़दीकी बताने के लिए 'by' का भी प्रयोग होता है।

Examples

(a) I met him by the temple.
वह मुझे मन्दिर के पास मिला।

(b) They met each other by hotel Star.
वे एक दूसरे को होटल स्टार के पास मिले।

(c) My house lies by the lake.
मेरा घर झील के निकट स्थित है।

(G) जब हम कभी किसी रास्ते के बीच ही में हों, जिसे अभी पूरा न किया गया हो, तब 'on' शब्द का प्रयोग होता है।

Examples

(a) **On the way back home, I saw a peacock dancing.**
अपने घर वापस लौटते हुए मैंने रास्ते में एक मोर नाचता हुआ देखा।

(b) He met me on the way.
वह मुझे रास्ते में मिला।

(H) जब हम कहीं खुले कस्बे में हों, तो भी 'on' लगेगा।
On the fields, he felt cheerful when he saw the crops dancing in the air.
खेतों पर हवा में लहलहाती फसलों को देख कर वह बहुत खुश हुआ।

(I) कई बार नज़दीक बताने या किसी के साथ होने के लिए 'beside' का प्रयोग होता है।

Examples

(a) She was sitting beside her father.
वह अपने पिता के साथ बैठी थी।

(b) I sat beside the window.
मैं खिड़की के पास बैठा था।

(J) कई बार 'beside' का अर्थ 'दूर हटकर' भी होता है। जैसे—Your words are beside the mark. अर्थात्, आपके शब्द बात से हट कर हैं।

EXERCISE 1

नीचे दिये गये वाक्यों का अंग्रेजी में अनुवाद करें:

1. वह एक गांव में रहता है।
2. मोहित शहर में रहता है।
3. मैं दिल्ली में रहता हूँ जो कि भारत में है।
4. वह नम्बर 301, पॉकेट 5, रोहिणी में रहता है जो कि दिल्ली में है।
5. रास्ते में वह मुझे मिला।
6. वह फर्श पर सोया हुआ था।

7. वह मुझे बस स्टैंड पर मिला।
8. तुम मुझे कल चर्च के पास मिले थे।
9. वह अपने पिता के पास सोया।
10. वह जंगल में रहता है।
11. वह मुझे समुद्र तट पर मिला।
12. इस कालोनी की सड़क टूट चुकी है।
13. क्या इस गली में लाइट नहीं है?
14. वह एक होटल में काम करता है।
15. वह स्टेशन के पास, गली न० 7, मकान न० 46 में रहता है।

2. Prepositions used for Time

(A) Point of time के लिए 'at' का प्रयोग किया जाता है। सही समय बताने के लिए भी 'at' का प्रयोग होता है।

Examples

(a) Rosy arrived at five O'clock.
रोज़ी पांच बजे आई।

(b) Mukesh went at nine O'clock.
मुकेश नौ बजे गया।

(B) Time Period को बताने के लिए 'in' का प्रयोग होता है।

Examples

(a) I visited this place in December last.
मैं यहाँ पिछले दिसम्बर में आया था।

(b) She was born in 1981.
वह 1981 में पैदा हुई थी।

(C) किसी भी त्यौहार के नाम पर 'at' का प्रयोग होता है।

Examples

(a) Lucky was very happy at Deepawali.
लक्की दीपावली पर बहुत खुश था।

(b) He goes quite busy at Deepawali.
वह दीपावली वाले दिन बहुत व्यस्त हो जाता है।

परन्तु निम्नलिखित वाक्य को पढ़िये:

He was very happy on the day of Deepawali.
वह दीपावली के दिन बहुत प्रसन्न था।

(D) ऐसे ही किसी खास दिन या Date को बताने के लिए 'on' का प्रयोग किया जाता है।

Examples

(a) I saw him riding a horse on Monday.
मैंने उसे सोमवार को घोड़े पर बैठे देखा।

(b) He was very busy on January 5th.
वह पांच जनवरी को बड़ा व्यस्त था।

Remember

(i) 'Night' शब्द के साथ हमेशा 'at लगता है—'at night.'

(ii) Morning के साथ हमेशा 'in' लगता है—'in the morning.'

(iii) Afternoon के साथ 'at' लगता है—'at afternoon.'

(iv) Lunch के साथ 'at' लगता है—'at Lunch.'

(v) Dinner के साथ 'at' लगता है—'at dinner.'

(vi) Evening के साथ 'in' लगता है—'in the evening.'

(vii) Dawn के साथ 'at' लगता है—'at down.'

(viii) 'in time' का मतलब है निश्चित समय से पहले पहुँचना तथा 'on time' का अर्थ है, समय पर पहुँचना।

EXERCISE 2

नीचे दिये गये वाक्यों का अंग्रेजी में अनुवाद करें:

1. बस ठीक समय पर पहुँची।
2. वह 1968 में पैदा हुई थी।
3. मैंने उसे पांच बजे मन्दिर जाते देखा।
4. मेरा भाई शुक्रवार को आयेगा।
5. उसने मुझे दोपहर के भोजन पर बुलाया है।
6. मैंने उसे रात के भोजन के लिए निमंत्रण दिया है।
7. यह किताब जून में छपेगी।
8. मैंने अपना सारा काम रात को ख़त्म किया।
9. हम शाम को सैर पर जायेंगे।
10. वह जनवरी में चेन्नई गई थी।

3. Prepositions Used with Nouns, Adjectives and Verbs

कुछ ऐसे Prepositions होते हैं जो किसी Noun, Adjective अथवा Verb से मिलकर एक नयी ही Meaning निकाल देते हैं।

1. Affection for स्नेह होना

2. Afflicted with — दुखी होना (प्राय: रोग से)
3. Aim at — लक्ष्य या उद्देश्य रखना
4. Angry at — क्रुद्ध होना (व्यवहार आदि पर)
5. Apply to — प्रार्थना पत्र देना
6. Angry with — क्रुद्ध होना (व्यक्ति से)
7. Agree to — स्वीकार करना (सुझाव आदि)
8. Agree with — सहमत होना (व्यक्ति से)
9. Alive to — सचेत होना
10. **Anxious about** — **चिंतित होना**
11. **Apologize to** — **क्षमा मांगना**
12. Afraid of — भयभीत होना
13. Accused of — दोष लगना
14. Abound in — भरा हुआ होना
15. Absorbed in — मग्न होना
16. Ashamed of — लज्जित होना
17. Attend upon — सेवा करना
18. Aware of — सचेत होना
19. Begin with — आरम्भ करना
20. Believe in — विश्वास करना
21. Beg of — मांगना
22. Bent upon — तुला हुआ होना
23. Blind of — अंधा होना
24. Born of to (parents) — पैदा हुआ
25. Born in (family) — पैदा हुआ
26. **Chnage for** — **रेज़गारी, गाड़ी बदलना (*e.g.*, change here for Kolkata)**
27. Charged with — दोष लगाना
28. Compete with — मुकाबला करना
29. Compare with — तुलना करना

30. Complain against शिकायत करना
31. Deal with व्यवहार करना
32. Deal in व्यापार करना
33. Dispose of फेंक देना, निपटा देना
34. Differ with सहमत न होना
35. Eligible for चुने जाने के योग्य होना
36. Eager for उत्सुक होना
37. Engaged in मग्न होना
38. Escape from भाग जाना
39. Faithful to आज्ञाकारी होना
40. Familiar with परिचित होना, पता होना
41. Familiar to मिलता जुलता होना
42. Famous for प्रसिद्ध होना
43. Fond of शौकीन होना
44. Greedy of लालची होना
45. Guilty of दोषी होना
46. Gifted with गुणी होना
47. No hope of (success) आशा न होना
48. Hope for (the best) आशा रखना
49. Ill of बीमार होना
50. Inferior to घटिया
51. Introduce to परिचय कराना
52. Innocent of मासूम
53. Liable to सम्भावना होना
54. Liable for ज़िम्मेदार
55 Match for तुल्य
56. Married to ब्याहा जाना
57. Necessary for (life) अनिवार्य
58. Necessary to आवश्यक

59. Notorious for — बदनाम
60. Obliged to — कृतज्ञ होना
61. Obedient to — आज्ञाकारी होना
62. Open to — उदार, बात के लिए तैयार
63. Parallel to — समानान्तर
64. Peculiar to — विशिष्ट होना
65. Prefer to — अच्छा समझना
66. Proud of — घमण्डी होना
67. Pray to — प्रार्थना करना
68. Quick of — तेज़ (फुर्तीला)
69. Refer to — हवाला देना
60. Regard for — आदर होना
71. Responsible to — उत्तरदायी होना
72. Reward for — पारितोषिक देना
73. Respect for — आदर करना
74. (In) Search of — ढूंढना/की खोज में
75. Shocked at — धक्का लगना
76. Slow at — सुस्त होना
77. Succeed in — पास होना, सफल होना
78. Superior to — बढ़िया होना
79. Surrender to — अधीन होना, हार मानना
80. Stand by — साथ देना
81. Slow of (hearing) — कम सुनाई देना
82. Trust in — विश्वास रखना
83. Tired of — तंग आ जाना
84. Thankful to — आभारी होना
85. Tremble with — काँपना
86. Unuseful — अनुपयोगी
87. Useful for — उपयोगी

88. Victim to शिकार होना
89. Warn of सावधान करना
90. Wonder at हैरान होना

कुछ याद रखने योग्य तथ्य इस प्रकार हैं:

1. Use of by, with

'by' Word का प्रयोग अधिकतर 'doer' को Denote करने के लिए किया जाता है जबकि 'with' Instrument को Denote करता है।

(i) He was struck down by his brother with a rod.

Note: इस Sentence में 'by' शब्द 'his brother' से सम्बन्ध रखता है जबकि 'with' शब्द 'a rod' से।

2. Use of at, in, on

(i) I got up at 5 O'clock.
मैं पांच बजे जागा।

(ii) He died on Friday.
वह शुक्रवार को मरा।

(iii) My grandfather died in 1990.
मेरे दादाजी 1990 में मरे।

3. Use of at, on

(i) I sat *at* the table.
मैं मेज़ पर बैठ गया (अर्थात् मेज के पास बैठ गया या बैठा)।

(ii) I sat *on* the table.
मै मेज़ पर बैठ गया या बैठा था।

Sentence No. (i) का अर्थ है कि मैं कुर्सी पर बैठा था जो कि मेज के पास पड़ी थी। लेकिन Sentence No. (ii) का अर्थ है कि मैं मेज़ के ऊपर बैठा था।

4. Use of since, for

'since' Proposition के तौर पर जब किसी Noun या Phrase से पहले प्रयोग होता है तो यह Point of Time को सम्बोधित करता है जब कि 'for' शब्द Period of Time को सम्बोधित करता है।

(i) It has been raining since morning.
सुबह से वर्षा हो रही है।

(ii) It has been raining for two hours.
दो घण्टे से बारिश हो रही है।

5. Use of in, into

'in' Word किसी वस्तु के आन्तरिक Action या State को दर्शाता है जबकि 'into' शब्द बाहर गिर रही या पहुँच रही दूसरी वस्तु के Action की व्याख्या करता है।

(i) He was walking in the room.
वह कमरे में चल रहा था।

(ii) The crocodile jumped into the river.
मगरमच्छ ने नदी में छलांग लगा दी।

Note: अगर हम ध्यान से दोनों Sentences को देखें तो अन्तर पता चल जाता है। Sentence No. (ii) में मगरमच्छ नदी से बाहर था तथा उसने नदी में छलांग लगा दी। यह Sentence उसकी दो स्थितियों को बताता है जब कि Sentence No. (i) से केवल यही पता चलता है कि वह कमरे में था और घूम रहा था। इस वाक्य में 'he' की एक ही स्थिति प्रकट होती है।

6. Use of till/by

'till' शब्द का भाव है **'not earlier than'** तथा **'by'** का अर्थ होता है 'not later then'.

(i) He will come by 5 O'clock.
वह पांच बजे तक पहुँच जायेगा।

(ii) We will wait for him till he comes.
हम उसके आने तक उसका इन्तजार करेंगे।

7. Use of during for

'during' का प्रयोग, Time को Express करता है जबकि 'for' समय की लम्बाई बताता है।

(i) During the rainy season, you should go out with an umbrella.
बरसात के दिनों में तुम्हें छाता लेकर बाहर जाना चाहिए।

(ii) I am terribly busy for the next week.
मैं अगले सप्ताह में बहुत ही व्यस्त हूँ।

8. Use of on, upon

'on' शब्द का प्रयोग जो काम आराम से किया गया हो, उसके लिए किया जाता है 'upon' Word का प्रयोग जो काम मेहनत से या हलचल से किया जाए, उसके लिए किया जाता है।

(i) I sat *on* the table. (ii) I jumped *upon* the horse's back.
मैं मेज़ पर बैठ गया। मैंने घोड़े की पीठ पर छलांग लगा दी।

Note: 'on' शब्द के प्रयोग से Sentence No. (i) के दो अर्थ बन गए हैं।

(i) मैं मेज़ पर बैठ गया।

(ii) मैं मेज़ पर बैठा था।

परन्तु Sentence No. (ii) का एक ही अर्थ निकलता है।

9. Use of before, for

'before' शब्द Point of Future Time को Denote करता है। लेकिन 'for' शब्द Negative Tense में Period of Future Time को Denote करता है।

(i) He is able to do this work before the next month.
वह अगले महीने से पहले इस काम को करने में समर्थ है।

(ii) You will have to wait for a week for the decision to come.
आपको निर्णय के लिए एक सप्ताह इंतजार करना पड़ेगा।

10. Use of on, over

'on' शब्द Object से Contact व्यक्त करता है जब कि 'over' शब्द ऐसा नहीं करता।

(i) I put my book *on* the shelf. (ii) The horse jumped *over* the wall.
मैंने अपनी पुस्तक शैल्फ पर रख दी। घोड़े ने दीवार के ऊपर से छलांग लगा दी।

11. Use of in, after

'in' Word Period of Time in Future को Denote करता है लेकिन 'after' शब्द Period of Time in Past को Denote करता है।

(i) I will talk to him in a couple of days.
मैं उससे एक-दो दिनों में बात करूंगा।

(ii) He left the place after a few minutes.
वह कुछ मिनटों के बाद वहां से चला गया।

12. Use of in, within

'in' शब्द का प्रयोग 'at the end of' को Denote करता है जबकि 'within' का प्रयोग 'before the end of' को Denote करता है।

(i) She will come in a week.
वह एक सप्ताह में आ जायेगी (अर्थात् सप्ताह के अन्त तक)।

(ii) She will come within a week.
वह एक सप्ताह के अन्दर ही आ जायेगी (अर्थात् सप्ताह खत्म होने से पहले पहले)।

13. Use of at, about

'at' शब्द का प्रयोग जहां पर समय का पूरा पता हो वहां होता है जबकि 'about' एक अनुमान के तौर पर प्रयोग में लाया जाता है।

(i) I shall get up at 5 O' clock.
मैं पांच बजे उठुँगा।

(ii) I am about to go there.
मैं बस वहां जाने ही वाला हूँ।

14. Use of between, among

'between' शब्द का प्रयोग वहां होता है जहां किसी वस्तु का बंटवारा दो व्यक्तियों में किया जा रहा हो। लेकिन अगर दो से अधिक व्यक्ति हों, तो 'among' का प्रयोग होता है।

(i) Divide this orange *between* Mohan and Lucky.
यह संतरा मोहन व लक्की में बांट दो।

(ii) Distribute these sweets *among* the girls.
लड़कियों में यह टाफियां बांट दो।

Note: यहां 'among' लगाने से पहले यह स्पष्ट है कि लड़कियां दो से अधिक हैं।

15. Use of beside, besides

'beside' का अर्थ है 'पास' (near): 'besides' का अर्थ है 'के अतिरिक्त'।

(i) Besides a rabbit, a dog is also there in his house.
खरगोश के अलावा उसके पास उसके घर में एक कुत्ता भी है।

(ii) My house is situated beside a temple.
मेरा घर एक मन्दिर के पास है।

Note: 'beside' का एक और अर्थ सीमा को पार कर जाना भी है।
He was beside himself with joy (or sorrow or rage)
उसे अत्यन्त प्रसन्नता (दुःख या क्रोध) हुई।

EXERCISE 3

नीचे दिये गये वाक्यों को Prepositions के प्रयोग द्वारा अंग्रेज़ी मे लिखें:

1. मैं सुबह पांच बजे उठता हूँ।
2. मेंढक ने पानी में छलांग लगा दी।

3. उसने तीन बजे खाना खाया।
4. हम आज दोपहर के भोजन के लिए होटल पार्क में जायेंगे।
5. वह खेतों पर ही सो गया।
6. बिल्ली मेज़ के नीचे छिप गई।
7. वह घोड़े पर बैठ गया।
8. सोहन रुड़की में रहता है।
9. मोहन दिल्ली में रहता है जो कि भारत में है।
10. वह मुझे रास्ते में मिला।
11. कल से ठण्डी हवायें चल रही हैं।
12. दो घण्टे से वह मेरी बात नहीं सुन रही है।
13. वह कल रात चार बजे तक लौट आयेगा।
14. वह कल शाम तक लौट आयेगा।
15. वह शाम को घर लौटा।
16. उसने मुझे आज रात के भोजन के लिए आमंत्रित किया है।
17. वह आज दस बजे तक यहां होगा।
18. वह कमरे में टहल रही थी।
19. संगीता मकान न० 40, गली न० 23 में रहती है।
20. इस गली में गंदगी के ढेर लगे पड़े हैं।

EXERCISE 4

1. वह मेरे साथ आया था।
2. वह अपने भाई के साथ सो रहा था।
3. उसके पास घोड़े के अतिरिक्त एक गाय भी है।
4. मैं अपने अंकल के साथ बैठा था।
5. वह मुझे पहाड़ी के पास मिला।
6. वह मुझे सिनेमा हाल के पास मिला।
7. वह मुझे समुद्र तट पर मिला।
8. वह 1987 में पैदा हुआ था।
9. उसके पिताजी का देहांत 1997 में हुआ था।
10. वह सोमवार को बाज़ार नहीं गया।
11. वह सुबह जल्दी काम पर चला गया।
12. वे पानी में तैरने लगे।
13. वह सड़क के पार भागा।
14. वह सुबह होने से पहले जा चुकी थी।
15. मेरा घर एक होटल के पास है।
16. मैं उसको एक हफ्ते के बाद मिला।
17. वह नदी में गिर गया।
18. उसने मेरी बात का बुरा नहीं माना।
19. वह सुबह होने तक आपके फैसले का इंतजार करेगा।
20. वह छत पर चढ़ गया।
21. आओ, अपने देश के कानूनों का पालन करें।
22. भिखारी ने मुझसे एक रुपया मांगा।

23. उसने मुझ से पानी मांगा।

24. कुत्तों से बचकर रहो।

25. उस पर कत्ल का दोष लगाया गया।

26. हमें निर्धनों पर हँसना नहीं चाहिए।

27. कृपया इस मामले की ओर ध्यान दो।

28. उसे अफीम खाने की आदत है।

29. निर्धनों से घृणा मत करो।

30. गाय घास पर निर्वाह करती है।

31. कीड़े पेड़ों के पत्ते खाकर गुजारा करते हैं।

32. मुझे निर्धनों से बहुत सहानुभूति है।

33. वह आपके मुकाबले में कुछ भी नहीं।

34. आप उसका मुकाबला नहीं कर सकते।

35. यह मेरी समझ से बाहर है।

36. अधिक काम की वजह से उसका स्वास्थ्य बिगड़ गया।

37. उसकी हैज़े से मृत्यु हुई।

38. क्या उसे कम सुनाई देता है ?

39. वह एक आंख से अंधा है (अर्थात् काना है)।

40. हमें अपने देश के प्रति स्वामिभक्त होना चाहिए।

41. क्या आप मुझसे सहमत हैं?

42. मैं आप के सुझाव से सहमत नहीं हूँ।

43. वह मुझसे बहुत क्रुद्ध है।

44. मैं आपके काम से संतुष्ट हूँ।

45. संतरे दर्जन के हिसाब से बिकते हैं।

46. क्या गाड़ी स्टेशन पर ठीक समय पर पहुँच गई ?

47. आप किस गाड़ी द्वारा वहां गये ?

48. मैं स्कूल पैदल जाता हूँ।

49. मैंने उसे डांटा।

50. अपनी जिह्वा को लगाम दो।

51. दूसरों के धन पर बुरी नज़र मत डालो।

52. उसने एक नई योजना सोची।

53. उसे उसके शब्दों के आधार पर मत जांचो।

54. मुझे उस पर कोई विश्वास नहीं।

55. मैं उसकी चालाकी को ताड़ गया।

56. उच्च न्यायालय ने निचले न्यायालय का फैसला रद् कर दिया है।

57. भगवान पर विश्वास रखो।

58. उसने कार्यभार मुझे सौंप दिया है।

59. आप इतने उदास क्यों दिखाई देते हैं ?

60. आप का नया सुझाव आपके पहले सुझाव के विपरीत है।

Chapter 26

Interjections

(विस्मयादिबोधक शब्द)

Interjection वह शब्द होता है जो अकस्मात् किसी भाव को व्यक्त करता है। Interjection के बाद Mark of Exclamation (!) लगता है।

Examples

(a) Hurrah ! — यह अत्यन्त प्रसन्नता (Joy) के भाव को प्रकट करता है।

(b) Ha ! Ha ! — यह भी प्रसन्नता को अभिव्यक्त करता है।

(c) Alas ! — यह अत्यन्त दु:ख (Sorrow) की अभिव्यक्ति करता है।

(d) Bravo !—यह अत्यन्त प्रशंसा (Applause) के भाव को व्यक्त करता है।

(e) Fie !

(f) Pshaw !

(g) Pooh !

(h) Oh !

} ये शब्द अत्यधिक घृणा (Contempt) को प्रकट करते हैं।

(i) What !—ये शब्द असीम हैरानी (Surprise) को प्रकट करते हैं।

(j) Hello!—(a) इसके द्वारा हम प्राय: अभिवादन को प्रकट करते हैं। या (b) Telephone Call का उत्तर देते हैं।

(k) Halloo !—इसके द्वारा हम

(a) चिल्लाते हैं या (b) कुत्तों को आवाज देते हैं।

(l) Hallo!

(m) Hello!

Hello !—(a) इनके द्वारा हम चिल्लाते हैं, या

(b) किसी को नमस्कार या उसका स्वागत करते हैं।

(n) By God !

(o) By heaven !—

ये एक प्रकार की सौगन्धें हैं।

इस प्रकार और भी कई Interjections हैं। यह प्राय: लिखित में किसी वाक्य में पृथक् ही नजर आते हैं।

EXERCISE 1

निम्नलिखित वाक्यों का English में अनुवाद करें:

1. चुप रहो! बच्चा सो रहा है।
2. छी! छी! उसकी क्या बात करते हो?
3. वाह! क्या विचार है?
4. हुर्रा ! हम मैच जीत गये।
5. कितना दु:ख है! वह बर्बाद हो गया।
6. शाबाश ! बहुत अच्छा किया।
7. खेद है! उसका अपमान हुआ।
8. धिक्कार है! तुम मल्लाह होकर पानी से डरते हो?
9. हे भगवान! यह क्या हो गया?
10. हे परमात्मा! अब मुझे क्या करना चाहिए?

Hints for Translation

1. Hurrah! **2.** Chi! Chi! **3.** Eh! **4.** Hurrah! **5.** Alas! **6.** Bravo! **7.** Ah! **8.** Fie! Oh God! **10.** Good God!

EXERCISE 2

नीचे लिखे वाक्यों का अंग्रेज़ी में अनुवाद करें और अनुवादित वाक्यों में विभिन्न प्रकार के Parts of Speech बतायें:

1. अच्छी बात है! आगे बढ़ते जाओ।
2. मैं उसे यहां नहीं देखना चाहता।
3. भूख बड़ी मुसीबत है।
4. उसे दूर रखो।
5. मुझे यह काम करने दो।
6. कितनी घृणापूर्ण बात है! तुम इतने घमण्डी हो।
7. आपका क्या हाल है?
8. मुझे आप पर गर्व है।

Hints for Translation

1. well **2.** Hunger is a great calamity **4.** Keep him at an arm's length. **6.** Pshaw ! (or Pooh!) **8.** proud of you.

Chapter 27

Idiomatic Sentences

(मुहावरेदार वाक्य)

1. सच्चाई कड़वी होती है।
   Truth is bitter.
2. मेरी बातों का बुरा न मानना।
   Do not take offence at my words.
3. झूठ के पांव नहीं होते।
   A lie has no legs to stand on.
4. यह बात तुम्हारे और मेरे मध्य है।
   It is between you and me.
5. बहती गंगा में हाथ धो लो।
   Make hay while the Sun shines.
6. उसके मस्तिष्क में गड़बड़ है।
   He is nuts.
7. मुझे आज भूख नहीं है।
   I have no appetite today.
8. इधर-उधर की मत हांको।
   Do not beat about the bush.
9. दूसरों के दोष मत निकालो।
   Do not find faults with others.
10. समय सारे घाव भर देता है।
    Time is a great healer.
11. यह सुनी-सुनाई बात है।
    It is a hearsay.
12. तुम मुँह क्यों बनाते हो?
    Why do you make faces?
13. इस मामले को दबा दो।
    Hush up this matter.
14. उसने मेरे जख्मों पर नमक छिड़क दिया।
    He added insult to my injury.
15. इस डिब्बे में और जगह नहीं है।
    There is no more room in this compartment.
16. बस खचाखच भरी हुई थी।
    The bus was packed to capacity. or
    The bus was jam-packed.
17. उन्होंने लज्जा बेच खाई है।
    They have no sense of shame. or

They are lost to all sense of shame.

18. वह छटा हुआ बदमाश है।
He is a rogue of the first water.

19. वह मेरे झांसे में आ गया।
He fell into my trap.

20. मैं अन्त तक आपका साथ दूंगा।
I will stand by you to the last.

21. वक्त गुज़रते देर नहीं लगती।
Time has wings.

22. हमने उसे उल्लू बनाया।
We made a fool of him.

23. तुम मेरे पीछे क्यों पड़े हो?
Why are you after me?

24. उसकी आशाओं पर पानी फिर गया।
His hopes were dashed to the ground.

25. तुम सारे काम अधूरे करते हो।
You do things by halves.

26. यह बूढ़ा कुछ दिनों का मेहमान है।
This old man's days are numbered.

27. आपकी दाल यहां नहीं गलेगी।
Your scheme will not work here. or
Your tricks will not work here.

28. दाल में कुछ काला है।
There is something wrong at the bottom. or
I smell a rat.

29. इश्तहार लगाना मना है।
Bill-sticking is prohibited.

30. बीता वक्त कभी हाथ नहीं आता।
Time once lost can never be recalled.

31. आओ हम अपने मतभेद मिटा दें।
Let us sink our differences.

32. आजकल मेरा हाथ तंग है।
I am hard up these days.

33. बुराई को शुरू में ही दबा दो।
Nip the evil in the bud.

34. मैं ये अपमान सहन नहीं कर सकता।
I cannot pocket this insult.

35. उसने अफसर की मुट्ठी गर्म की।
He greased the palm of the officer.

36. आप मेरे विरुद्ध उसके कान भरते हो।
You poison his ears against me.

37. जो गरजते है वो बरसते नहीं।
Barking dogs seldom bite.

38. जब तक सांस है तब तक आस है।
Hope sustains life.
or
Hope springs eternal in the human breast.

39. चोर रंगे हाथों पकड़ा गया।
The thief was caught red-handed.

40. वह नमक हलाल है।
He is true to his salt.

41. वह बाल-बाल बच गया।
He had a narrow escape.

42. तुम तो ईद का चांद हो गये।

Your visits are few and far between. or
You visit only once in a blue moon.

43. मौत का कोई समय नहीं होता।
Death keeps no calendar.

44. बाप बेटे की आपस में नहीं बनती।
There is no love lost between the father and the son.

45. मुझे घर की याद आती है।
I feel home-sick.

46. वह मोटा होता जा रहा है।
He is putting on flesh.
or
He is growing fat.

47. वह खुशी से फूला नहीं समाया।
He was beside himself with joy. or
He was overjoyed.

48. वह अपना निर्वाह कठिनाई से करता है।
He lives from hand to mouth.

49. मैं हैरान हूँ क्या करूँ।
I am in a fix.
or
I am at my wit's end what to do.

50. उसने अपना दोष मान लिया।
He made a clean breast of his fault.

51. उसकी बातों ने जलती पर तेल डाल दिया।
His words added fuel to the fire.

52. वह मेरा जानी दुश्मन है।
He is my sworn enemy.

53. कठिनाई के समय में सभी रिश्तेदार मुँह मोड़ लेते हैं।
All the kith and kin fall off in adversity.

54. लाड़-प्यार से बच्चा बिगड़ जाता है।
Indulgence spoils the child.

55. इस बात की नगर में चर्चा है।
It is the talk of the town.

56. वह सूख कर कांटा हो गया।
He was reduced to a skeleton.

57. उसने जीवन में बहुत उतार-चढ़ाव देखे हैं।
He has seen many ups and downs in his life.

58. वह ऊँचा सुनती है।
She is hard of hearing.

59. मौत का कोई इलाज नहीं।
Death defies all treatments.

60. उसे अपना उल्लू सीधा करना है।
She has her own axe to grind.

61. वह अपना सा मुँह लेकर रह गया।
He felt wry.

62. मेरा छोटा भाई बहानेबाजी में उस्ताद है।
My younger brother is an expert in making excuses.

63. मैंने दुख-सुख में उसका साथ दिया।

I stood by him through thick and thin.

64. उसने कई जगह पैर फंसा रखा है।

He has too many irons in the fire.

65. उसके हाथों के तोते उड़ गये।

He was non-plussed.

or

He was flabbergasted.

66. दीवार में एक कील गाड़ दो।

Drive a nail into the wall.

67. वे एक ही थाली के चट्टे-बट्टे हैं।

They are chips of the same block.

68. वह सदा अपनी ही तूती बजाती है।

She always blows her own trumpet. or

She always harps on her own tune.

69. मेरा घर बस स्टैण्ड से थोड़ी दूरी पर है।

My house is at a stone's throw from the bus-stop.

70. दोनों भाई एक दूसरे के जानी दुश्मन हैं।

The two brothers are at daggers drawn with each other.

71. अपनी आय से अधिक खर्च न करो।

Do not spend beyond your means. or

Cut your coat according to your cloth.

72. तुम्हारा चेहरा उतरा-उतरा क्यों है?

Why do you pull a long face?

73. फौज ने पूरे ज़ोर से शत्रु का मुकाबला किया।

The army fought tooth and nail against the enemy.

or

The army fought the enemy with might and main.

74. तुम जीवन में कुछ न कुछ ज़रूर कर दिखाओगे।

You are sure to make a mark in your life.

75. मेरे कामों में अपनी टांग मत अड़ाओ।

Do not poke your nose into my affairs.

76. वह सदा अपनी मनमानी करता है।

He always has his own way.

77. गले पड़ा ढोल बजाना पड़ता है।

What cannot be cured must be endured.

78. वह एड़ियां रगड़-रगड़ कर मरा।

He died by inches.

79. आपने अपने लड़के को बहुत सिर चढ़ा रखा है।

You have pampered your son too much.

80. यह दुकानदार सदा कम तोलता है।

This shop-keeper always

uses (or gives) short measures.

81. मुझे इस बात का आभास हो गया है।

I have got the wind of this matter.

82. वह दिन दुगुनी रात चौगुनी तरक्की कर रहा है।

He is progressing by leaps and bounds.

83. घमण्ड का सिर नीचा।

Pride hath a fall.

84. एक हाथ से ताली नहीं बजती।

It takes two to make a quarrel.

85. दूसरों से वैसा व्यवहार करो जैसा कि आप चाहते हैं कि आपके साथ हो।

Do unto others as you wish to be done by.

86. वह छिपा रुस्तम है।

He is a dark horse.

87. वह भेड़ के वेष में एक भेड़िया है।

He is a wolf in sheep's clothing.

88. उसकी टांग में मोच आ गई है।

He has sprained his leg.

89. सौन्दर्य को किसी आभूषण की आवश्यकता नहीं होती।

Beauty needs no ornaments.

90. सौंदर्य नौ दिन का मेहमान है।

Beauty is a nine days' wonder.

91. वह पक्का निशानेबाज है।

He is a crackshot.

92. उसने मुझे निशाना बनाया।

He trained his guns at me.

93. वह विश्वशनीय नहीं है।

He is a broken reed.

94. वह नगर में एक महत्त्वपूर्ण व्यक्ति है।

He is a big gun of the town.

95. उसे कोई आशा नहीं है।

He has lost all hopes.

96. वह आशा के विरुद्ध आशा कर रहा है।

He is hoping against hope.

97. आओ, सर्वोत्तम (घटना) की आशा रखें।

Let's hope for the best.

98. अन्त भला सो भला।

All's well that ends well.

99. भगवान पर विश्वास रखो और ठीक काम करो।

Trust in God and do the right work.

100. ईश्वर सब कुछ देखता है।

God sees everything.

Chapter 28

Translation Exercise (I)

MIXED TENSES

EXERCISE 1

नीचे दिये गये वाक्यों का अंग्रेजी में अनुवाद करें:

1. वह आज ही दिल्ली चला गया है।
2. वह क्यों रो रहा था?
3. उसके पिताजी का निधन हो गया।
4. कल सुबह होने से पहले क्या आप लौट आयेंगे?
5. आपको किसने निमन्त्रण दिया है?
6. वे कहां चले गये?
7. वह 1990 से इसी शहर में रह रहा था।
8. आज बारिश होगी।
9. तुम उसे कैसे जानते हो?
10. वह आपसे पूछे बिना कहां जा रहा है?
11. मैंने उसे कभी भी रोते हुए नहीं देखा है।
12. वह अपना घर का काम कर चुकी है।
13. उसका भाई तुमसे क्यों लड़ रहा था?
14. वह पांच बजे का बाज़ार गया हुआ है।
15. वह चांद निकलने से पहले घर आ जायेगा।
16. उसने कई लड़ाइयां लड़ीं।
17. आपने मेरी बात क्यों नहीं मानी?
18. वह आपको अच्छी तरह जानता है।
19. उसका इस दुनिया में कोई सगा-सम्बन्धी नहीं रहा।
20. वह बहुत तेज चलती थी।

Hints for Translation

1. left for **3.** died. **4.** return **5.** invited **12.** home-work **15.** before the moon appears **16.** fought, battles. **19.** kith and kin. **10.** very fast.

EXERCISE 2

नीचे दिये गये वाक्यों का अंग्रेजी में अनुवाद करें:

1. वह पहले से ही बहुत दु:खी था।
2. तुम इतने दिन से कहां थे?
3. मैं पांच दिन से अम्बाला गया हुआ था।
4. चोर चोरी करके भाग गया।
5. सिपाही हाथ मलता ही रह गया।
6. कल एक सांप ने सोहन को डस लिया।
7. यह उसकी कॉपी है।
8. वह तुम्हारी बात जरूर मानेगा।
9. मेरे स्टेशन पर पहुँचने से पहले गाड़ी जा चुकी थी।
10. तुम्हारे वहां पहुँचने से पहले बारिश शुरू हो चुकी होगी।
11. वह सुबह-सुबह नहाता है।
12. वह बहुत अच्छा गाना गाती है।
13. तुमने हमारी बात पर विश्वास क्यों नहीं किया?
14. वह तुमसे क्या कह रहा था?
15. उसने कल नई किताब खरीदी।
16. उसने आज तक कभी भी सच नहीं बोला।
17. उसके नये जूते उसे काट रहे होंगे।
18. मोहन उदास हो गया होगा।
19. आज से हम दोनों पक्के मित्र हैं।
20. वह आपकी बात पर विश्वास नहीं करता।

Hints for Translation

1. miserable **17.** pinching **18.** sad **19.** fast friends

EXERCISE 3

नीचे दिये गये Negative Sentences का अंग्रेजी में अनुवाद करें:

1. तुम हंस क्यों नहीं रहे हो?
2. रमाशंकर यादव आज से हम से नहीं बोलेगा।
3. वह 1950 से वहां नहीं रहता होगा।
4. क्या सुबह से बर्फ नहीं पड़ रही होगी?
5. वह आपका कहना नहीं मानता।
6. क्या तुमने आज तक चिड़ियाघर नहीं देखा?
7. वह तुम्हें अपना दोस्त नहीं मानेगा।
8. उसने झूठी कहानी क्यों नहीं सुनाई?
9. वह कभी अपने से बड़ों का कहना नहीं मानता।
10. भला वह आपसे आकर क्यों नहीं लड़ेगी?
11. संगीता को समझ क्यों नहीं आ रही?

12. तुम मीठी आवाज में क्यों नहीं गाते?
13. वह तुमसे प्यार से नहीं बोला।
14. वह आपके पैसे क्यों नहीं चुरा सका?
15. वह दिनेश का भाई नहीं है।
16. वह काफी दिनों से दिखाई नहीं पड़ा।
17. उसने आज तक किसी का उधार वापिस नहीं किया।
18. तुम्हारी टांग ठीक क्यों नहीं हो रही है?
19. वह एक अच्छा इन्सान क्यों नहीं बन जाता?
20. तुमसे बात करना मुझे अच्छा नहीं लगता।

Hints for Translation

4. snowing **6.** zoo **8.** cooked up story **9.** obey or carry out the orders of **17.** borrowed money **18.** getting cured

EXERCISE 4

नीचे दिये गये वाक्यों का अंग्रेजी में अनुवाद करें:

1. मुझे घूमना बहुत अच्छा लगता है।
2. मैं जानवरों से बहुत प्यार करता हूँ।
3. मुझे फूलदार व अन्य पौधे बहुत अच्छे लगते हैं।
4. मुझे बाग में बैठकर हवा में लहराते फूलों को देखना अच्छा लगता है।
5. रंग-बिरंगे फव्वारे भी अच्छे होते हैं।
6. फूलों पर सुन्दर-सुन्दर तितलियां आकर बैठती हैं।
7. कई बार आकाश में इन्द्रधनुष भी दिखाई देता है।
8. सूर्यास्त का दृश्य बड़ा सुहावना होता है।
9. काफी कम लोग बाग में होते हैं।
10. मैं वहां पर हल्की-फुल्की कसरत करता हूँ।
11. घास ओस के कारण गीली होती है।
12. घास काफी नर्म सी लगती है।
13. कई बार माली पौधों को पानी दे रहा होता है।
14. वह घास को काट कर व्यवस्थित करता है।
15. माली किसी को फूल नहीं तोड़ने देता।
16. मैं सीमेंट के बैंच पर बैठता हूँ।
17. पक्षी पेड़ों में चहचहा रहे होते हैं।
18. सूर्य की किरणें धरती पर पड़ रही होती हैं।
19. छोटे-छोटे बच्चे भी वहां घूम रहे होते हैं।
20. हर चेहरे पर खुशी की लहर दौड़ रही होती है।

Hints for Translation

1. wandering **4.** garden **5.** colourful fountain **8.** pleasant **10.** light exercises **11.** dew **14.** pruning **15.** to pluck **16.** cement bench **17.** chirping **19.** walking **20.** a wave of joy.

EXERCISE 5

नीचे दिये गये वाक्यों का अंग्रेजी में अनुवाद करें:

1. तुम यहां क्या कर रहे हो?
2. मैं अपने भाई को ढूँढ रहा हूँ।
3. मेरा भाई आज प्रातः घर से भाग गया।
4. वह कहां गया?
5. मैं नहीं जानता।
6. क्या आपने उसे रेलवे स्टेशन पर ढूंढा?
7. हां, पर वह वहां नहीं मिला।
8. क्या आपने उसे बस स्टैण्ड पर ढूंढा?
9. हां, पर वह वहां भी नहीं मिला।
10. वह ज़रूर स्कूल में जाकर छुप गया होगा।
11. या फिर वह खेल के मैदान में होगा।
12. वह इनमें से किसी भी जगह पर नहीं है।
13. चलो, छत पर देखें।
14. कोई लाभ नहीं।
15. क्या उसने खाना खाया है?
16. उसने कुछ भी नहीं खाया।
17. मम्मी व पापा उसके लिए काफी बेचैन हैं।
18. कहीं वह अपने अंकल के पास दिल्ली न चला गया हो?
19. यह हो भी सकता है।
20. ठहरो, मुझे भी एक आवाज़ लगाने दो।
21. तुम भी कोशिश कर लो।
22. मोहन तुम कहां हो? आओ क्रिकेट खेलें।
23. मैं अपने कमरे में रजाई के नीचे छुपा हूँ।
24. शैतान! यह तुमने क्या किया?
25. भैया! मैं बहुत शर्मिंदा हूँ।

Hints for Translation

2. searching for **6.** look for **11.** playground **13.** roof. **14.** no use **17.** restless, **23.** quiet. **24.** naughty **25.** much ashamed.

EXERCISE 6

नीचे दिये गये वाक्यों का अंग्रेजी में अनुवाद करें:

1. वह आप पर हंस रहा था।
2. वह क्यों रो रही थी?
3. वह आपकी बात ध्यान से सुन रहा था।

4. आपको क्या हुआ है ?
5. मुझे किसी से बात नहीं करनी है।
6. आप कहां चले गये थे ?
7. तुम झूठ मत बोलो।
8. भगवान की कसम ! मैं सच बोल रहा हूँ।
9. वह आपका क्या लगता है ?
10. वह चोर है।
11. तुमसे किसने इतनी घटिया बात कही ?
12. तुम्हें वे कहां पर मिले थे ?
13. आप का भाई बहुत शरारती है।
14. उसे कल अध्यापक ने पीटा।
15. बकवास बन्द करो।
16. बत्ती बुझा दो।
17. दरवाजा बन्द कर दो।
18. नल चला दो।
19. कान में ऊँगली मत डालो।
20. रोज़ दांतों पर ब्रश करो।

Hints for Translation

1. laughing at **8.** By God ! **9.** What is he to you? **13.** naughty **15.** stop this nonsence. **16.** Switch off the light **17.** shut **18.** turn on

EXERCISE 7

नीचे दिये गये वाक्यों का अंग्रेज़ी में अनुवाद करें:

1. शोर मत करो।
2. सदा हंसते रहो।
3. मत रोओ।
4. आंखें खोलो।
5. दांतों पर ब्रश करो।
6. सुबह हो गई है।
7. हवा चल पड़ी है।
8. जूते पालिश करो।
9. खाना धीरे-धीरे खाओ।
10. स्नान करके स्कूल जाना।
11. अपना बस्ता चैक करो।
12. अखबार पढ़ो।
13. खाना खाते समय कम बोलो।
14. बच्चों को खूब दही व मक्खन खाना चाहिए।
15. शर्म मत करो।
16. डट कर खाओ (या पेट भर कर खाओ)।
17. बच्चे चाय नहीं पीते।
18. अपना काम करो।
19. मेरी बातें ध्यान से सुनो।
20. रोज सैर के लिए जाओ।
21. खाना खूब चबा कर खाओ।

Hints for Translation

8. polish **9.** slowly. **14.** curd and butter. **16.** Have your fill **21.** Chew your food well.

EXERCISE 8

नीचे दिये गये वाक्यों का अंग्रेज़ी में अनुवाद करें:

1. स्कूल में अध्यापक की बात ध्यान से सुनें।
2. स्कूल समय पर पहुँचें।
3. काम से जी मत चुराओ।
4. क्लास में शोर मत करो।
5. स्कूल की दीवारों पर कुछ मत लिखें।
6. पार्क में गन्दगी मत डालो।
7. स्कूल की कोई भी वस्तु न तोड़ें।
8. लाइब्रेरी में चुपचाप पढ़ें।
9. खाने की छुट्टी के समय ही खाना खायें।
10. अध्यापक के क्लास में दाखिल होते ही खड़े हो जायें।
11. पढ़ाया जा रहा पाठ ध्यान से पढ़ें।
12. शोर करने वाले विद्यार्थी की शिकायत अध्यापक से करें।
13. पेंसिल व पैन हमेशा अपने पास रखें।
14. श्याम-पट पर कुछ मत लिखें।
15. सदैव मुस्कुराते रहें।
16. किसी से मत लड़ो।
17. मिलजुल कर रहें।
18. मिलजुल कर रहने से खुशी मिलती है।
19. सदा सच बोलें।
20. कभी झूठ न बोलें।

Hints for Translation

3. Don't shirk work **9.** interval

EXERCISE 9

नीचे दिये गये वाक्यों का अंग्रेज़ी में अनुवाद करें:

1. गरीबों पर दया करें।
2. भगवान ने सभी को एक जैसा बनाया है।
3. कमज़ोरों से नफरत न करें।
4. ताकतवर के सामने झुके नहीं।
5. बड़ों का सम्मान करें।
6. किसी की चुगली न करें।
7. जुल्म के सामने मत झुको।
8. सभी से प्यार से बात करें।
9. सदा साफ कपड़े पहनें।
10. बच्चों से मत लड़ो।
11. कमज़ोर को मत दबायें।
12. क्लास में न सोयें।
13. क्लास में बिजली की चीज़ों को मत छुएं।
14. घर आकर मुँह एवं हाथ धो लें।
15. खाना खूब चबाकर खायें।
16. अपनी कापी-किताबें सही ढंग से रखें।

17. वस्तुओं को इधर-उधर मत बिखेरें।
18. सदा चुस्त बन कर रहें।
19. खाना खाने के बाद थोड़ा सो जायें।
20. शाम को अपने स्कूल का कार्य खत्म करें।
21. फिर अपने मित्रों के साथ थोड़ी देर खेलें।
22. सूर्य ढलने से पहले घर वापिस आ जायें।
23. थोड़ी देर टी० वी० देखें।
24. टी० वी० सदा उपयुक्त दूरी से देखें।
25. कम रोशनी में मत पढ़ो।

Hints for Translation

1. pity **2.** alike, created **3.** the weak, look down upon **4.** bend **6.** back-biting **7.** tyranny **11.** suppress **16.** in order **17.** scatter **19.** have a nap **22.** sun-set

EXERCISE 10

नीचे दिये गये वाक्यों का अंग्रेजी में अनुवाद करें:

1. बहुत ज़्यादा रोशनी में भी मत पढ़ें।
2. रात को सोने से पहले अपने माता-पिता के चरण छुएं।
3. रात को दूध पीकर सोयें।
4. कॉफी या चाय मत पीयें।
5. साफ बिस्तर पर सोयें।
6. खुले कपड़े पहनें।
7. सिरहाना ज्यादा ऊँचा मत लें।
8. गर्मियों में पंखा चला कर सोयें।
9. सर्दीयों में पंखा मत चलायें।
10. बिस्तर बहुत ज्यादा सख़्त नहीं होना चाहिए।
11. शराब का सेवन मत करो।
12. सिगरेट मत पियें।
13. रात को चाय या कॉफी भी नहीं पीनी चाहिए।
14. सोने से पहले अपना बैग ठीक से लगा लें।
15. सारा सामान सही ढंग से देख लें।
16. कोई वस्तु गुम हो गई हो तो उसे ढूंढें।
17. दिमाग पर वजन रखे बिना सोयें।
18. सोने से पहले भगवान का नाम लें।
19. अच्छा सपना आने पर सुबह सबको बतायें।
20. मां-बाप बच्चे को खुश देखकर खुश होते हैं।

Hints for Translation

6. loose cloths **7.** pillow **11.** hard **17.** weight or tension **19.** dream

EXERCISE 11

नीचे दिये गये वाक्यों का अंग्रेज़ी में अनुवाद करें:

1. मैं हर रोज सुबह कार्यालय जाता हूँ।
2. मैं सदा ठीक समय पर जागता हूँ।
3. मैं समय का बड़ा पाबंद हूँ।
4. मुझे देर से आने वाले इन्सान अच्छे नहीं लगते।
5. मैं अपना नाश्ता करके कार से दफ्तर पर जाता हूँ।
6. रास्ते में कार कई बार रोकनी पड़ती है।
7. सड़क पर बहुत भीड़ होती है।
8. लोग यातायात के नियमों का पालन किये बिना गाड़ियां चलाते हैं।
9. कभी-कभी दो वाहन आपस में टकरा भी जाते हैं।
10. कई बार कई लोग मर जाते हैं।
11. मैं सड़क के कानूनों को मानता हूँ।
12. मैं कभी भी दुर्घटना का शिकार नहीं हुआ।
13. मैं कार के शीशे बन्द रखता हूँ।
14. चारों तरफ धुएं के बादल उड़ते हैं।
15. कभी-कभी सांस लेना मुश्किल हो जाता है।
16. मैं कार सही स्पीड पर चलाता हूँ।
17. मुझे आप कभी जल्दी में नहीं देखेंगे।
18. ज़्यादा तेजी दिखाना खतरनाक है।
19. इससे इन्सान का मानसिक सन्तुलन बिगड़ सकता है।
20. तब वह पागल भी हो सकता है।

Hints for Translation

3. punctual. **4.** late-comers **5.** by car **9.** run or ram into each other **12.** accident **18.** dangerous **19.** mental balance **20.** go mad.

EXERCISE 12

नीचे लिखे वाक्यों का अंग्रेज़ी में अनुवाद करें:

1. काम से कभी जी न चुराओ।
2. मैं आपके लिए क्या कर सकता हूँ?
3. बुरी संगति से अकेला भला।
4. नाच न जाने आंगन टेढ़ा।
5. एक गंदी मछली सारे जल को गन्दा कर देती है।
6. हाथ पर सरसों नहीं उगती।
7. कभी डरो नहीं।

8. आपको किससे डर है?
9. आप डरते क्यों हैं?
10. दाल में कुछ काला है।
11. उसकी चिकनी चुपड़ी बातों में मत आओ।
12. इधर-उधर की मत हांको।
13. काम की बात करो।
14. क्या वह मान गया?
15. क्या आपने उसे मना लिया?
16. सांच को आंच नहीं।
17. दो और दो चार होते हैं।
18. समय किसी की प्रतीक्षा नहीं करता।

Hints for Translation

1. shirk **11.** oily talks **18.** wait

Chapter 29

Translation Exercise (II)

PASSAGES IN HINDI (SOLVED)

PASSAGE 1

भारतीय संविधान के अनुसार भारत एक संम्प्रभु, धर्मनिरपेक्ष, समाजवादी, लोकतांत्रिक गणतंत्र है। परन्तु वास्तविक स्थिति क्या है? भारत में 100 करोड़ लोग रहते हैं। क्या उनमें तीव्र आर्थिक असमानतायें नहीं हैं? अधिकतर लोग निर्धनता की चक्की में पिस रहे हैं और केवल कुछ मुठठी भर लोग अत्यंत विलासपूर्ण जीवन बिता रहे हैं। तो हमारा देश किस प्रकार का समाजवादी देश है। हमारे प्रतिनिधि, जो बहुत अच्छे भी माने जाते हैं और संवैधानिक सुरक्षा और पाबंदी की शपथ लेते हैं, उन्होंने धनियों और निर्धनों की आय के अन्तर को कम करने के लिए अब तक क्या किया और वह अभी भी इस बारे में क्या कर रहे हैं? यह अन्तर तो दिन-प्रतिदिन बढ़ रहा है। फिर हम इन प्रतिनिधियों को इतना सम्मानजनक और ईमानदार कैसे मान लें जबकि वह अपने सब से महत्त्वपूर्ण कर्त्तव्य (अर्थात् संविधान को सच्चाई से लागू करना) का पालन ही नहीं कर रहे?

TRANSLATION

According to the Indian Constitution, India is a sovreign, secular, socialist, democratic republic. But what is the real situation? 100 crores of people live in India. Don't they have sharp economic inequalities? Most of the people are grinding under the wheels of poverty while only a handful of people are leading an awafully luxurious life. Then what kind of socialist country is ours? What have our representative who are even considered quite good people and who take an oath to defend and uphold the Constitution, have so far done to diminish (or lessen) the gap between the incomes of the rich and the poor and what are they doing even now in this respect? This gap is rather increasing day by day. Then how should we regard these representatives so honourable and honest when they are not performing their most significant duty (*ie*, implementation of the Constitution in a truthful manner).

PASSAGE 2

स्वयं मशीनें और जो शक्ति मशीनों ने हमें दी है, सभ्यता नहीं है अपितु सभ्यता के सहायक अंग हैं। गाड़ी में चढ़ने में विशेष रूप में कोई सभ्यता वाली बात नहीं है। परन्तु आपको याद होगा कि हम आरम्भ में इस बात पर सहमत थे कि सभ्यता का अर्थ है सुन्दर वस्तुएं बनाना तथा उन्हें पसन्द करना, स्वतन्त्रतापूर्वक सोचना, और ठीक ढंग से रहना, तथा मनुष्यों में न्याय कायम रखना।

TRANSLATION

The machines themselves and the power which the machines have given us are not civilisation but are aids of civilisation. There is nothing particularly civilised in boarding into a train. But you will remember that we agreed at the beginning that being civilised meant making and liking beautiful things, thinking freely, living properly, and maintaining justice for the entire mankind.

PASSAGE 3

जहां तक मेरा सम्बन्ध है, अपनी अस्थियों के मुट्ठी भर भाग को इलाहाबाद के स्थान पर गंगा नदी में प्रवाहित करने के बारे में मेरी इच्छा का कोई धार्मिक महत्त्व नहीं है। इस विषय में मेरी कोई धार्मिक भावना नहीं है। इलाहाबाद के स्थान पर गंगा तथा यमुना नदियों से मेरा संबंध शिशुकाल से ही रहा है और जैसे ही मैं बड़ा हुआ, मेरा यह स्नेह भी बढ़ता गया। मैंने ऋतुओं कें बदलने के साथ-साथ इन नदियों की बदलती हुई मुद्राओं को भी देखा है तथा प्राय: उस इतिहास, पौराणिक वार्ताओं, परम्पराओं, गीतों तथा कथाओं के बारे में सोचा है जो लम्बे युगों से इनके साथ जुड़े हुए हैं तथा उनके जल प्रवाह का एक भाग बन गये हैं।

TRANSLATION

My desire to have a handful of my ashes thrown into the Ganges at Allahabad has no religious significance, so far as I am concerned. I have no religious sentiment in this matter. I have been attached to the Ganges and the Yamuna rivers in Allahabad ever since my childhood and as I have grown older, this attachment has also grown. I have watched their varying moods as the seasons changed, and have often thought about the history, myths from the *Puranas,* traditions, songs and stories that have remained attached to them through the long ages and have become a part of their flowing waters.

PASSAGE 4

एक बार एक पंजाबी सिपाही जहाज पर एक भयानक बीमारी का शिकार हो गया और डॉक्टर ने उसे समुद्र में फेंक देने के मृत्यु-दण्ड देने की घोषणा की। सिपाही को इस बात का पता चला। साधारण मनुष्यों में भी बहादुरी की कुछ चमक आ जाती है जब उन्हें विपत्ति का सामना करना होता है। वह असीम शक्ति के साथ उछला और निर्भय हो गया। डॉक्टर ने तुरन्त उसे कुशल होने का प्रमाण-पत्र प्रदान किया। निराशा निर्बलता है। इससे बचो। सारी शक्ति निर्भयता से प्राप्त होती है।

TRANSLATION

Once, a Punjabi sepoy was down with some fatal disease on board a ship and the doctor passed the capital sentence on him and announced to throw him overboard. The sepoy come to know of it. There are flashes of fearlessness even in ordinary beings when they face tough times. He sprang up with unbounded energy and become fearless. The doctor immediately gave him a certificate of health. Despair is weakness. Avoid it. The entire strength comes from fearlessness.

PASSAGE 5

मेरी इच्छा है कि जब मेरी मृत्यु हो जाए तो मेरे शरीर का दाह-संस्कार किया जाये। यदि कहीं विदेश में मेरी मृत्यु हो तो मेरे शरीर का वहीं दाह-संस्कार कर दिया जाए तथा मेरी अस्थियों को इलाहाबाद भेज दिया जाए। इन अस्थियों का एक छोटी मुट्ठी-भर भाग गंगा में प्रवाहित कर दिया जाए और इसके अधिकतर भाग का निम्नलिखित ढंग से निपटारा किया जाये। इन अस्थियों का कोई भी भाग बचाया न जाये अथवा सम्भाल कर न रखा जाए।

TRANSLATION

When I die, I would like my body to be cremated. If I die in a foreign country, my body should be cremated there and my ashes sent to Allahabad. A small handful of these ashes should be thrown into the Ganga and the major portion of them disposed of in the manners indicated below. No part of these ashes should be retained or preserved.

PASSAGE 6

अपनी इतिहास की पुस्तकों में तुम राष्ट्रों के जीवन में आने वाले महान समय के विषय में पढ़ते हो। हम महान् पुरुषों और स्त्रियों और उनके द्वारा किये गये महान् कार्यों के विषय में पढ़ते हैं और कई बार हम अपने स्वप्नों तथा दिवा-स्वप्नों में अपने आपको उन्हीं युगों में अनुमानित करते हैं तथा पुराने समय के नायकों तथा नायिकाओं की तरह बहादुरी वाले कार्य करने की कल्पना करते हैं। क्या तुम्हें याद है कि जब तुमने जोन ऑफ आर्क की कहानी पहली बार पढ़ी तो तुम कितनी आकर्षित हुईं थीं, और तुम्हारी आकांक्षा थी कि तुम उसी की तरह कुछ कर दिखाओ?

TRANSLATION

In your history-books, you read of great periods in the life of the nations. We read of great men and women and great deeds performed by them and sometimes, in our dreams and reveries, we imagine ourselves back in those times and doing brave deeds like the heroes and heroines of the old ages. Do you remember, how fascinated you were when you first read the story of Joan of Arc, and that your ambition was to do something like her?

Chaper 30

Translation Exercise (III)

(UNSOLVED WITH HINTS)

PASSAGE 1

गुस्से[1] को एक भयानक विष[2] कहा जाता है। विष और क्रोध में मुख्य अन्तर यह है कि विष जिस बर्तन में हो, उस बर्तन अथवा बोतल को हानि नही पहुँचाता परन्तु गुस्से का विष जिसमें हो, वह सबसे पहले उसी मनुष्य को जलाता है[3]। संसार में सभी हत्याओं, दंगों[4] और झगड़ों का कारण गुस्सा ही होता है। इस प्रकार गुस्सा सभी बुराइयों की जड़[5] है। इस पर हमें काबू पाना[6] होगा।

Hints for Translation

1. गुस्सा = anger **2.** भयानक विष = a dangerous poison **3.** जलाता है = burns **4.** दंगे = riots **5.** जड़ = root cause **6.** काबू पाना = to control.

PASSAGE 2

यह आप ठीक ही कहते हैं कि मुझे धन भी मिला और यश[1] भी। परन्तु मुझे एक बहुत कीमती[2] चीज़ नहीं मिली और वह है मित्र। अगर मुझे अपना जीवन फिर से शुरू करना पड़े तो मैं मित्रों की तलाश करूंगा[3]। मेरे धन ने मुझे लोगों के दिलों से मिलने नहीं दिया और अब मैं अनुभव[4] करता हूँ कि मेरा इस जीवन में कोई भी सच्चा मित्र नहीं है। मैं आज कुछ अच्छे मित्रों के बदले[5] अपना सारा धन और मान देने को तैयार हूँ। सच्चे मित्रों की प्राप्ति से बढ़कर दुनिया में दूसरा सुख[6] नहीं है।

Hints for Translation

1. यश = fame **2.** कीमती = precious **3.** तलाश करना = search for **4.** अनुभव करना = feel or realise **5.** बदले में = in exchange for **6.** सुख = happiness, joy.

PASSAGE 3

विद्यार्थी जीवन मनुष्य जीवन का स्वर्णकाल[1] है। यही वह समय है जिसमें मनुष्य अपने भावी जीवन[2] को सफल बनाने के लिए शक्ति और योग्यता संचित[3] कर सकता है। देश, जाति और समाज का भविष्य आज के विद्यार्थियों पर निर्भर[4] है। हमारी संस्कृति[5] हमें स्वार्थी होना नहीं सिखाती। विद्यार्थियों पर देश, जाति और समाज के अनेक उपकार हैं। अतः विद्यार्थियों को भी चाहिए कि उन उपकारों के बदले में देश, जाति और समाज के प्रति अपने कर्त्तव्यों का पालन करें।

Hints for Translation

1. स्वर्णकाल = golden period **2.** भावी जीवन = future life **3.** संचित करना = to gather **4.** निर्भर होना = depend upon **5.** संस्कृति = culture.

PASSAGE 4

हमारे देश की ही नहीं, संसार भर की सबसे बड़ी आवश्यकता[1] शांति है। यह आवश्यकता विकसित देशों[2] से भी कहीं अधिक विकासशील[3] देशों की है। ऐसे देश कई क्षेत्रों[4] में पिछड़े हुए[5] हैं। गरीबी प्रत्येक जगह पर है। आवश्यक वस्तुओं[6] की उपज कम है। शिक्षा सीमित[7] है। युद्ध का मतलब है कई वर्षों की उपजाऊ वस्तुओं का थोड़े समय में नाश[8]। युद्ध में सबसे अधिक हानि विकासशील देशों की होती है। इसलिए वे बहुधा[9] शान्ति के लिए चेष्टा करते[10] हैं।

Hints for Translation

1. आवश्यकता = necessity **2.** विकसित देश = doveloped countries **3.** विकासशील = developing **4.** क्षेत्र = field **5.** पिछड़े हुए = backward **6.** आवश्यक वस्तुएं = essential commodities **7.** सीमित = limited **8.** नाश = destruction **9.** बहुधा = mostly **10.** चेष्टा करना = to try.

PASSAGE 5

स्वतंत्रता एक मुधर ध्वनि[1] वाला शब्द है। लगभग[2] हम में से सभी इसका प्रयोग करना चाहते हैं और इसका प्रयोग सुनना चाहते हैं। चाहे हमें इसका अर्थ पूरी तरह से समझ न आये, परन्तु हम समझते हैं यह किसी सुन्दर और साहसपूर्ण[3] धारणा का प्रतीक[4] है, यह किसी कीमती वस्तु के लिए है जिसके लिए संसार के प्रत्येक भाग से पुरुष व स्त्रियां संघर्ष[5]

करते आये हैं। स्वतंत्रता के लिए उन्होंने कष्ट सहे[6] हैं और मृत्यु को भी प्राप्त[7] हुए हैं। यदि आज हम स्वतन्त्रता का आनन्द लेते[8] हैं, यह सब उनके कारण ही हुआ।

Hints for Translation

1. मधुर ध्वनि = sweet sound **2.** लगभग = almost **3.** साहसपूर्ण = courageous **4.** प्रतीक = symbol **5.** संघर्ष करना = to struggle **6.** कष्ट सहना = to suffer **7.** मृत्यु को प्राप्त होना = to die **8.** आनन्द लेना = to enjoy.

PASSAGE 6

न्यूटन ने बड़ी आयु पाई और बहुत प्रसिद्धि[1] प्राप्त की। उसे पार्लियामेंट का सदस्य[2] बनाया गया। किन्तु वह सांसारिक[3] प्रसिद्धि की कुछ परवाह नहीं करता था और उसे अपने ज्ञान की असीमितता पर गर्व नहीं था। उसने जो कुछ ज्ञान प्राप्त किया, उससे वह यही अनुभव करता था कि जो कुछ उसने सीखा है, वह उससे बहुत कम है जो सीखना बाकी है। ''मैं अपने आपको एक बच्चे की तरह समझता हूँ।'' उसने कहा, ''जो कि समुद्र के किनारे[4] खेल रहा हो और इधर-उधर से पत्थर का एक सुन्दर टुकड़ा[5] उठा रहा हो, जब कि सत्य का अथाह[6] समुद्र मेरे सामने अनजाना[7] पड़ा है।''

Hints for Translation

1. प्रसिद्धि = fame **2.** सदस्य = member **3.** सांसारिक = worldly, **4.** समुद्र का किनारा = sea-shore **5.** पत्थर का टुकड़ा = pebble **6.** अथाह = infinite **7.** अनजाना = unknown.

PASSAGE 7

हमारे देश को स्वतंत्र हुए 50 वर्ष से अधिक हो गए हैं। हमने काफी उन्नति[1] की है परन्तु यह उन्नति कहीं अधिक[2] होती यदि हम ईमानदारी से कार्य करते। अभी तक हमने स्वतन्त्र लोगों की भांति आचरण करना नहीं सीखा। हममें बहुत से लोग स्वार्थी[3] हैं। आपस में छोटी-छोटी बातों[4] पर लड़ते हैं और अपनी शक्ति[5] व्यर्थ खोते[6] हैं। हमें भूलना नहीं चाहिए कि संगठन में शक्ति[7] है और फूट में विनाश। सबकी भलाई[8] में ही हमारी भलाई है।

Hints for Translation

1. उन्नति = progress **2.** कहीं अधिक होती = would have been greater **3.** स्वार्थी = selfish **4.** छोटी-छोटी बातें = trifles **5.** शक्ति = energy **6.** व्यर्थ खोना = waste **7.** संगठन में शक्ति है = union is strength **8.** भलाई = welfare.

PASSAGE 8

प्रत्येक स्त्री को ऐसा करना चाहिए जो समाज के लिए लाभदायक[1] हो। यदि कोई व्यक्ति ऐसा नहीं करता तो वह स्वार्थी है। ऐसा व्यक्ति समाज पर बोझ[2] होता है। उसका जीवन में कोई स्थान नहीं है। यदि वह अपने दिल में झांक[3] कर देखे तो उसे पता चल जाएगा कि वह अपने समाज और देश के साथ धोखा[4] कर रहा है। प्रत्येक स्त्री व पुरुष को अपने देश की भलाई[5] के बारे में सोचना चाहिए क्योंकि आधुनिक युग[6] में विज्ञान ने समय और दूरी पर विजय प्राप्त[7] करके सारे संसार को पहले से बहुत छोटा[8] बना दिया है।

Hints for Translation

1. लाभदायक = useful, beneficial to **2.** बोझ = burden **3.** अपने दिल में झांकना = peer into one's own heartage **4.** धोखा करना = to betray **5.** भलाई = welfare **6.** आधुनिक युग = modern age **7.** समय और दूरी पर विजय पाना = to win over time and distance **8.** पहले से बहुत छोटा = much narrower.

PASSAGE 9

एक आदमी अपने घर बैठा अपने एक रिश्तेदार[1] को ख़त लिख रहा था। उसी समय उसका एक मित्र आकर उसके पास बैठ गया। जो कुछ वह व्यक्ति लिख रहा था, उसका मित्र उसको पढ़ता गया। यह बात उस आदमी को अच्छी नहीं लगी। पर वह खुलकर कुछ भी ना कह सका। उसका मित्र बड़ा ही बेशर्म[2] तथा निडर[3] निकला[4]। वह खत पढ़ता ही रहा। आखिर में वह आदमी बहुत नाराज़ हुआ। उसने यह लिख कर बंद कर किया, "मैं बहुत कुछ लिखना चाहता था पर एक मूर्ख मित्र मेरे पास बैठा है। जो मैं लिखता हूँ वह पढ़ रहा है।" इस पर उसका मित्र बड़ा शर्मिंदा हुआ[5] और कहने लगा, "बड़ी खुशी से लिखो[6]। मैंने कुछ नहीं पढ़ा।" तब उसने उत्तर दिया, "क्या किसी और प्रमाण[7] की अभी आवश्यकता[8] रह गई है ?"

Hints for Translation

1. रिश्तेदार = relative **2.** बेशर्म = shameless **3.** निडर = fearless **4.** निकला = proved to be **5.** शर्मिंदा हुआ = felt ashamed **6.** खुशी से लिखो = write with pleasure **7.** प्रमाण = proof **8.** आवश्यकता = need, necessity.

PASSAGE 10

स्कूल में विद्यार्थियों के पुस्तकें पढ़ने का एक कारण[1] है–अपने अध्यापकों को प्रसन्न करना[2]। क्योंकि अध्यापक ने कहा है कि यह पुस्तक, वह पुस्तक या अन्य पुस्तक अच्छी

है और उसे पसन्द करना अच्छे शौक[3] की निशानी[4] है, इसलिए अधिकांश[5] लड़के-लड़कियां, जो अध्यापक को प्रसन्न करने के उत्सुक[6] होते हैं, वास्तव में वह पुस्तक प्राप्त कर लेते हैं और उसे पढ़ डालते हैं। फिर वे अध्यापक के प्रति कृतज्ञ[8] होते हैं कि उसने उन्हें उस पुस्तक के बारे में बताया[9]। परन्तु अधिकांश उसे सच्चे दिल[10] से पसन्द नहीं करते या फिर वह अपने आपको समझाने[11] का यत्न करते हैं कि वे उसे पसंद करते हैं। इससे बहुत हानि[12] होती है।

Hints for Translation

1. कारण = reason **2.** प्रसन्न करना = to please **3.** शौक = taste **4.** निशानी = sign, token **5.** अधिकांश = most of **6.** उत्सुक = eager **7.** वास्तव में = in reality **8.** कृतज्ञ = grafeful **9.** बताया = told, guided **10.** सच्चे दिल से = sincerely **11.** अपने आपको समझाना = persuade oneself **12.** हानि = harm

PASSAGE 12

मैंने कहा कि रोशनी चली गई[1] लेकिन शायद मैं भूल कर रहा था क्योंकि जिस रोशनी ने इस देश को प्रज्वलित किया[2] था वह कोई मामूली[3] रोशनी नहीं थी। वह रोशनी तो आगे भी बहुत सालों तक इस देश को ज्योतिर्मय करती रहेगी। लोग हजार सालों बाद भी इस रोशनी को देख सकेंगे। उसे सारा संसार देखेगा और वह असंख्य हृदयों[4] को शांति प्रदान करेगी। वह रोशनी तात्कालिक वर्तमान की ही नहीं, अपितु भविष्य की भी प्रतिनिधि[5] है। वह हमें ठीक मार्ग का स्मरण[6] कराती थी। वह हमें देश की आज़ादी की तरफ लाई[7] थी।

Hints for Translation

1. चली गई = has gone out **2.** प्रज्वलित किया = illuminated **3.** मामूली = ordinary **4.** असंख्य हृदय = innumerable hearts **5.** प्रतिनिधि = representative **6.** स्मरण करना = remind **7.** लाई थी = guided us.

Chepter 31

Practice Passage

UNSOLVED WITH HINTS

नीचे दिये गये गद्यांशों का अंग्रेजी में अनुवाद करें:

I

बड़ी पुरानी बात है एक राजा का केवल एक ही बेटा था। उसका नाम था—राजकुमार[1] दिनेश। दिनेश बहुत ही सुन्दर[2] व प्रभावशाली[3] इन्सान था। वह चतुर[4] व राजनीति[5] में निपुण[6] भी था। दूर-दूर तक कोई उसके मुकाबले का नौजवान नहीं था। वह तलवार चलाना, धनुष-बाण[7] चलाना इत्यादि भली-भांति[8] से सीख चुका था। राजा को पूर्ण विश्वास था कि दिनेश का कोई बाल भी बांका[9] नहीं कर सकता। इसीलिए एक दिन उसे अकेले[10] ही वन[11] में शिकार[12] के लिए भेज दिया गया।

अभी राजकुमार दिनेश कुछ ही कदम[13] आगे बढ़ा ही था कि उसको झाड़ियों[14] में से सरसराहट की आवाज़[15] आई। वह चौकस[16] हो गया। उसकी पकड़[17] तलवार पर और मज़बूत हो गई। वह घोड़े से नीचे उतर[18] आया। मुश्किल से[19] वह पांच ही कदम चला होगा कि एक शेर ने दिनेश पर धावा बोल दिया[20]। दिनेश बड़ी बहादुरी से[21] लड़ता रहा लेकिन वह शेर को नहीं मार सका। अचानक उसकी तलवार उसके हाथ से छूट गई तथा झाड़ियों में ही कहीं गुम हो गई[22]। दिनेश को पूरी तरह से आभास हो गया[23] कि अब उसका बचना मुश्किल है। मौत उसको अपने काफी निकट नज़र आने लगी लेकिन एक सच्चा बहादुर होने के कारण वह जरा भी भयभीत न था। न ही उसने वहां से भागने[24] की कोशिश की। लेकिन उसकी हैरानी का उस समय कोई ठिकाना न रहा, जब शेर उस पर जैसे ही झपटने लगा, एक बाण कहीं दूर से शांय-शांय करता हुआ शेर के माथे में आ धंसा तथा वह थोड़ा छटपटाने के बाद वहीं ढेर[25] हो गया। राजकुमार दिनेश ने इधर-उधर[26] देखा। उसे कोई दिखाई नहीं दिया। लेकिन ठीक एक मिनट के बाद उसे एक हल्की सी रोशनी दिखाई

दी। वह उसको बड़े ध्यान से देखने लगा। रोशनी धीरे-धीरे आकार[27] में बड़ी होती जा रही थी। जैसे ही वह उसके पास पहुँची राजकुमार दिनेश की आंखें चुन्धिया गईं[28]। थोड़ी देर के लिए उसे दिखाई देना बन्द हो गया। राजकुमार बेहोश[29] हो गया। उसे जब होश आया[30] तो वह अपने महल में बिस्तर पर लेटा पड़ा था। वह घर कैसे पहुँचा उसे कुछ याद नहीं था।

II

एक बार की बात है चुन्नू नामक एक लड़का एक गांव में रहता था। वह बेहद शरारती था। वह सारा दिन खेलता रहता था। उसका मन पढ़ाई में न लगने के कारण वह अक्सर स्कूल का काम नहीं करता था। इसलिए कई बार वह अपने अध्यापक के द्वारा पीटा जा चुका था। एक बार दोपहर को वह अकेला पहाड़ी के पास घूम[1] रहा था। चारों तरफ झाड़ियां ही.झाड़ियां थीं। गर्मी के कारण कोई भी पक्षी वहां नहीं चहचहा रहा था। चारों तरफ सन्नाटा[2] छाया हुआ था। तभी चुन्नू की नज़र एक बूढ़े बाबा पर पड़ी जो कि उसी की ओर चले आ रहे थे। चुन्नू ने बाबा को नमस्ते की। बाबा ने उसकी नमस्ते का कोई उत्तर नहीं दिया। चुन्नू यह देख कर बेचैन[3] हो गया। उसने बाबा से पूछा कि उन्होंने उसकी नमस्ते का जवाब क्यों नहीं दिया। बाबा ने अपनी आंखें बंद करते हुआ कहा कि मैं गंदे बच्चों से बात नहीं करता। चुन्नू की जिद्द[4] पर बाबा ने उसे अच्छा बच्चा बनने के कई ढंग बताए—जैसे कि, रोज़ सुबह जल्दी उठना, हर रोज़ स्नान करना, बड़ों का कहना मानना, सदा सच बोलना, किसी से झगड़ा नहीं करना, रोज स्कूल का काम करना तथा मन लगाकर पढ़ाई करना।

चुन्नू ने ऐसा ही किया और उसी वर्ष वह क्लास में प्रथम आया। जब उसके मुख्याध्यापक पुरस्कार[5] दे रहे थे तो उसे बाबा की याद[6] आ रही थी। वह पुरस्कार लेने के बाद सीधा पहाड़ी की तरफ बाबा को ढूँढने चला गया लेकिन उसे बाबा कहीं नहीं मिले। शायद बाबा अपना कार्य सम्पूर्ण[7] करके कहीं दूर जा चुके थे। दूसरों को कामयाबी[8] के रास्ते पर डालना ही अच्छे इन्सान का धर्म है।

III

एक छोटा सा घर था। उसमें एक नन्हीं सी गुड़िया रानी[1] अपनी मां व भाई के साथ रहती थी। वह गुड़िया रानी बड़ी सयानी[2] थी। वह घर का सारा काम[3] करती थी—जैसे घर की सफाई, बर्तन साफ करना[4], खाना बनाना[5], चाय बनाना आदि। एक दिन उसने अपनी मां से कहा कि वह स्कूल में पढ़ना चाहती है। उसकी मां को गुड़िया की बात बहुत अच्छी

लगी, तथा उसने गुड़िया को स्कूल जाने की आज्ञा दे दी। गुड़िया के भाई को ये सब अच्छा न लगा। वह नहीं चाहता था कि गुड़िया भी पढ़े। उसका विचार था कि लड़कियों का दिमाग कम होता है और इसलिए, उन्हें पढ़ने की बजाय घर का ही काम करना चाहिए। लेकिन उस वर्ष का परिणाम निकला तो सभी लोग यह सुनकर दंग रह[6] गये कि गुड़िया प्रथम आई थी तथा उसका भाई जो अपने-आपको बहुत कुछ समझता[7] था, पास भी न हो सका था।

IV

एक बार रात को न जाने मेरे मन में यह विचार क्यों आया कि मैं थोड़ी सी सैर के लिए अपने घर से कहीं दूर जाऊँ। मैंने अपने-आपको समझाने की बड़ी कोशिश की कि यह बात मुझे मंहगी[1] पड़ सकती है परन्तु यह विचार एक ऐसा तीव्र व शक्तिशाली तूफान था जिसके सामने मैं बेबस था। यहां तक कि अपना खाना आधा छोड़कर मैं उठकर[2] चल दिया। जैसे ही मेरा पहला कदम ज़मीन पर पड़ा, मैंने सिर उठाकर दूर-दूर तक नजर दौड़ाई[3] ताकि अपने आसपास की दुनियां को मैं बीस बरस बाद देख सकूँ कि वह किस तरह की दिखाई देती है। वहां से कोसों दूर[4] मुझे कहीं प्रकाश नज़र आया। शायद यही मेरी मन्ज़िल[5] थी। मेरे इर्द-गिर्द पेड़ बड़ी जोर-जोर से हिल रहे[6] थे। जो थोड़े छोटे थे वो कुछ ज्यादा ही प्रभावित नजर[7] आ रहे थे। मैं अपने-आप में खुशी से फूला नहीं समा[8] रहा था। ज्यादा खुशी हैरानगी[9] का रूप धारण[10] कर चुकी थी। मेरी आंखें नम हो रही[11] थीं। मेरे होंठ ने जाने क्यों फड़फड़ा[12] रहे थे। मुझे वह बीस बरस से पहले की सारी घटनाएं[13] याद आ रहीं थीं। किस तरह मैंने और मेरे साथियों[14] ने दुश्मनों को गोलियों से भून[15] दिया था! किस तरह हमारी बटालियन[16] ने दुश्मन के दांत खट्टे किये थे! किस तरह अफसर ने मेरे कंधे[17] पर तगमे[18] ही तगमे सजा[19] दिये थे। लेकिन यह क्या? मेरे कानों तक केवल धड़ाम की आवाज[20] पहुँच सकी और मैंने अपने आपको मिट्टी में लोटते[21] हुए पाया। शायद मेरा पांव फिसल गया[22] था। मैंने जैसे ही उठने[23] की कोशिश की, फिर गिर गया। शायद रास्ता साफ न था। मैंने फिर कोशिश की और फिर गिर गया। ओह! मुझे याद आ गया कि मेरी एक टांग गोली लगने के कारण काट[24] दी गई है। मैंने ठीक चीज़ की खोज अंधेरे में शुरू की—वह थी बैसाखी[25] जो कि वहीं कहीं पड़ी थी और मुझे मिल गई। मैंने आगे बढ़ने का इरादा बदल दिया और वापिस अपने घर चला आया।

V

आधुनिक युग[1] में अखबार पढ़ना शायद खाना खाने से भी ज़्यादा जरूरी है। हर इन्सान अपने आपको नई से नई खबरों से अवगत करवाना[2] चाहता है। कुछ स्त्रियां नये-नये फैशनों को अपनाना[3] चाहती हैं। विद्यार्थी नई नौकरियां के बारे में एवं व्यापारी लोग नये व्यवसायों[4] के बारे में जानना चाहते हैं। शेयरों का काम करने वाले लोग या इस धन्धे में रुचि रखने वाले लोग सुबह चाय पीने से पहले अखबार देखना पसंद करते हैं। देश विदेश के ताज़े[5] व विस्तृत[6] समाचारों को जानने के इच्छुक[7] भी इस सस्ती चीज को खरीद लेते हैं। मैंने तो कई कंजूस लोगों[8] को भी एक या दो रुपये की अखबारें खरीदते देखा है। यहां तक कि एक चाय की दुकान पर एक भीख मांगने वाले को भी कई खबरों में रुचि[9] लेते देखा है। तो आप क्या समझते हैं, हमारे देश के मंत्रीगण उस सस्ती सी वस्तु का लाभ[10] नहीं उठाते होंगे?

Hints for Translation

I

1. राजकुमार = prince 2. सुन्दर = handsome 3. प्रभावशाली = influential (here, impressive) 4. चतुर = smart 5. राजनीति = politics 6. निपुण = adapt, well-versed 7. धनुषबाण चलाना = archery 8. भली-भांति = well, thoroughly 9. बाल-बांका करना = harm, do harm 10. अकेले = alone 11. वन = jungle, forest 12. शिकार = hunting 13. कदम = steps 14. झाड़ियां = bushes 15. सरसराहट की आवाज = rustling sound 16. चौकस = alert 17. पकड़ = grip 18. नीचे उतरा = got off 19. मुश्किल से = hardly 20. धावा बोल देना = assault, attack 21. बहादुरी से = bravely 22. गुम हो गई = was lost 23. आभास हो गया = realised 24. भागना (डर कर) = to flee 25. वहीं ढेर हो गया = collapsed there and then 26. इधर-उधर = here and there 27. आकार = shape 28. चुन्धिया गईं = were dazzled 29. बेहोश = unconscious 30. होश आना = regain consciousness.

II

1. घूम रहा था = was wandering 2. सन्नाटा = silence 3. बेचैन हो गया = got (or become) restless 4. जिद्द पर = on his insistence 5. पुरस्कार = prize 6. याद आ रही थी = was reminded of 7. कार्य सम्पूर्ण करके = having completed his work

8. कामयाबी के रास्ते पर डालना = to guide a person on the path to success.

III

1. गुड़िया रानी = a small girl 2. सयानी = intelligent 3. घर का काम = household work 4. बर्तन साफ करना = to clean untensils 5. खाना बनाना = to cook food 6. दंग रह गये = were surprised 7. अपने आपको बहुत कुछ समझता था = thought much of himself.

IV

1. बहुत मंहगी पड़ सकती है = can cost me dearly 2. अपना सिर उठाकर = raising my head 3. नजर दौड़ाई = cast my eyes 4. कोसों दूर = several miles (or kilometres) away 5. मन्ज़िल = destination 6. हिल रहे थे = were swinging 7. प्रभावित नज़र आते थे = seemed to be affected 8. खुशी से फूला नहीं समा रहा था = was beside myself with joy 9. हैरानगी = amazement 10. रूप धारण कर चुकी थी = had assumed the shape of 11. नम हो रही थी = were getting moist 12. (होंठ) फड़-फड़ा रहे थे = (lips) were twitching 13. घटनाएं = incidents 14. साथी = companions 15. गोलियों से भून दिया था = had perforated the enemy with bullets 16. बटालियन = battalion 17. कंधा = shoulder 18. तगमे = medals 19. सजा दिये थे = decked 20 .धड़ाम की आवाज = the sound of a thud 21. मिट्टी में रौंदते = wallowing in dust 22. फिसल गया = slipped 23. उठना = get up 24. (टांग) काट देना = amputate (the leg) 25. बैशाखी = crutches.

V

1. आधुनिक युग = modern age 2. परिचित करवाना = familiarise with 3. अपनाना = adopt 4. व्यवसाय = occupations, professions 5. ताजा समाचार = latest news 6. विस्तृत = detailed 7. इच्छुक = interested in, desirous of 8. कंजूस लोग = miserly people 9. रुचि लेना = take interest in, 10. लाभ उठाना = take advantage of, make use of.